Advance Praise
for Open Admissions

Bachus is a clear-eyed and likable protagonist and his hard-earned reflections on the way humans learn from one another are worth a read. A valuable and thoughtful work from a professor at the end of his teaching career.

—*Kirkus*

I loved this book. Ned Bachus can really write. This memoir is brilliant, engaging, and instructive. *Open Admissions* is both moving and personal; it is serious without being sanctimonious. Bachus is never pious and he is always inspiring, whether he's talking about the students he's teaching or about his own experiences and family life. A must read, not only for those who teach at community colleges or at public institutions, but for all teachers and all administrators. I recommend *Open Admissions* with a full heart.

— Gina Barreca, Professor of English, University of Connecticut, contributor to *Chronicle of Higher Education*, and author of *Babes in Boyland: A Personal History of Coeducation in the Ivy League*

In a time of crumbling infrastructure, education budget cuts, and spiraling college debt, Ned Bachus finds hope and possibility in our country's community colleges. *Open Admissions* is a love song to the promise and accessibility of affordable higher education. Weaving a narrative tapestry from the threads of his own search within and abroad, Bachus discovers that while he thought he taught writing to nontraditional students, what he really was teaching was independence.

— Roger LaMay, General Manager, WXPN

With humor and compassion, Bachus reveals the transformational work that occurs in community colleges in helping students reach their educational goals. He intertwines his own mishaps in a foreign culture with the challenges that students face as they enter the new world of academia. Teaching and learning occurs by *both* faculty and students in this must-read book for anyone employed at a community college.

— Kathleen Hetherington, President, Howard Community College

To Al and Betty

OPEN
ADMISSIONS

My fellow Italians —
Brother + Sister of the Chalk
Raiser of _awesome_ children and
Changers of lives for the better.
Love
Ned

Published by Wild River Books
PO Box 672
Lambertville, NJ 08530
www.wildriverconsultingandpublishing.com

Distributed by Wild River Consulting & Publishing, LLC.

Design and composition by:
Tim Ogline / Ogline Design for Wild River Consulting & Publishing, LLC.

Publisher's Cataloging-In-Publication Data
Bachus, Ned
  Open Admissions: What Teaching at Community College
  Taught Me About Learning
ISBN: 978-1-941948-04-0

Printed in the United States of America

First Edition

OPEN ADMISSIONS

What Teaching
at Community College
Taught Me About Learning

by Ned Bachus

WILD
RIVER
BOOKS

CONTENTS

IN MEMORY OF
Hélene Pellerin Bachus and Max W. Eirich

FOR
Vince Castronuovo

*"I never teach my pupils, I only attempt
to provide the conditions in which they can learn."*
–Albert Einstein

Prologue

March 2011: Community College of Philadelphia

Every Honors student has arrived early for the 8:00 a.m. midterm essay exam. I distribute copies of the essay prompt along with sheets of loose-leaf paper, conscious that these students want to make full use of the next two hours. The normally chatty group quietly shuffles through the two-page prompt, their faces creased in contemplation.

I stand at the front of the Community College of Philadelphia classroom like a proud papa, surveying the motley group at work before me. Mostly in their late teens or early twenties, some of them have reached their forties. Black, white, Hispanic, Asian. My teaching partner Vince Castronuovo and I are both in our sixties and have seen many strong students in our decades in the classroom. It's seven weeks into the semester, and already we suspect that this might be the most talented and dedicated group we've ever guided through our linked Honors section of English 101 and Psychology 101.

Sudden shouts down the hall startle everyone away from their papers, and we all turn toward the din as if we could see through the walls. The noise of people running and screaming out in the hallway echoes even more loudly now. "Just do your work," I say, and rush to the door. *This noise is going to stop. Nobody is trashing my students' exam time.*

My office is a few classrooms down the hall, and just beyond it two young men are pummeling each other on the marble floor. Yelping students line the narrow hallway but stand back. A woman I assume is a teacher shrieks from a classroom doorway for the combatants to stop. The larger of the two fighters rolls on top of the other. They trade punches as onlookers hoot and scream. All along the hallway, doors have opened to gapers.

I rush to the scene, knowing only that I must think of something. Reaching them, I kneel beside them and scream as loudly as I ever have screamed: "Get UP!"

They flinch.

"NOW!" I yell, then stand up. As they pick themselves up, I step between them. "It's over."

"Fuck you up!" the muscular teenager in the white T-shirt screams at the bigger man who'd been on top of him. He tries to shift around me, working to get a clear line toward his taller, beefier opponent.

I turn briefly to the man behind me, who is keeping his distance but not taking his eyes off his opponent. "Walk away!" I yell at him.

The younger one dodges around me and lands a punch on the more reluctant fighter. The big man drops him with a massive swing. Stunned for a moment, the teenage student rolls away and is up and landing karate kicks before I can do anything. He yanks his T-shirt off and tosses it to the floor. The two bob and weave, again to the crowd's apparent mixture of horror and delight, and I see a smear of blood on the marble floor. They each land pounding blows, but the shirtless guy is backing his opponent along the wall. I position myself behind the younger man and inch closer. When he pauses between jabs, I clamp my arms around him from behind, pinning his arms to his chest.

The larger man stands his ground, alert but no longer in the fight. "It's over," I say, shifting my head so that I'm out of range, should the younger guy in my grip decide to head-butt me. *If he breaks loose, he could make quick work of you, old man.* He goes all out against my grip but backs off a bit when he fails. "I'm not going to hurt you," I say. I pivot him around so he no longer has direct sight of his opponent.

"Walk away now!" Turning, I see the other man, books and jacket in his grasp, heading toward the stairs at the end of the hallway.

"It's over, " I repeat, more quietly.

"Nobody says that shit to me!"

Some people have left the hallway but many remain, watching us.

"It's okay," I say.

"I can't breathe, man!"

I loosen my grip. His resistance continues but with less urgency. "You don't want to get kicked out of college," I say. We continue our awkward dance along the hallway wall. "I'm going to let you go. If you walk down to Security with me, I'll be able to tell them that you stopped, that you took your foot off the gas."

He grumbles, but his words are not intended for me.

"You don't want this to be your last day as a student. I'll go with you."

He stands still, no longer actively resisting.

"Okay," I say and let him go.

He picks up his shirt and pulls it back on, cursing. He shows no intention of harming me. He keeps shaking his head and muttering. "Not going down there."

"Could make a difference," I say.

"Shi-it," he drawls out, then storms off in the opposite direction.

Down the hallway, two faces are peeking from my classroom's open door. They scurry back inside when we make eye contact. I walk into the classroom and collapse into my chair with a sigh. My students are writing away at their desks.

Maria raises her hand. I nod. "You have blood on your shirt, Mr. Ned," she says gently. "You should wash it off."

In the men's room at the quieter end of the hallway, I look at the grizzled face in the mirror as I dab water on the small bloody section on my blue dress shirt, then wash my hands. In nearly four decades here, first as a student then as a faculty member, I have heard about maybe one such incident. In a piece of fiction that I set at a school much like this one, one of my characters, a young female teacher, breaks up a fight between students, sparking dramatic plot lines, but that was purely my imagination at work.

When Vince relieves me at nine, I step outside to briefly tell him what happened then go to Security, where I find the larger student talking with the police. He'd gone down on his own immediately after leaving the hallway. Like him, I fill out a statement and speak with the police and Security. No, I tell the police, he had not been the aggressor in the hallway. The student apologizes to me. Officers are on their way to the address of the other student. The young men are classmates in a developmental English class, both have prison records, and this one is fearful that today's incident might destroy his efforts to right his life. "I'm passing *everything*," he tells me. His eyes flash anger, maybe fear.

I feel that drive again. "I can meet with you for the rest of the term, tutor you, be your academic advisor," I say, the words rushing out of my mouth as unplanned as those that I'd yelled in the hallway. "You've dug yourself a hole today."

"He may need you to go to court, if you're willing," an officer tells me.

"As long as it's not during an exam."

At home, Kathleen and I are joined for dinner and a TV series by Michael Napoletano, my friend since sixth grade and de facto uncle to our now-grown kids, whom he remembers when they were tiny and napped in a drawer on our dining room table. I tell them the story. Kathleen hugs me for what feels as long as the time I'd held onto the less wise of the two students.

"Promise me you won't do that again," Michael barks at me, echoing the words I'd heard from one of my colleagues that afternoon at the copy center.

I can't answer him without going into the hundred things that still run through my brain.

"You get that, don't you?" He jabs his finger in the air.

Perhaps if I taught at one of the nation's most dangerous high schools, I would have remained with my students and not gone out into the hallway. Our campus might be one of the safest places in the city, where students build on their hopes—an oasis for those who return to dangerous streets. It's been that way since I walked in its doors as a freshman from a single-parent, working-class family nearly half a century ago.

"You said the one guy claimed he'd seen a knife in the other guy's hand," Michael continues.

"He thought the guy held something shiny, and he had been cut, bruised. I didn't see anything like that. Nobody else did," I say.

"Not smart," he smirks then turns to Kathleen. "Talk sense to him!"

We open up the bottle of red wine that Michael had brought, then talk about other things during dinner, but I suspect that we all still have the incident on our minds. After the show, Michael rises to leave, knowing that it is a work night for those who have not yet retired. A stack of midterm exams awaits me in the small bedroom I use as an office.

Later, I bring an opened College envelope to bed, where Kathleen sits propped up with a book. "You know what this is," I say, showing her the letterhead.

"I saw the envelope in the mail. What you were expecting, right?"

I nod.

"Great timing," she says, closing her book.

In the last few months, I'd been awarded sabbatical leave for the 2012 spring semester. More good news followed when I learned that I'd been granted an artist's residency to spend that April writing in a cliff-side cottage on the west coast of Ireland. Today's letter acknowledges that I have accepted the College's offer of early retirement—a year's salary. The contract offers no such incentives for employees who stay past age sixty-three, so my window is about to close. I still can rescind my decision, but barring that, I will teach my final semester next fall.

"Quite a day," she says, putting her eyeglasses and book on the nightstand.

I climb into bed and stare at the letter. "Some people would see today as a clear sign," I say.

"But you're not sure you can leave all that, are you?"

I hear no sarcasm or irony in her voice. "I'm not looking for another day like today," I assure her.

"That's not what I mean." She squeezes my hand.

I want time to write full time, to play music with my friends, to explore life with Kathleen in a completely different place. To do all those things before my body won't allow it. But today reminds me how much Community College of Philadelphia is in me, in my blood. Could I even *be* me if I left this place?

"You'll know when you know," she says.

I turn back to the letter, sure that it stated the final date that I could change my mind, but Kathleen turns off the light.

"You can't do any more tonight," she says.

In the dark, I toss the letter onto the floor and roll over beside her, my mind still awake and buzzing.

Fall Semester, Week One

Wednesday, September 7, 2011: Philadelphia

On the first day of the 2011 fall semester at Community College of Philadelphia, five minutes before class time, my English 101 students waited in classroom S2-12B.

I picked my way through the hallway's boisterous traffic then paused to rest my stack of texts and handouts atop the large blue plastic recycling bin near my classroom, relieved to see that I had brought the correct set of syllabi. I rummaged around in my jacket pocket for two other classroom essentials: cough drops and fresh sticks of chalk, then ran a finger down the list of students on my sheets. *Who are they?* As the semester went on, I would amass pages of notes about conferences and progress and grades, but right now, I knew these students only as names on a page. That was about to change. Suddenly, butterflies swarmed in my chest, the same swirl of dread and drive that had attacked me on every opening day since I first began teaching in September of 1970.

The hallway crowd swerved around each other like figure skaters. Everyone shouldered a backpack, and some toted plastic bookstore bags or containers of food from the trucks that lined 17th Street. The air was filled with the smell of onions, jerk chicken, and tomato sauce and the sounds of loud conversations in English, Russian, Spanish, and Cambodian or Vietnamese. I imagined the same type of energy pulsing more quietly through hallways at Harvard. Their noise didn't bother me. It sounded like hope.

Their teachers felt hope as well. Few of us failed to experience some form of opening-day anxiousness. I remembered long ago reading that legendary *Tonight Show* host Johnny Carson admitted to becoming nervous before every show. That this raised the eyebrows of the interviewer surprised me far more than hearing that an experienced entertainer also got the jitters before going on stage. When I'd entered my office that morning, I had felt enough hope to share some with everyone in the whole building. I told my teaching partner and friend Vince, a most optimistic teacher, "If every day felt like this one, I might teach forever."

"The other days aren't like this," he replied pragmatically.

But on opening day, no one had failed, confidence ran high, and, as some of my more jaded colleagues might add, the idea that pigs can fly remained a distinct possibility.

I thought of two wise, seasoned colleagues, both veteran fishermen, who still got as charged up about a new semester's drama as they did about trout season's first day. I imagined them over the break between semesters, alternately tying flies and reviewing syllabi, readying to begin anew their rhythmic efforts to lure both fish and learners. Patience marked good fishermen and teachers alike.

Community college students resembled anglers too, though not the catch and release sort. They fished for jobs, homes, cars, clothes, and everything else that honestly earned money could buy. Some of them also fished for accomplishment, meaning, career identity, and prestige. I watched these strangers dart around one another, all headed for the classes where they were expected to spend this hour three times a week for the next fifteen weeks. Their compatriots filled classes across the country in far greater numbers than most Americans realized. Nearly half of American undergraduates were community college students. [1]

I gathered up my materials and headed straight for S2-12B, swept along by the hallway's energy. Opening day, and I hardly could wait for the first cloud of chalk dust to settle all over my clothes.

I pulled open the door and swept into the classroom. Except for a repeating student from one of my previous spring's comp classes, all these students looked new to me. Like dancers paired for a waltz, teachers and students worked closely for fifteen weeks until a new semester gave them different partners. The music was cued up. It was time to dance.

I scanned the faces before me but did not want to make them feel self-conscious. About half of them studiously ignored me, including a young woman in pajama pants, not yet a standard wardrobe choice at commuter schools like ours. A few students smiled at me, and I smiled back. They knew less about me than I did about them. Simply seeing their faces, academic records, or placement scores did not enable me to accurately predict which ones would succeed or fail. My smile lingered, sustained now by the intruding thought that no, they needed no reassurances that I was old enough to teach them.

Their youth startled me, most of this group in their late teens or early twenties. Two earbud-wearing young men, one black and the other Mediterranean-looking, took adjacent seats, nodding gently to music I could not hear. A young woman dressed in black landed behind them. They appeared even younger than the uniformed kids who now drove police cruisers and darted about hospitals in long white jackets. However, a few of my students had neared retirement age and others appeared to have reached what one might characterize as mid-career age. A photographer, looking for a camera-ready image of classroom diversity, would do no better than my class in S2-12B. In short—a typical CCP English 101 class.

I plopped down my materials on the table at the front of the classroom and went to the board to write my name and office number. Even though that information jumped out from page one of the syllabus, it felt more personal this way. The chalk broke in half with my first stroke—the same cheap stuff that the College always provided. I caught the broken piece in midair, tucked it into my pocket, and continued writing.

"Bachus," a voice called. "You play Mr. Magoo back in the day?"

I turned and located an eighteen-year-old white man, slouched back in his seat and sporting a "Dallas Sucks" T-shirt. "He spelled it with a K," I said.

His quizzical expression intact, the wiry young man nodded slightly.

"Jim," I said.

"Damn," he said, sitting up in his seat. "How'd you know that?"

"I just remember it."

"I never met you, man," he countered. Muscles tensed, he fixed on my eyes, as if he were ready to launch out of his desk in my direction.

"Jim B-A-C-K-U-S," I said.

His glare softened and he returned to his far more comfortable position. "Yeah, yeah," he said. "I knew that. I'm Jim too."

I nodded. "Glad to meet you, Jim."

A middle-aged black woman seated in front of him rolled her eyes. The other twenty students busied themselves with the contents of their backpacks, as if nothing had happened.

I knew that over the next fifteen weeks Jim and his classmates would occasionally reveal some of the reasons they found themselves in my classroom on this September day. Their long-term plans varied tremendously, but they had one thing in common: Like most other entering college students, they needed to pass freshman composition.

Most Americans had come to expect college as a standard rite of passage into adulthood. Though the door to college might swing wide open to let these students enter, once inside they run into a second door, English 101, which looks to them more like a great locked gate.

While many of my students had to pass remedial English before they could even attempt tackling this class, almost all college students, regardless of their major, paid their dues in English 101 or the equivalent before moving on to courses in their chosen fields, which was almost never English at community colleges. Not all students planned to transfer to a four-year institution, but even those headed for a two-year associate's degree or a certificate in a career field had to pass English 101.

Basic requirements existed at all colleges, but at community colleges, open access sometimes became a cruel joke, a come-on, a lie. English 101 lurked in the small print that students did not often bother to read, and for many of them, it would shine a bright light on their least attractive academic features. For students at all manner of colleges, this proved the most determinant course they took, a make-or-break experience. In general, they entered less academically prepared for this course than did previous generations' freshmen, facing at least as many nonacademic challenges. Teachers at public and private four-year institutions assured me that poorly prepared students appeared on their rosters far more often than they had in the past.

My students would leave this course either as seasoned college writers who held a reasonable chance of succeeding in their whole endeavor or as struggling students left to decide between leaving school or retaking the course—pending the vagaries of financial aid eligibility/personal financial resources and college policy on the number of times students could repeat a course.

For enormously varied reasons, almost all of these students would show up for our next class. I did not represent to them a beloved and inspiring leader, charging ahead with red pen held aloft. To them, I was no one. Worse, I might have reminded them of a familiar stereotype of the most discouraging sort. Except for any repeating students, in English 101 we all started off as strangers who knew little, if anything, about each other. On the first day of the fall semester, these students saw standing before them a bald, stocky white guy with a grizzled goatee, an old man with whom they must somehow pass an hour three times a week until just before Christmas but who, alas, was not Santa Claus. Like most professors I knew, I saw myself as firm but fair, not necessarily endearing but energizing—clearly a common faculty delusion. The previous semester, a timid Jamaican student, who I would have sworn thought the world of me and would gladly spend endless hours in my company, finally confessed to me, "You can be very scary." Santa Claus indeed.

I directed the students to rearrange their desks into a large oval with my long table at the front of the room near the chalkboard. They did so noisily while I distributed Syllabus Plus, a bound document that ran close to eighty pages long. "We will always begin class by answering an attendance question," I announced. "You can find the question in the weekly schedule at the end of the syllabus, but I'll say it out loud too."

They remained quiet, watchful. With some groups, chaos took over at this point. "Where did you attend high school?" I asked, beginning the roll call. "And tell me now if I mispronounce your name. If you don't help me, you may end up with a completely new name."

A couple of them laughed.

Not all students came from Philadelphia, so I asked for the location of any unfamiliar schools. When a second person named West Catholic High School, I commented on it, but otherwise I mostly nodded at their answers and placed a stroke mark beside their name on the class list. I had the information about their high schools on my data sheets, but asking the question provided an easy way to get each student to say something in the first class. "Saying *anything* in class, especially in the beginning of the hour," I told shy students who came to my office, "makes it easier to say something later. I do not know why this is true, but try it, and let me know what you find."

Some students laughed nervously as I moved through the roll. "Lincoln," Jim said when I reached *James Dunn*. "I mean, I started at Judge but finished at Lincoln." As a Philadelphian, I knew that he meant Father Judge High School, a Roman Catholic diocesan school in the city, and that his one-sentence explanation might be shorthand for a complicated saga.

When brown-skinned Chelsea answered the attendance question, two other young black women to my left exchanged disapproving groans that segued into words. I looked up from my class list without making eye contact with the chatters. "I can't help you if I don't hear you, so I need you to speak clearly and one at a time. I'll try to remember that too. Okay?" In both verbal and nonverbal ways, teachers always tried to make certain things very clear on day one. From the first day on, they would hear me describe both classroom discussion and academic writing as conversational, usually a new concept and experience for them. If they learned one thing about me today, it should be that I took seriously everything we did in the classroom.

A young white man in a baseball cap and sweat suit entered the classroom while his classmates were answering the question, and when I reached the bottom of the class list, I gave the newcomer the day's materials, asked him the attendance question, and marked him present. "Everybody is looking for the right room today, so you're all fine," I told the class, "but from now on, when I finish asking the attendance question, I will put a Do Not Enter sign on the door." I held up the sign.

Most of them looked puzzled.

"I'll never start taking roll early. If you arrive while I am still taking answers, come in quietly and take your seat—like Ryan did. I will mark you present when I hear your answer. The question will usually have something to do with what you're studying, and sometimes hearing everybody's answer will take five minutes or so. But if you find the door closed and the sign posted, you cannot come in. I will mark you absent."

I saw something like horror spread across several faces—for them, our honeymoon had ended. "We can't afford distractions of any sort. We only have an hour. If you arrive after the sign goes up, you may sit silently outside the door and take notes, though you will be marked absent."

Two women in the rear had gone slack-jawed. My draconian measures, established practice in the College's Honors curriculum, risked losing some of them; however, most students quickly became grateful for the respectful climate that this created and took it seriously. I could not know for sure what students thought, but I suspected that seeing their teacher finish the roll then pause at the door to allow a breathless classmate to scamper in from the hallway before posting the Do Not Enter sign and shutting the door would suggest to them that this teacher would stick to his word on other issues as well.

"You can be dropped if you miss six or more classes," I said. "College rule."

Jim smiled wryly, as if his worst fear about teachers had just been confirmed. I told the class that since I taught the same course across the hall an hour later, they could come to that session any time they missed the 11:15.

"Would we still be marked absent if we come to the 12:20 class?" a black man in a FedEx uniform asked.

"No," I said.

Rashid looked as if he was waiting for the "but ..." clause that contained some cruel exception to this policy. It didn't come.

Ryan's eyes narrowed, perhaps suggesting that he possessed the same lackadaisical attitude toward attendance that I'd had when I started college. I had seen cuts as a personal right. Only years later, taking graduate classes in folklore at the University of Pennsylvania while also working full time as a counselor, did I grasp how each course session that I paid for constituted *my* time, a unique opportunity that I cherished, a few special hours per week that I would not allow myself to miss unless I were deathly ill. Now, each class I taught included students who shared such a sensibility, but other students resembled my seventeen-year-old self, who blithely registered for sixteen credit hours, then worked numerous weekly shifts at the A&P Supermarket, played basketball under the lights when not working, listened to Beatles and Lovin' Spoonful records with old high school buddies, or spent hours ruminating about the latest girl of my dreams. Back then I cut class anytime that I thought I could get away with it. Occasionally, in conferences or in class, these students would hear about the forces that ultimately prevented me from slipping completely off my professors' grade books. These influences tended to be social in nature—people often were at the root of both problem and solution.

"As you'll read in the syllabus and as I'll say again before the hour is over, you don't have to stay in this class if you don't want to," I said, continuing my introductory spiel. "You are welcome to try to drop and add into a different section if this class doesn't feel like the right fit for you. But if you want to do that, you will need to move on it today. You don't want to get behind in class."

Rules, rules, rules. Enough to send a shiver down the spine of a student taking any college course today, but these rules were especially relevant in a dreaded gateway course that some of these students already had taken and failed. A few students shared looks of concern. *How did I get registered in the Hotel California section of English 101? Have any of his students ever made it to 102?*

Students took turns reading aloud sections from the syllabus. The text informed them that they should think of their classmates as their fellow writers and of me as their editor, and that they might learn as much from each other and each other's writing as they would from me.

"I am a writer too," I said. "And I get help all the time, as a writer and as a teacher. For instance, I got the idea of asking a daily roll question from Vince Castronuovo, who got it from Clint Gould, both professor friends with whom I taught for a long time."

One after the other, they worked their way through the syllabus, uncovering more rules that I knew might cause discomfort. Barring medical excuses, once in the classroom, they must remain in their desks. They must not eat in the classroom. Then we got to a course practice that always puzzled and sometimes irked students. Some of them would gripe about it all semester long.

"Each major writing assignment goes through a draft and revision process. Drafts receive no grade but must be turned in on time, and likewise the final revisions. Those revisions will be returned with corrections and comments but no grade. To learn your grade, you must see me privately and walk through the paper with me. When you show me that you understand the meaning and purpose of my comments, I will ask you what grade you believe the paper received. Then I'll tell you the grade I recorded. So you'll need to spend some time with me outside of class."

They nodded, but many of them looked disturbed.

They filled in schedule grids, accounting for all of their week's anticipated activities, from sleeping to working to checking Facebook. I walked around the perimeter, stopping to study what they had produced so far. A wiry Eastern European–looking woman's grid included chunks of hours for "job" but indicated almost no time for sleep. Another's featured forty hours for watching TV. A couple of them had written finely detailed schedules, blocking off time for commuting, working jobs, attending church, chatting on the internet.

"Count the number of hours you've allotted for out-of-class academic work," I called out.

"Homework?" Jim asked.

"Papers, reading assignments," I said, nodding. I stood beside his desk, waiting for him to say something. "For the week."

"Four?" he said, as if desperately trying to guess the correct answer.

I offered him nothing. "And for you?" I said, turning without expression to Lourdes, the petite Nigerian woman whom I'd taught the previous semester. *Let the bidding begin.*

"Six," she said.

I walked halfway around the oval to the middle-aged black woman who hadn't hidden her disdain for Jim's poor manners. "Charisse?" I said.

"I've got eight," she said, hopefully.

"Hold onto these," I announced. I directed them back to the syllabus booklet and pointed out where they could find the reading and writing assignments that they must complete for the second class. I started to explain them, but I stopped before the bell rang to remind them that they could seek escape from this section if it did not feel right to them. "However," I said, "if you want to stay, show up on Friday with all the assigned work done." Glancing at my watch, I grabbed all of my materials and headed for the classroom across the hall. I could not tell what to make of this group. Each class had its own personality, always. So far, I'd seen no signs that this section would become a nightmare, but the semester was very young.

Once again, I was beginning an academic year confident that I was better equipped than I'd been the year before. As in previous years, I spent part of the summer reworking my courses in the light of recent successes and disasters, work that I enjoyed the way some people loved solving crossword puzzles. Some people end up in jobs they aren't suited for, but I couldn't imagine a job more suited to me than this. Like my favorite athletes, I played the game for love.

I'd just begun my seventy-fifth semester as a faculty member at my alma mater, but it already felt different because there was a very good chance that it could be my last. Why leave my dream job? Maybe I would stay, despite the College's offer of one year's salary as a goodbye present. For years, I'd squeezed writing into the time that the teaching life allowed, which was far more than most other jobs. But leaving my job would open up days and months for writing and for the other things Kathleen and I might do. I had to decide before the fall semester ended, so Kathleen and I had little time left to crunch numbers and wrestle with the profound questions that this decision raised.

Sometime at the beginning of the past hour, my pre-class edginess had morphed into drive, like what Roux, our Border Collie/ miniature American Eskimo dog, apparently felt every time we threw a ball in her presence. Like an athlete charging out onto the field,

I hustled toward the adjoining classroom, eager to get going again. I'd been through these opening-day emotions many times, so all of this felt familiar in a reassuring way. *But is this my last rodeo?*

As happened every first day, my voice had started to go, and I reached for one of my cough drops. "Another opening, another show," I'd cracked to a colleague on the stairway earlier. It was a joke, but it wasn't.

Spring Sabbatical,
Day One

Tuesday, April 3, 2012: Ireland

Jack McCarthy, son of the old sod and taxi driver supreme, screeched his unmarked van to a halt in front of Cottage 8 at the Cill Rialaig (pronounced Kill Rill-ig) artist retreat near Ballinskelligs, County Kerry, Ireland, one of the remotest places in Europe—my new home for the next four weeks. Though close by the fabled Ring of Kerry—the loop of roads that every year drew millions of visitors to the scenic lakes and mountains of Ireland's majestic southwest coast—hardly any travelers knew about or ventured near this craggy nook, where the sheep population vastly outnumbered the handful of year-round resident humans.

"Ah," said Jack. "The key would be hiding under a rock by the door."

"Thanks." I took in the eight humble stone buildings, wedged into a slightly wider spot than the rest of the cliff-skirting road. Across from the string of reconstructed Famine Era cottages, a red Toyota sat in a gravel lot, or "car park," as the Irish put it.

I saw no other signs of life. "Pretty deserted," I said.

"Michael's the caretaker for the village. You'll see him from time to time."

Just beyond the lot, the land dropped away, leaving a panoramic view of Ballinskelligs Bay. The wind whipped up over the cliff's lip and smacked my face.

"Best be getting inside now," confided Jack, grabbing my monstrous rolling suitcase. His gravelly voice suggested that he might easily play the role of pirate captain Long John Silver, but he'd been nothing but kind to me.

I gathered up my briefcase and two backpacks and followed Jack to the heavy wooden door, slammed open by the wind. We staggered into the cottage, dropping the luggage quickly so I could push the door closed behind Jack, who headed back to the car. A paint-splattered linoleum floor distinguished a rear studio from the clean and tidy main area. A peat-burning stove, flanked by a loveseat, created a focal point for the main floor's one large room. A peat or firewood box, a dresser, a black boom box flecked with the same paint that dotted the floor, an easel, two tables, and three straight chairs rounded out the furnishings. I had no telephone, television, or internet access.

The door slammed open again as buccaneer Jack reappeared, lugging the grocery bags from my Caherciveen shopping spree.

"Mind the wee stairs," rasped Jack, nodding toward a steep stairway, more ladder than stairs, which led to the loft at the cottage's front. Half of each stair was full-sized, the other half much smaller. The large halves alternated from left to right all the way to the loft, making clear how people negotiated these odd stairs.

I clambered to the loft. The only things that fit up there were a good-sized bed beneath a tiny window and a straight chair beside the head of the bed like a nightstand.

I picked my way back down the steep stairway and checked out the bathroom's sink, toilet, and curtain-less shower area before proceeding to the kitchen. Swinging open cupboard doors, I found pots and pans, plates and silverware, then took in an electric stove and refrigerator. The fridge, though plugged in, did not seem to operate.

"No peat," Jack called from the main room. "None at all."

I had no idea what to say, let alone what to do, about this problem. I heard Jack mumble something that sounded like "mo-bile."

Returning to the main room, I found Jack standing beside the empty fuel box.

"The peat man will come around nine," he creaked, pocketing his cell phone.

"Thank you," I said, nearly calling him Captain. "For everything." I pulled out my wallet and paid him.

He nodded. "At your service," he said. "Just ring me any time." Then he took his leave.

I was three thousand miles away from home and my life the previous semester teaching at Community College of Philadelphia. I'd always told people that teaching at a community college—my alma mater—meant that I was living the teacher's dream. I'd come here to write about that life. Settled into a little cottage in a village of artists, I was living the writer's dream.

Now, even though I was in this cottage planning to write about those months of teaching, I already sensed that *this* experience in Ireland had to find its way into the book. Every story had backstory. Even when writers think they have just begun, they probably already have reached the middle of something. Last summer, I'd started keeping a journal, knowing that I'd be writing about my fall semester during my sabbatical. The files in my computer, which sat temptingly on the loveseat, held the record of those days of teaching. Listening to sheep baaing to each other, I sat down and opened the laptop.

Every hour and every mile since the plane had landed in Shannon had brought me closer to perfect isolation and cultural difference. My adjustment hadn't been entirely smooth. The bus station's closed ticket office, the noncompliant ticket machine, the three-hour discrepancy between the online and printed bus schedules. Even procuring the proper currency had been a challenge.

"Would the bus driver make change for a fifty?" I'd asked the grim operator of the bus terminal's snack bar.

She sneered, not taking her eyes off the tabloid she had laid out on the counter.

"Would you change it?" I asked, holding out the fifty.

In that lilting but nearly incomprehensible Irish singsong that I hadn't heard since my previous trip to the Emerald Isle, she launched into a litany of her life's woes, not complying with my request until I made a purchase.

This was no time to stop keeping a journal.

I roused myself from my reverie and stood from the loveseat. I tinkered with the cottage's radio until the FM worked, but it offered few options. A classical station provided background music while I wedged sweaters, long-sleeved shirts, and jerseys into the dresser's rickety drawers, already glad that I had heeded Kathleen's advice and brought more layering possibilities than I'd thought I would ever need.

During the bus ride here, I'd thought about how college must seem foreign and foreboding to my students when they first walked into a classroom. Nontraditional community college students were the first in their families to attend college, and they entered the experience without the benefit of an appropriate sendoff. At home, they never heard talk about withdrawal dates, learning lab specialists, teachers' office hours, and so on. In my head, I started drafting an account of the day's quirky adventures, hardly the make-or-break challenges my nontraditional students faced on day one of the semester.

After unpacking, I decided to eat my first meal at my new residence alfresco, despite the window-rattling April wind. Toting a kitchen chair in one hand and a ceremonial peanut butter sandwich in the other, I stepped outside and walked toward the lot's edge that dropped in several severe steps to the sea. A rainbow rose out of the water, creating a tableau completed by the rugged islands and the waves' shimmery whitecaps. I let the enormity of it all wash over me. At seven in the evening, the defiant April sun still hovered at the vast horizon. The red car I'd seen earlier was gone. I neither heard nor saw any signs of human life. Finally, the fierce cold wind forced me to head back inside, but not before I met a threesome of visitors, two sheep and a lamb, that stopped in the road to pay their respects.

Inside, I dragged one table to the cottage's studio section and matched it up with the one already there before sitting down and opening my laptop. By eight o'clock, I had finished entering a brief description of the day's journey. The night of the transatlantic flight, the day of bus rides, the night in the Killarney hotel, and today's final legs in the trip to the cottage all blurred together in my mind. *What beginning had I expected?* Like the screeching gulls outside, and like community college freshmen, I'd landed in the middle of things.

I decided to take a walk to stretch my travel-cramped legs and capitalize on the evening's continuing light. In a watch cap and several zippered layers, I started off to the right of Cottage 8, heading further uphill. The rocky road zigzagged up and up before disappearing into the sky. You couldn't have built a road closer to the sea, but in many places it still left steep grazing land between water and the road.

Climbing slowly, I followed the twisting little barbed wire-lined road, stopping frequently to take in the view below that changed every time I turned. A few house lights twinkled far across the bay, but I neither saw nor heard a soul. Sheep, however, appeared to have no trouble finding this place. Sheep-filled hills like these covered similar swaths of Scotland, New Zealand, and other parts of the world. Farmers had spray-painted a flash of red on some of their backs, blue on others. They chorused back and forth to one another from opposite sides of the path. As I walked, I imagined an audio version of Google Earth, featuring a cacophony of sheep chatter.

"Who's that odd fellow in the cap?"

"It's steep."

"I'm shitting."

"Can you hear me now?"

I followed a ewe and her lambs, who scurried ahead each time they glanced around at me, and tried not to tailgate. After about twenty-five minutes, we reached a roadside marker: End of Route, Please Turn Around. "I take this as a sign!" I bellowed ahead to my fellow travelers, then about-faced and started back. Some other day, I told myself, I would explore beyond the sign.

After a few descending turns in the road, I glimpsed the little row of eight stone cottages below. I recalled what I'd read about Cill Rialaig and learned from Jack during the drive. "They'd gone derelict," he'd told me in a hushed voice. I pictured sheep and perhaps a buccaneer's parrot poking about the ruins.

Modernity had transformed virtually every such road along Europe's western coast, save this one. When eccentric, impulsive, and successful former fashion journalist and magazine editor Noelle Campbell-Sharp learned of plans to turn the village road into a tour bus thoroughfare along the lines of the Ring of Kerry, the Irish woman bought the "village." The gallery owner's plan was to save this tract of land, strengthen the arts in Ireland, and create a sustainable resource for the community. The practical visionary had the cottages faithfully reconstructed, numbered rock by numbered rock. Her platoon of local workers turned them into an artist colony: a cottage for meetings, a small hut for a laundry facility, and seven residences for visiting musicians, visual artists, and writers to live in, drawing inspiration from the awe-striking surroundings. And she created a gallery, café, and printmaking center down the hills in Ballinskelligs. Artists from all over the world now served residencies in the reconstructed village, often donating fresh work to Cill Rialaig Project as a witness to their stay.

Clomping down the redeemed road, I heard only the wind's whistle and sheep's calls and responses. During the whole walk, I passed just two dwellings, only one of which could possibly have inhabitants. Back at the village, other than the now-returned red Corolla, signs of human life had yet to appear. I chased away my disappointment, figuring that they must all be working away on their own projects and that we'd meet soon enough.

I wasn't alone for long. Inside Cottage 8, I sat at the computer and found my journal entry from the first day of the fall semester. I'd taught two sections of English 101, along with an Honors section that was linked in terms of schedule, content, and assignments with Vince Castronuovo's Honors Pscyh 101. I'd also taught an Honors English 102 course linked with Vince's developmental psychology course. My fall semester had introduced me to dozens of students, and I'd introduced them to questions about learning. *What had I tried to do to them?*

Study about the phenomenon of learning invites the nature versus nurture debate, and my English 101 classes focused on the nurture side. I familiarized students with content from psychology about the role that other people played—for better or worse—in one's learning. But while the 101 course—linked with Psych or not—gave *environment's* influence its due, our second-semester Honors link, with its biology-heavy content, opened the door to *heredity's* limitations. There, continuing students who'd already learned about learning's social factors found out about the biological backdrop against which the forces of nurture did their best. Many of these 102 students had already worked with me, but otherwise, my students were strangers to me. Seeing their names in my journal and on class lists brought faces and stories back to me.

Around 9:15 that evening, I heard a knock at the door and opened it to a ruddy-faced man, wearing a long coat and Wellingtons, who loomed under the light, his idling truck behind him. Ridges lined his face, exactly what I would expect on a man who spent most of his days outside in this weather.

"How much turf would you need?" he asked, sniffling.

Peat. Sod. Turf. Feeling about as confident as beginning community college students probably did when appearing for their first conference with a professor, I told him that I would be staying here for four weeks.

He nodded, tromped to the rear of his truck, then returned with a massive bag slung over his shoulder. He proceeded to lug in several more bags, setting them beside the wooden peat box. I paid him what he asked for and said goodbye. My predecessor had left behind several boxes of matches, and I had brought matchbooks collected over the years at weddings and restaurant outings; however, I lacked kindling: the cottage contained no newspapers or fire-starters to set off these hairy, wood-like chunks of sod. "My kingdom for a Sunday *Inquirer*," I muttered in my best Ricardian accent. I would have to scrounge for kindling in the morning. If somehow my students could see me here desperate to start a fire, they'd roar.

The Cill Rialaig Project acceptance letter had mentioned the presence of a convenience store located three or so miles away. Newspapers and fire-starters shot to the top of my shopping list, bringing home the reality that tomorrow demanded a hike down the hills if I ever wanted to feel warm again.

Despite the cold, I pinched myself. What would my writer friends say if they could see this small village of artists' cottages? I was surrounded by the ocean, the mountains, and beautiful solitude. I had food and a roof over my head. Except for kindling, I had everything I needed to do the work I was anxious to begin. Hell, I'd landed in Brigadoon. But a nagging restlessness sent me to the window. *Where are the others?*

Stepping outside, I saw another car at the far end of the lot, and instantly felt relief. The two cottages next to mine remained dark, but the third one down the line had lit up. I introduced myself to two women from Limerick, a choreographer and a dancer, who had stepped outside to bargain with the peat man. Their names sounded like Sinead and Shannon; I did not quite catch them.

"We're just settling in," one of them sighed, as her companion bustled off to the car. She told me that they had met the painter with the red car who lived in Cottage 2.

I wished them both a good evening, walked up to Cottage 2, and knocked on the door to introduce myself to Deirdre.

"Sorry," the slim thirty-something woman said, through a barely cracked door. "Working right now. Maybe we can take a walk together tomorrow."

Awkward. I returned to my place and planned a sequence of meals, but one by one, students that I hadn't thought about for months came to mind. In last semester's courses, experienced and inexperienced students came together, like the artists here. I'd read that many "villagers" returned to Cill Rialaig, and I had gotten the distinct impression on my ill-fated social venture that I was among such veterans. It was my turn to learn the ropes.

I turned off the downstairs lights and climbed the funny ladder to the loft. As the wind thump-thumped the outer door against its frame, I gazed out the small window above my bed. The now-black sky showed a wash of stars and enough moonlight to reveal a shadowy hint of the white-capped sea below.

Fall Semester, Week One

Wednesday, September 7, 2011: Philadelphia

Lourdes, the sweet and quiet Nigerian student who had not passed my course the previous semester, appeared in my doorway during my first office hour of the semester, as I'd requested. My office was roughly the size of the audio-visual storage closet down the hall, but today it felt anything but claustrophobic in the late summer light from the blessed window. I smiled and gestured for her to sit in the chair beside my desk. I'd passed an earlier office hour without visitors and was glad to see someone break the ice. Appointments and visits left me knowing more about my students, and usually smiling, but I could not remember Lourdes having visited during the previous semester.

"What did you want?" she asked.

"You saw on the syllabus that we're doing mostly the same assignments as last spring?"

She nodded.

"As I said in class, you're welcome to stay in the course, but I thought it was worth discussing your options."

Another nod. She looked at me with those sad eyes that I remembered.

"I am happy to work with you, if you decide you want to stay, but a fresh start often helps. I wanted to make sure you knew your options. It's your decision." I explained again that other instructors taught the course at the same time, that going into a section with a new teacher would mean different texts, new assignments, and that she might find such an arrangement more interesting.

She shook her head.

I recalled agonizing over her final grade in the spring, wishing she'd done enough quality work to earn a C but realizing that passing her would only doom her to a disaster at the next level. "The same books," I repeated.

"Oh, I didn't read all those books last semester."

"Oh." She had apparently gotten enough from the discussion to make me believe she had read them. I felt like a fool. Could I create a system that somehow would let me know if they'd read everything? What would *trying* to do such a thing say about me?

"I really need to pass now," she said.

Do you think this is about me? She must see that she needs to try a different approach?

I felt a flash of anger, but it passed. *Surely I'll think of something useful to say.* Instead, I merely nodded.

She rose from the chair. "Okay?" she said.

I felt flatfooted, inadequate. I thanked her for coming and wished her the best. "I'll be glad to go over your work with you, whether you stay in my class or not. And you probably know people in the lab who can help you a lot."

She vanished as silently as she'd arrived. No *esprit d'escalier* insight arrived once she'd left my office. Instead of savoring some sage advice that I might share with her if she did show up at Friday's class, I tasted the bitterness of my own limits and feared that she might be doing the same.

Will she settle in this time? I knew very little about her life and of the people and circumstances that might have contributed to her performance. Teachers rarely did. When I'd been a counselor, I often heard what students seldom told teachers. Such things provided the content and focus for the work counselors did with students; but as much as personal problems affected a student's performance, academics—not personal issues—provided the primary focus for the student-teacher relationship. Still, when a student felt so inclined, teachers heard plenty about nonacademic interferences.

So far, things had not gone smoothly for her, but she still saw college as the right place for her. For various reasons, all of my students did. In time, I would learn more about their skills as well as about their reasons for attending, gaining insight into how they understood the world to operate. That so many of them possessed erroneous views about the role that college could play in one's life or, indeed, about the way that college worked disturbed but did not surprise me.

I stretched out in my office chair, admiring the still-tidy desktop and listening to students scurrying to and from classes. My two neighbors in the cul-de-sac off the third-floor hallway were both teaching. Earlier I'd chatted briefly with Vince about our shared students and traded barbs with Gary, who happily observed that again laughter rang in our little alcove. In previous years, I'd taught with Gary, but this fall my semester was tethered to Vince's. Three days a week, Honors students worked with me for one hour then with Vince. They knew us as a team and seemed to enjoy learning about each of us from the other. The name Ned regularly appeared in Vince's test questions or case studies, and I had just mentioned to our shared students that Vince had completed the Labor Day mile-and-a-half Pageant Swim in deep water off Atlantic City.

Our wives referred to Vince and me as academic spouses, an accurate assessment. If the phone rang when one of us was with his actual spouse, no one wondered who was calling. During our annual shore getaways, trim, athletic, and silly Vince and I effortlessly embarrassed our wives. Like two wound-up first graders, we laughed while they groaned, and vice versa. In the surf, we were Seal and Whale. Standing in my doorway, I looked at his name on the adjacent door, grateful that I again had a teaching teammate. Faculty collaboration worked to our students' advantage. I was certain that working with him and with my other sisters and brothers of the chalk had made me better when I taught alone.

Just as I already had met almost all of the students assigned to me this semester, so too those students had gotten their first look at their teachers, taking our measure and forming first impressions. If my grasp of the stacked odds facing my students was all I had to go on, I would have found entering the classroom difficult, but I knew some other things about them and about the enterprise that we had embarked upon. They didn't know it yet, but they already had started becoming students of learning. I was about to immerse them in a new world, and over the next fifteen weeks, I planned to share with them as much as I could about it.

Among the reasons that my students found the task they faced so daunting was the way that so many of them thought about and understood the learning process. My course would force them to reconsider their understanding of the very nature of a learner. They did not register for English 101 thinking that it would involve this sort of thing. In my courses, students would read explanations of the ways people learned given by respected researchers and theorists.

Once they realized that they even had preconceptions, they would see their own preconceived assumptions, beliefs, and practices lined up against those of the experts.

A few years ago when Desmond had registered, he surely anticipated something different from what he encountered. "What ingredients add up to success in our course?" I had asked him the day we'd spoken about his attendance.

"Am I supposed to know this from the syllabus? Eighty pages. You didn't leave something important out?"

I laughed, prompting nervous laughter from him. "What behaviors help you learn?" I pushed. "What kinds of activities stop you or slow down your learning?"

"I don't study enough," he blurted, looking relieved that he'd found the appropriate confession.

"Suppose you spent eight hours every day reading and rereading, going over notes, writing and rewriting papers. Besides those activities, what in your life would be helping or hurting you as a student?"

His expression contorted. I imagined him thinking, *Balancing workloads is one thing, but where is this professor going?* "I'm sorry," he said. "I don't know what I'm supposed to say."

Learning about learning and taking a long look in the mirror that a professor held up to your face was not what he expected from college. "The things you do and the people you deal with outside of here affect your work as a student," I said. "Doing well in school can affect the rest of your life too. We're going to read about this very thing and talk about it in class." I feared that I would blather on and that he would gloss over, so I stopped and asked if that made sense.

"Yes," he said.

When he left, he seemed more settled, but maybe he simply was relieved that I'd stopped asking questions. Later, I realized that the one thing I hoped he took away from what likely felt like an unexpected interaction was the belief that together, he and I and the rest of the class could take some useful steps. So much of what he and his classmates faced involved strange and intimidating newness.

This class probably would be the first time something had forced my students to examine the nature required of a learner. Like Desmond, most of them would dislike or feel uncomfortable finding themselves in that position. I knew that the same ingrained patterns of beliefs, values, and practices that impaired so many of them also affected students at other types of colleges and universities, but more traditional college students probably had less vulnerability because they faced fewer hindrances, had greater support systems, and possessed a somewhat clearer grasp of a learner's nature. Failure and underachievement did not belong exclusively to community college students or students from society's lower economic levels though. Thousands of entering college students across the country would find failure waiting for them just around the next corner.

I had tried to help Desmond. The disappointments stung, but my optimistic side had pushed me to figure out how to best use my time with students and how they could best use their time. Teachers might try to infer the level of a student's work based on results, but they knew only so much about their students, and I believed Desmond had given his best effort. Other Desmonds might be waiting for me in this semester's classrooms, and I hoped they might accept the help that we at the College could offer.

However, I could only deal with today's opening day, the honeymoon period. Most of my students were not thinking about giving up. And even though I knew very well the odds against them, I wasn't considering it either. As on every other opening day, I entered the classroom knowing that students must acquire the unnatural discipline of productive academic behavior and that few of them would want to buy what I was selling.

I knew not to guarantee results because I understood that teaching comprised only one part of the learning equation and that what would matter most must occur on the other side of the classroom. I believed that the role teachers played in students' learning, while delicate and important, mattered far less than what went on in students' lives, much of which paved a smooth road to a failure to learn. But for fifteen weeks I got to try my best. I believed, with my friend and colleague Tom Ott, that unless my students learned, all I was doing up there was talking.

What my students tried to do mattered. Soon I would come to know these students as people, and then it would become personal. I could not help that. I had learned to see the phenomenon of entering my students' lives as a privilege. For years, students had come to my office to work on making their dreams happen. Their successes kept me coming back with optimism. I'd tried to use their failures to improve my game, and theirs.

Nontraditional students might begin college relatively unaware that they needed to learn more than course content. "It takes a while to learn the ropes," I had told Desmond. "You don't want to know how long it took me." Helping beginners was never easy, but I'd become experienced at it. Perhaps because I'd been a bad student, I took great satisfaction in helping others gain traction, since I knew how at risk they were. Every semester I got to watch fledglings figure it out.

But by necessity, something had felt different since the beginning of this first day because if I accepted the early retirement offer, it might be the last time I would ever teach. *Are you really ready to give this up?* I just wasn't sure.

Dreams moved students to take college courses, and dreams were working on me, and Kathleen too. A former preschool teacher of the Deaf, Kathleen earned her RN at Community College of Philadelphia—saying, "It was more difficult than graduate school"—while I took our second-grader Stephan to school and cared for three-year-old Anna during my first sabbatical leave in 1988. Kathleen dove into the variety of experiences that nursing offered, working first in hospital Med-Surg units then in traditional labor and delivery, evolving to birthing suite work alongside midwives. She then became a visiting nurse for hospice patients in some of the poorest sections of the city, and now cared for elderly patients in a private skilled care facility. Every day she came home from her job with an empty tank but charged off the next morning eager to return to her patients.

Shifting to a position at a nearby facility that did not require her to drive all day had enabled our daughter to use her car to drive to her graduate school classes, and Kathleen predictably became more than just a charge nurse at St. Catherine's Infirmary in Germantown, caring for aging and infirm Vincentian priests and brothers. Accepting the college's retirement offer could affect the *where* as well as the what of our own dreams. Kathleen's job flexibility and mobility had benefited our family, but my position was the one that held the bulk of our retirement funds. My retirement would topple dominoes, including Kathleen's work situation. The closeness she had developed with people at St. Catherine's became yet another connection we would lose if we moved from Philadelphia.

No one would be more affected by a move than our grown children, Stephan, age thirty, and Anna, age twenty-six. My retirement in itself would create no problems for either of them, but its financial implications for Kathleen and me were another matter. Long ago, my quarterly financial calculations and projections became monthly, then weekly. For the last seven years, working out scenarios and their costs had become something of a hobby, one that I turned to when the day's last paper had been graded or when the cleaned pots and pans and the leftovers had been put away. I had found ways to retire by taking the College's incentive, but none that involved remaining in our current home. We couldn't afford it without my full salary.

Kathleen and I saw our future being spent somewhere else, thus putting miles between us and our children. They were both fairly independent, and we knew we'd never go too long without returning to spend time with them, but a move from Philadelphia would alter their lives. They'd grown up in this house and had no other relatives in the area. Anna had moved back to her third-floor room when she'd returned from Pittsburgh to attend graduate school, but surely she would prefer her own apartment when she could afford it? Stephan was apt to pop in unannounced, but didn't he always seem eager to return to his West Philly digs? Wouldn't a gentle nudge toward even greater independence do them good?

My head spun with the possibilities, but I had time. On opening day, I didn't have to make final decisions either about my retirement or about these new students' grades for English 101; in fact, at this point, I could not make those decisions. If I had not come across as a complete jerk, almost all of the students I met today would go to the bookstore and purchase the books, an act of hope for many of them.

At this point in the semester, no one had failed yet. It was New Year's Day.

Spring Sabbatical, Day Two

Wednesday, April 4, 2012: Ireland

I rose early, nearly frozen but ready to face the first full day at Cill Rialaig. After quickly dressing in several layers, I surveyed the row of books I had arranged atop the dresser and over on the table, the notebooks filled with jotted-down ideas, and the laptop on the table, but I decided that before anything else, I had to procure kindling and fire-starters to ignite those straw-whiskered blocks of peat. And I was anxious to use the phone cards I'd bought back home so I could speak with Kathleen. The village of Ballinskelligs sat several miles down the twisty road that Jack had driven me up the evening before, a good hike down and a steady climb back.

Intermittent rain accompanied me on my downhill trek. The clouds swirling above made the view of the bay only more scenic. When I reached the bay, I stopped at Susie's Café to check e-mail and warm up with a cup of tea. Not so much a café as a snack bar with displays of postcards and vintage photos of the region, Susie's offered three or four small tables inside, as well as a few outside for the truly hardy.

I picked a table next to the only other customer, a young woman with a laptop who I realized was Deirdre. She seemed agreeable enough now, but I was not about to interrupt her again. Opening my laptop, I quickly got online. I read then replied to Kathleen's most recent message then started scanning through the other e-mails.

"Excuse me." Deirdre had risen and was standing beside my table. "If you're near ready to head back, I'd be happy to run you up the hill."

According to my map I had miles to go before I could head back: a one-mile walk to the Cill Rialaig Project gallery then a longer walk to the convenience store. "That's a great offer," I said, "but I've got to find out about the bus that goes to Caherciveen and I have a few other stops yet."

"Suit yourself," she said, smiling. I couldn't imagine an American using that expression in cheeriness, but she seemed entirely genuine.

When she'd left, Susie called out to me. "The market day bus to Caherciveen stops at the post office up the road. Mary there will tell you when you need to turn out to catch it. Friday, you know."

"Thanks," I called back. Good to know, but I could not wait several more days for a fire. "I don't see a pay phone," I said, rising to leave.

"You might find one at the post office," she said, pouring tea for a young couple that had joined us. "Try the pub as well. Cable O'Leary's."

"Right."

"Just down the road," she added, pointing in the direction I'd been headed.

"Down the road" seemed like the operative phrase here.

When I reached the post office, it was closed for lunch. A passerby informed me that there was no phone there anyway. After I reached the gallery, I introduced myself to the staff and to Noelle, the red-haired dynamo behind the whole Cill Rialaig Project. They got nowhere trying to use my international phone cards. Because of Good Friday, the weekly Caherciveen market bus would make its run tomorrow, Thursday; this looked like my best option. I explored the gallery a bit and ate lunch there, sitting as close as I could get to the tantalizing peat fire burning in the hearth.

Leaving the gallery, I pressed on in the suddenly colder air to the inconvenient convenience store. If not an Irish rover, I was at least a rover in far-away Ireland. I smiled at the thought of my students' reaction to their teacher tramping through the foggy dew. *You mean he does something besides think up assignments for us?* At the equivalent point in their semester, students acquired textbooks, pens, and notebooks; I was acquiring fire-starters and the thickest newspapers I could find.

When I reached the village pub, no cars sat in its lot, but I stopped in. Finding no phone in the empty entrance area, I headed to the bar at the rear of the large building. Two ancient souls sat under equally ancient tweed caps at the bar. I saw no sign of workers or other patrons.

The space between the bar and the back wall of windows that looked out onto the bay could accommodate quite a crowd. What a place for a gig, I thought, picturing the Sacred CowBoys, the New Orleans–style roots rock band I'd played with for decades, setting up at the end of the room. We rarely ventured beyond the friendly confines of our favorite bar, so I knew this was a pipe dream. I headed back to the pair at the bar.

"Hello," I called.

They nodded without comment then returned to their pints.

"Is there a pay phone here by any chance?"

They seemed to mull that over for a bit. "I don't think so," said the man closer to me. His strained facial expression indicated that this might have been the trickiest question he'd fielded all day.

I heard no sounds to suggest that staff might be in the back, moving boxes of potato crisps or napkins. "Bartender?" I said.

They shrugged their shoulders. Perhaps the barman and the postal worker were out on a nature hike together.

The first man turned toward me again. "I think the owner removed the pay phone some time ago."

"Thanks, " I said, and resumed my chilly walk.

Five hours after departing the cottage, I returned and opened the door, cold but sweating, sure that I'd read somewhere that a well-preserved pay phone had been discovered in a Donegal peat bog alongside the remains of a mastodon. I had not spoken with Kathleen, but soon I would have fire! I studied the stove manual that I found in a kitchen drawer. The only kindling that I could forage consisted of dead straw-like plant stems from behind the cottage, which I broke off and stacked in the stove on top of a few crumpled sheets of the newspaper's Gaelic language section. I lit the fire-starter. *Voila*. After monitoring the gorgeous little fire for five minutes, I felt confident enough to head to the kitchen to sauté chicken legs and boil carrots and potatoes.

Once the vegetables had started cooking, I popped back into the living space only to find my fire had gone out. "Damn!" I shouted at the still, black remains in the silent stove. "Okay," I muttered, "I see what you're doing here. Divide and conquer?" I stormed off to the kitchen and turned off the burners, the need for heat trumping my hunger. I crumpled a section of the newspaper then wedged it along with fresh fire-starters and the last of the scavenged brush into the cursed stove. This time, I went for a small but steady fire. I coaxed the little flames, prayed over them, threatened them. An hour later, I returned to the kitchen, with a reliable fire burning steadily in the stove.

After dinner, I stared at my computer screen, bleary-eyed after two hours of writing about the previous fall. I scrolled back to the beginning of the file and discovered to my dismay that I had completed only one page. As I started reading it, I immediately began deleting and changing words. "Sweet Jesus," I groaned, trying to stifle my inner editor and just read to the end of what I had typed without touching the keyboard.

It was crap and must be crap because all first drafts are crap, but writers must endure producing such crap to give them something stationary that they can tinker with as they try to figure out exactly what they want to say. Intending to write about last fall, I ended up mostly writing about the previous twenty-four hours instead. Thinking about my new physical and social surroundings now sent my mind back to the previous fall's events. I slid my laptop to the side and started scribbling in my frayed notebook, and before I knew it, I'd filled two pages. Writers' reasons for preferring to draft in longhand or on the computer or while smoking cigarettes or while not smoking cigarettes were no more logical than the reasons that baseball players offered for their batting or pitching rituals. I gladly switched one superstition for another as long as one appeared to work.

Creating a first draft was always a problem, but for me it was a familiar one. Gazing at the steady fire in the little stove, I recognized that when I'd faced the writing problem I had mustered greater patience than when I'd furiously sought to set fire to blocks of peat or had gone in search of a pay phone. The challenges and frustrations of writing had to feel screamingly alien and unwelcome to my students.

Despite shutter-shaking wind outside, the cottage was warm. I had food and a comfortable bed, and I hadn't yet hit my head on the loft's low ceiling. My laptop computer knew all of my favorite songs and remembered everything I typed. In daylight, the studio's glass roof let me watch sheep pick their way across the steep rise directly behind the cottage. At night, when I turned off the lights, stars splayed across the black sky above me.

Sure, I lacked internet access and, for the moment, a phone that would connect me with Kathleen, but I was living the writer's dream. I was physically isolated, yet writing about classroom life somehow kept me connected to the social experience of teaching. These cottage-bound rewards tasted different than those I'd appreciated throughout decades of teaching, and holing up here with notebooks and journals was like discovering a new flavor of ice cream. This reminded me of a text that my students used near the end of every semester when we explored positive psychology, the relatively new subfield that measured and studied happiness or well-being in its various forms and that explored the question of meaning and happiness in life.

Ice cream connotes happiness for most people, but the journal article coauthored by University of Pennsylvania's Martin Seligman, a psychologist, uses it to make a point about kinds of happiness and how people worked to achieve it. Sitting back from the worktable, I thought about how students' goals, no matter how practical they believe them to be, transcend the purely mundane.

Students with what one might call an instrumental approach to learning—seeing education solely as a means to an end, as the instrument they would use to obtain goals like a good-paying job that would net them a nice house and creature comforts—follow what Seligman calls the first or most basic route to happiness. Its goal is pleasure or positive affect. I raised my level of this kind of happiness every time I grabbed an ice cream cone at Penn State's Creamery or a crisp Belgian ale at McMenamin's Tavern in Mount Airy. But it isn't all taste bud–driven. Research shows that nurturing the sense of forgiveness or gratitude also can affect one's positive emotion about the past. [1]

Gratification, the second route to happiness, involves and requires engagement, more than the fairly passive involvement of imbibing a snack or beverage.[2] Simply put, this means it takes work. In discussions with students, I paraphrased a definition of work I'd learned early in my career: Work is conscious effort aimed at producing good for oneself or others.[3] In other words, work turns out to be most of what we do when we're not sleeping, eating, or very passively relaxing. Fixing a flat or painting a portrait or a bathroom wall might not be my job, but when I do those things, I'm doing work. These kinds of activities might not always feel good at the time, much like training for a marathon. They require use of character strengths. And there are no shortcuts on this route to happiness—these are activities in which we get lost in time and forget about everything else around us.[4]

I'd gotten the first kind of happiness from eating dinner and the second kind from preparing it. Now banging on the keyboard was giving me more of the second kind. I'd gotten that from teaching too—some days more than others, of course. But teaching also had the potential to provide the third kind of happiness: meaning and purpose. This kind also entails use of character strengths but with one critical difference: it involves using personal skills in service to people, ideals, or our idea of God—in other words, to something greater than ourselves.[5]

"I envy you," one of my more well-to-do neighbors told me once. He volunteered in his spare time, going out of his way to find meaning as a balance to a successful and lucrative career that left him short in one area that he obviously believed to be important. "Your work is so meaningful," he gushed.

"I got meaning and purpose out the wazoo," I replied.

He looked confused. Was I joking? Yes. And no. So many college teachers unblessed by the secure kind of position that I'd had since my first day on the job might have hit the guy.

Highly educated people run colleges and universities. They tend to project the image of being on the cutting edge in terms of social justice and human decency, yet they pay equally well-educated and accomplished teachers in a very inconsistent way. Only a small percentage of their instructors receive a good salary. Thousands of other adjuncts—often no different in their qualifications, experience, and talent—teach a course at one college and two more across town, patching together a life fraught with meaning but short on adequate and rewarding financial compensation. Yes, it was their decision to go into (and continue) teaching, knowing the scarcity of secure full-time positions. Yes, colleges have to do what they must to stay afloat. But at major universities, administrators look aghast as tuition costs rise at a level that far exceeds other kinds of inflation, all while apparently believing that a larger football stadium or a better basketball coach is just the ticket for making a university more efficient and more appealing. Surely we can come up with a way to run colleges that pays teachers more equitably.

I sat before my computer screen, wrestling with the jumble of ideas that came to me. For all this field's inconsistencies and imperfections, I'd been blessed to work in it. I'd had years of gratification, meaning, and plain old satisfaction. I recalled hearing a friend say, "If it's fun then it's not work." I still thought it was work, but work doesn't have to be a dirty word. People were at the heart of the worst experiences I'd had as a teacher, but they also provided the main reasons I'd gone back every semester with hope and passion. No matter how long I'd taught, that perfect semester never came around. But I'd also walked away from every semester believing that I'd gotten better at teaching, that I'd helped people, and that I probably couldn't find a better way to use my strengths—in short, believing that I'd been doing the stuff of my vocation.

I closed my laptop, flicked off the lights, and let my eyes take in the world of sky above me. I sat as still as I could and evened my breathing. I squinted—*Shadow? Cloud?*—then shifted slowly to one side. Blurry shadows parted, leaving blackness and one, two, then three small lights. Stars became brighter and bolder by the minute. I sat there and breathed them in.

I wondered what my French Canadian mother, Hélene, would have made of this place. She'd dreamed of traveling to England, loved the Royal Family, and considered Winston Churchill as great a hero as Franklin Roosevelt and John F. Kennedy. When her cancer went into remission the year she died, I'd asked her if Kathleen and I could arrange such a trip for the three of us, but she smiled and said no. It was okay. It wasn't the right time.

She comfortably managed being both an Anglophone and a Francophone. Growing up a Canadian citizen, she had been proud to think of herself as a British subject, and she was equally proud of her French heritage and her American citizenship. "So lucky," she'd crow. "What do you say, grand slam?" She had not lived among Irish people until she came to Philadelphia. Her awareness of Ireland came from her coffee shop coworkers, whose pride in all things Irish came as something of a surprise. That was all nice, but England had the Queen. She shared with the Irish American waitresses her belief that President Kennedy could do no wrong.

"If I could write," she used to say, "I'd write a whole book." She would have loved the idea that her son was across the ocean, writing a whole book in a cottage. Captured in an old photograph was an elegant, determined, and pleased-looking young woman, standing on the hills above the wide Saint Lawrence River, but I pictured her here, the Hélene from the forties, in her navy blue beret, billowing scarf, and long coat, walking on these winding hilly roads, looking like a character right out of *The Quiet Man*.

The next morning, I huffed back down the hill to the Ballinskelligs post office in time to catch the weekly market bus to Caherciveen, sixteen kilometers away. By noon, I ought to have a damn phone. I hoped.

I had arrived in this wild southwestern part of the Emerald Isle fully anticipating its inconsistent public transportation, but I had not prepared myself for a route that operated only once a week. I hopped into the long van, a fourteen-passenger affair, and sat behind the only other passenger, a man seated beside the driver, the two engaged in lively conversation. Down the road, the bus stopped to take on a woman clutching shopping bags. She settled behind me, and the van scooted down a road that seemed far too narrow for two-way traffic.

The male chatter from the front continued unabated as the bus jounced past fields of grazing cattle and sheep. We turned onto an even narrower road. Suddenly, the driver stopped at the end of long driveway. He swung the vehicle's nose out into the road then reversed all the way up the farm's driveway, stopping where the driveway met a path to the farmhouse. The driver and his friend continued chatting as the engine ran. Five minutes later, the driver finally said, "She might not be interested in the market today."

"Well, so," his friend said. The van pulled back onto the road. When we reached Caherciveen, the driver pointed out the pub entrance where he would pick up passengers at 2:30 for the only return trip before next Friday.

A sign posted in the phone store's window stated that the place should have opened two hours before I arrived, but the door was locked and the inside was dark. I quickly checked my e-mail in a tech store up the street. The clerk would gladly sell me a phone, but the store did not carry the SIM card it needed. That, the clerk informed me, I could buy at the phone store. I walked the main street, retrieved some cash from an ATM, then headed back to the phone store, which remained dark. Eating lunch in a quiet pub, I wondered if perhaps enough time had passed for the phone store staff to arrive, but after lunch, I found out that it hadn't. I had delayed grocery shopping until near the time that the van would depart, but now time had grown short. Racing my little shopping cart up and down the store's aisles, I prioritized based on need, weight, and, most importantly, the steepness of the hill I must climb after the bus ride.

A grinning woman waved wildly at me from the bread section. Deirdre bounded down the aisle. When she offered me a lift all the way home, my shopping list expanded, and my pace quickened.

In the car, Deirdre asked me about my teaching. I ran through the kinds of American colleges.

"Community college?" she asked.

I stammered through an explanation but suspected that I was not doing the task justice. "Many Americans are in the dark about community colleges too," I said. I found myself talking about something that had been on my mind since I'd arrived. "They're a place where people can discover their calling, and take steps towards doing that work." *Am I making any sense?* "Not just talk about it," I added.

She seemed to consider that for a moment. "And walk the walk," she said. She'd said it better than I could have.

Did I teach the kind of writing I was doing at the village? Sometimes, but mostly I taught academic writing.

"What's the biggest challenge your students face?"

I talked a bit about the skill level demanded in college writing compared to the competence that many entering students brought with them. "And so many of my students don't know the rules of the game, so to speak—nuts and bolts things like how to format an essay or how to express yourself to a professor in an e-mail. But other things too, like how they're not alone, that other people contribute to or interfere with their progress, that they can make good use of people around them."

"I had a hard time with writing in university, even though I had a good background," she said. "We're all used to talking all the time, but writing is a whole different animal."

"In a way, most writing's conversational, but academic writing especially," I said. "Students often think they're writing to me out of the blue, unconnected to anything that's been said or written about the subject. It's a one-time command performance."

She nodded.

"Are you on Facebook?" I asked.

"Of course."

"Well, all of my students are, and my daughter is," I said, sure that she had just taken me for the ancient dolt that I was. "You *Like* things," I went on. "That's what they do on essays. You get lots of opinions."

"And that's not good?"

I hoped my attempts writing about the subject during the rest of my stay would prove clearer than I sounded now. "Depends on the task. Most academic writing is in response to what's already been put out there, not just personal opinion."

"It's part of something."

"Yes." I pictured my students pausing in the midst of texting or Facebooking to do the academic equivalent of Liking something that an author had said, devoting as much critical thinking to the task as they would to Liking a friend's recently posted photograph of her kitten. I explained why I was half smiling and half frowning.

"I don't imagine they warm up to being told that they're missing the point."

"No one likes that," I said.

"No one *Likes* that," she laughed. "Why do they write that way?"

"It goes on in high school—secondary school. It's a big change for them." Thinking about what she'd said, I laughed again. "You made me think of something that would be good to share with students," I said. "The whole *Liking* example."

"It might help them understand what you're trying to get across."

I appreciated her interest in my work, but I wanted to move the conversation away from my teaching, so I asked her about her artwork. I followed most of what she said but suddenly wished I knew more about painting.

When we reached the village, I thanked her for the lift. I wanted to let her know that conversational moments like her joke were the kind of things that had helped me learn how to improve as a teacher, but I feared that might be a bit much to put on her, that it was almost too intimate a thing to say. I headed back to Cottage 8 feeling gratitude to the woman who'd shown her own level of dedication the night I'd arrived.

Back in my little kitchen, the conversation continued in my head, much the way that drafted scenes followed fiction writers even when they were away from their desks. Many first-year students began with their feet already pointed toward independence and success—but this did not describe most nontraditional students. Serving a population that did not fit such a profile was a large part of the community college mission. Because professors at more selective schools saw comparatively few such students, they likely saw college as a freshman's expected continuation of normal growth, not as an epic foray through unknown parts in the hope of reaching a better but somewhat vaguely understood destination. But I hadn't thought of this during the ride from Caherciveen. Arranging my groceries in the refrigerator and the kitchen cupboard, I wished my brain's shelves were as easily accessed.

I realized that an ambitious hike down the hills still separated me from having internet access, but at least I now had more food stashed in the cottage. I thought about the day's journey. Nothing fazed that bus driver. No sign announced the phone shop's closing, its darkness apparently sign enough. I lived in the midst of a new normal, like community college students on the first day of their first semester. I tried to reorient myself where I'd left off in my writing the night before, but the lunchtime pint had its way with me, and I nodded off.

A knock at the door startled me awake. Noelle had brought a writer friend up to the village and wanted to introduce her to me, the only writer in residence this week. Besides writing, her friend told me that she organized writing events, tended to her five children, and taught English. "I don't have time to make my own water," she chirped. We laughed about food, family, and writing until the woman calculated that her baby's full nappy needed replacement right about now, so my first human guests left before I'd gotten enough of the conversation. She'd be a great neighbor in the village. Perhaps another writer would move in during my stay.

Returning to my laptop, I tried to immerse myself in the manuscript but kept marveling about the Irish writer's unflappable attitude. Her way of seeing things enabled her to do a great many things in her busy life. *Does she ever lose focus?* Compared to her, I felt like a wastrel. And my students? No single way of seeing things characterized them, but decades of working with students had familiarized me with predictable student moves, of both the mental and behavioral sort.

Past experience gave students certain expectations. Their view of the roles of teachers and students most likely differed greatly from teachers' views of those roles. Soon after a semester began, those expectations, which concerned matters both large and small, came into play. They often concerned matters of time.

Students and teachers saw attendance very differently. The previous spring, Desmond had missed the semester's first five Fridays until he changed jobs. "I made sure I got to those Mondays and Wednesdays," he boasted in my office.

Imagine if you were paying someone to work on your house or car, and they proudly announced that they were only taking breaks for one out of every three hours on the job. I froze, not sure if I wanted to shove smelling salts under his nose or just scream.

"You look like you just saw a ghost," he exclaimed.

"Not yet!" I snapped. "But you might become one before you know it."

My own experience from both sides of the classroom had shown me that students needed very little time to head themselves in the wrong direction. Because college instructors tended to present the course's content in logical order, with one point fundamental to understanding the next, students who missed just one step rendered their ability to grasp the next point in the sequence difficult, if not downright mystifying. The damage they incurred by missing a class went beyond the specific gap in the process and into future class sessions, which they would find less clear and useful even if they did the outside assignments and remained alert and focused when they did attend class.

Desmond didn't realize how he had limited himself through his repeated absences. This guy's sincerity was endearing enough that

I smiled even as steam rose from my ears. He was alert and ambitious, but I saw that I had overestimated his capacity for being a student. His potential was undeniable, but like so many community college students, he desperately needed to develop a more realistic understanding of how this whole learning thing worked. For a student, being physically and emotionally present in the classroom was as basic as eating and drinking were to an animal's survival.

Maybe students with quick minds and extensive background knowledge could tolerate missing certain process steps in a semester's development, but Desmond, like many college students—especially community college students—hardly fit this description and could not afford to miss any steps. To his credit, Desmond upped his attendance game, but his papers reflected his limited exposure to the work.

I remembered *A Hope in the Unseen*, Ron Suskind's story of Cedric Jennings, a scholarship-winning graduate of one of the worst high schools in Washington, DC. Cedric had taken advantage of every educational experience that came his way; however, he discovered one month into his first college semester that his freshman classmates at Brown University had experienced a very different set of educational opportunities. Somehow and somewhere, they had gained enough knowledge to allow them to snooze through class or merely skim texts without falling behind, leaving Cedric feeling like a stranger in their mysterious land. [6]

Most community college students arrived with less academic background and far shakier work habits than Cedric Jennings had. Though they didn't find themselves alone in a sea of classmates with deep stores of academic and intellectual background, most community college students also had to meet challenging levels of performance and could ill afford to hurt their chances with spotty exposure to new information. Missing class or assignments came with as high a price as did missing a day's work at their job. Desmond was living proof.

As a student, I'd been as self-destructive, despite having been blessed with twelve years of education at good schools, unlike many of my students. Maturity might be the short answer for my own change—my mother's death and the birth of my children probably had more to do with my growth into a more responsible and engaged person than anything else. Teachers tried to create situations that caused the same effect, minus the mourning and the diapers.

Declaring another break, I ate the previous night's leftovers. Few things connoted home more than a meal cooked once and enjoyed twice, so this was surely a sign I was acclimating to this little cottage. I started the night's fire, then scrolled back to the previous night's last paragraph. Rereading the passage, I thought about the day in Killarney, when the incorrect online bus schedule left me with a nearly three-hour wait. While enjoying lunch, I had started seeing connections between ideas that I had not seen before, slightly more surprised than pleased at this revelation. The night before that, faced with a menu that featured nothing that my dietary restrictions allowed me to eat, I'd walked across the street and discovered a great place for mussels. Patience, not always my first impulse or practice, had served me well these last few days. By not following first impulses, I discovered things that might not have come about otherwise. I now saw what an extraordinary gift I had received: a month in this cottage. I would open it with care.

Fall Semester, Week One

Friday, September 9, 2011: Philadelphia

Classes began at eight. At seven o'clock on the second day of class, the hallway outside our little complex of three offices was still quiet. Indulging an urge, I lifted my feet on the top of the desk, sharing the space with neat stacks of materials for the morning's classes. Sometimes it was hard to remember whether I'd left a certain book here or in the tiny converted bedroom at home that I used as an office. "His other place," Kathleen called it.

Philadelphia being one massive small town, sometimes friends or acquaintances from the rest of life found their way here. Once, when someone had burglarized our three offices, I returned from class to find an Irish-born detective with whom I'd played rugby dusting my office door for fingerprints.

Few faculty offices had windows to the outside world, but I had a view of city traffic sputtering and honking its way up and down Spring Garden Street. I had a gargoyle, I told people—a grimacing creature perched on the ledge outside my window that some of my students probably found appropriate. Like the hallways' Italian white marble, the gargoyle was a remnant of the building's origins as home of the US Mint, built at the end of the nineteenth century. The College, originally housed in what had been Snellenburg's Department Store on South 11ᵗʰ Street in Center City (where my mother had once shopped), had relocated to the Spring Garden Street site in 1983, where new buildings had been constructed as extensions from two ends of the original Mint. The College had welcomed 700 full-time and 500 part-time students when it first opened, and now served well over 30,000 students from every corner of the city and offered over seventy degree and certificate programs.

"I grew up at CCP," I told people, then explained that I didn't mean my time as a student. The day after receiving my MA in counseling in Washington, DC, in 1974, I began working with CCP's program serving Deaf students. I was twenty-five and had been away from the College only six years, during which I'd finished my undergraduate degree at Temple, taught for two years at the Pennsylvania School for the Deaf, then spent two years in graduate school at Gallaudet College (now University), the liberal arts college for the Deaf that offered graduate programs for hearing as well as Deaf students.

Our state-of-the-art campus bore no resemblance to the eight-story department store building that we called Snellenburg U as undergraduates in 1966. A bank of elevators lined the far wall, but dominating the open space was the longest escalator I'd ever seen. It rose past the mezzanine with its warren of dimly lit, poster-covered English Department offices: D.H. Lawrence, Virginia Woolf, and the Jim Kweskin Jug Band. Offices occupied the top floor, but floors two through seven housed classrooms and laboratories, along with faculty offices.

It was tough squeezing a college into a tight space. The baseball team practiced in the enormous basement. Small groups of black students regularly sang doo-wop at the bottom of one of the stairwells—*You are my angel*—while their white counterparts used another such echo chamber—*From heaven above.* These groups harmonized, oblivious to my passing, but something stirred in me when I heard the magic in those stairwells. *I need your love.* It would be years before I had the guts and the occasion to try something like that myself. But that campus was where I first heard live bluegrass music and jazz, in particular the jazz bagpipe music of Rufus Harley, whom I recognized a week later when he was shopping in the A&P Supermarket where I worked part time.

Initially, open corners on the College's classroom floors were designated as student lounges. As the College grew and space became scarce, these spartanly outfitted nooks were converted into much-needed faculty offices. Two pinochle-playing friends invited me to join them and some friends in one of the second floor's windowless corner lounges between classes. I never played cards, but the future Lutheran minister and public high school teacher became my long-term friends.

When we found fresh drywall sealing off our hangout, we relocated to the last open corner on the second floor. More construction sent us packing to a corner of the fifth floor. Finally, when we discovered that the battered couches and coffee tables in the lounge had been removed and more construction begun, several members of The Second Floor Lounge Twice Removed, myself included, punched a hole in the condemned wall and scrawled angry epithets—and our first names on the walls. When hauled before the dean, we dodged drastic punitive action by agreeing to usher and serve lemonade at college functions for our final semester.

Six years later in 1974, my first CCP job interview took place with disabilities services director Aram Terzian, whose office was in the space we'd trashed. At the end of the hiring process, I met with the dean. Paul Sherwood slid a file of instantly familiar disciplinary paperwork across the table: photographs of the hole in the wall, our written apology and plea for adequate space for students to gather, the pledge to "volunteer" our services, my signature at the top of the other names. "How've you been?" he said, with a straight face.

"Great, Dr. Sherwood. I keep coming back to this place."

He gave me a half-smile.

The Spring Garden Street campus offered plenty of recreational and study space for students, though faculty office space still seemed to be at a premium. Like the original campus, the new one, 1.4 miles to the northwest, could be accessed by public transportation and likewise sat near historical and cultural sites. Over the years, the college campus had become a kind of home away from home, a place with its own personality, and the little office on the third floor was my teacher cave.

I loved my teaching life, with its intense semesters broken up by summers spent retooling courses, writing fiction, splitting firewood, and painting the neediest section of the house. But for nigh on a decade, I had cast my eyes down the line toward my eventual retirement. *A wide-open schedule in which I might work those scribblings into a book or two?* Downsized digs in a less pricey area with a smaller mortgage could spring us to a new adventure. We'd lived the urban experience since marriage; retirement could mean creating a new home in a very non-urban nook, like the ones that drew us every summer. The possibilities excited us. I regularly hit the internet in search of safe havens where Kathleen and I might settle.

Some of these places were in the region, but the ones that most appealed to us lay hours and hundreds of miles to the north: Kathleen and I wanted out of the Philadelphia summer heat and humidity. We loved our two grown children, our jobs, our neighborhood, and our friends, but something like the drive of students who registered for courses at the College worked on Kathleen and me. We too sought something different for the next stage of our lives. As our old friend Michael said, we were all getting closer to taking "the big dirt nap." So the search continued, along with the attendant financial calculations.

Almost daily in the summer of 2011, I had hunched over pages of financial calculations about real estate listings, imagining what life away from McCallum Street might look like—"scheming" I called it. In late July, Kathleen and I took a weeklong break from work and scheming. Perched on the ocean-view porch at our favorite hideaway on the coast of Maine, we read books, ate lobster, and watched the surf crash against the Bailey Island rocks. Occasionally though, I slipped away to meet with realtors, and on a rainy day, we drove to Portland, where we learned that those cute homes near the water were way out of our price range.

Back home, I continued my end-of-summer blitz through teaching materials and real estate sites. Sometime after our vacation, I'd broadened my research to include condos on the coast, and nearing the last weekend before the beginning of the semester, I proposed a fact-finding trip to Kathleen. She had the weekend off and two extra days to boot because of a previous holiday.

"That's nuts," she snorted, but the twinkle in her eyes said something else.

With Hurricane Irene blasting north across the Mason–Dixon Line, we pulled out of the driveway at 4:40 a.m. By the time the hurricane set its course straight north, slicing like God's own sword through Vermont and New Hampshire, we had already safely made it to Maine.

Even in the rain, Camden seemed perfect. We'd been there before and remembered the main street winding down past the town green and a string of shops and restaurants before it headed uphill again to the library and its view of the schooner-filled harbor below. The condo development sat within walking distance of the harbor, bookstores, post office, restaurants, drug store, banks, everything. Two minutes into our condo visit, I was pretty sure I didn't need to see any other places. A wall of windows. Skylights. All new appliances. A short walk to shops, the library, and the picturesque harbor. I knew from Kathleen's avoidance of my eyes that she was likewise smitten.

Over bowls of mussels and pints of Allagash White in Cappy's Chowder House, we gushed without restraint.

"This could be our neighborhood restaurant!" Kathleen exclaimed.

We drove home anxious to run numbers and face the cosmic question: did we really want to do this? By the New Hampshire line, we'd decided that we were dealing with a good problem, what psychologists called an approach-approach conflict. "Yeah," Kathleen said, "it's just that *conflict* part that I don't like."

By the time we reached Connecticut, the radio remained silent and we realized that mostly we'd been talking about Maine. "We don't have to know today," I said, "and we can cover a lot of points between here and Philly."

It was time to go to class. I was used to changing mental channels, shifting between thoughts about the immediate future and a more distant one. Kathleen and I had talked about the early retirement option for years. We'd been serious about this dream from the start, but the trip to Maine made the issue a lot less theoretical. I glanced at my watch then picked up my pace. This class hour was coming, ready or not. I'd signed on for early retirement months ago, but the date by which I could cancel was drawing closer.

Ready or not, that decision was coming too.

Spring Sabbatical, Day Four

Friday, April 6, 2012: Ireland

My first week at Cill Rialaig had begun three evenings ago on Tuesday, a night of many discoveries. Lingering daylight, the mysteries of peat, a cold shower. By now, I had discovered the little wall switch in the bathroom that controlled the shower's hot water. I also had gotten the refrigerator to function, so at last, all controls in the cottage had revealed their secrets. Like new community college students making sense of academic customs, I learned it bit by painful bit.

I woke up Friday morning with no illusions that I was back in Philadelphia. Ambient noise in the village was decidedly non-urban. The occasional cry of a gull pierced whatever quiet the sheep allowed. Descending the loft ladder, I felt sure that my ears were differentiating between at least five sheep of varying ages and sizes.

After breakfast, I went through the second version of chapter one again, the notes I'd brought, and the list of topics and questions I'd made since arriving. As my eyes locked on the top item on the list—time—an engine roar right out of the Indianapolis Speedway jolted me away from my laptop screen. I hustled to the door and glimpsed a small green truck rattling past the cottage and up the barren hill. Before its trailing cloud of dust and gravel settled, a grizzled Border Collie galloped behind it. Some dogs cared not a whit about other animals or people but couldn't make it through a day without pursuing a fast-moving vehicle. Our two rescue dogs back home, each part Border Collie, held full family membership rights, and the sighting on the dusty road brought on a quick pang of homesickness. Heading back inside, I wrote on until it was time to stop for more fuel.

When I'd finished lunch, I stuck my nose outside the cottage to catch the air. I creaked across the gravel road to the parking lot, the area's edge flat ground that suddenly gave way to sharply descending levels on which a few plucky sheep grazed. There I scanned the distant green heights beyond Balinskelligs Bay. Not a single boat dotted the choppy blue water below. A gust of wind shifted me in my place.

Turning back, I glimpsed a thin man of at least my own age walking deliberately up the road toward my end of the line of cottages. He wore a tweed cap and loose-fitting clothing. A poet? Filmmaker? "Hi," I called. Slight movement in the muscles around his mouth convinced me that he had replied in good spirit. "Brisk," I said, approaching him.

Stopping, he looked at me and mellifluously spoke for several seconds in what sounded more like English than anything else. My bafflement must have been apparent because he regarded me the way people do who suddenly realize that you do not speak their language. I froze, grasping that we were sharing a moment, though not through a common language. He mimed what I took to be painting motion. "You're a *painter!*" I exclaimed.

He laughed and shook his head, no. "You?"

"No, I write."

He spoke his name, prompting me to do the same. Thinking

myself denser by the moment, I put together that Michael was the custodian for the little village.

"American?" he said.

I nodded. Next I learned that he had a cousin in Chicago. I explained the distances that separated Chicago, Boston, and Philadelphia.

In the next few minutes, I picked out more and more English in the rolling, lilting cadence of his speech. It reminded me of the many times in childhood that I'd been vaguely surprised to hear people comment on my mother's French Canadian accent. To me, it was just Mom, speaking English her way. Maybe I would have noticed her speech if she suddenly broke out in nasal South Phillyese.

When I returned to work, writing about time and its challenges for students, I periodically heard Michael's footsteps or glimpsed him through the window, going on with his tasks in the same methodical and seemingly effortless way that he spoke. The gentle man outside seemed to have found his pace and was sticking to it—a skill I'd found my students often struggling to master.

Again and again, time proved to be an unfair match for students, and even talent coupled with commitment were not enough once time gained the upper hand. It happened every semester, but about five springs ago, when only thirty percent of our students finished with grades of C or better, Vince and I were flummoxed. Remembering what we could, we saw that issues with time either directly or indirectly impacted the experiences of those students. "So, what's the most determining factor in student success or failure?" I asked Vince.

"Time on task," Vince replied. "That's what the research shows."

"It's the fuel students run on," I said, "and their lives steal it every time they turn around."

Vince and I had previously cowritten several articles that served as both psychology texts and as prompts for writing assignments, and that day I'd gone home and begun drafting "It's About Time," which would become the fifth such article included in the ever-burgeoning syllabus booklet. Getting students to consider the time challenges after the semester had begun might already be too late, but our piece shot to the front of our collection of articles that became part of the huge syllabus.

Sitting in the cottage, I recalled reading Malcolm Gladwell's *Outliers*, a gift from former student Kehinde. Many readers celebrated the book for its unmasking of odd kinds of advantage, but to me its greatest value lay in reminding the reader of the role that individuals must play in their own story in order to find success. Gladwell recounts that early in the Beatles' career, the band performed for five to eight hours, day after day, in Hamburg. This intense immersion taught them how to perform, and he believes it explains much about their ultimate success. Gladwell makes much the same case in his analysis of Bill Gates. Put in 10,000 hours, and you might get good at something. [1]

While the formula of 10,000 hours hardly represented settled science, the takeaway for me concerned the importance of time on task—even for those possessing recognizable talent. Opportunities mattered, but even geniuses must follow through. Students seeking perhaps humbler goals must follow through as well.

Of course, not all students possessed the nose-to-the-grindstone approach of Bill Gates or the Beatles. Typically, my students' ideas of how much time they needed to study mirrored the practice of American high school students (about two hours per week), as opposed to their counterparts in other industrialized countries, who studied that much per day. [2]

As I kept pondering about time and writing about my experiences in trying to help students use it to their advantage, the hours flew by. One hour, I worked to classical music provided by RTÉ Lyric

FM; the next two, I listened only to my pecking on the keyboard. "Someday you're going to break that thing," Kathleen often said. I'd exchanged e-mails with her, so we each knew that the other was fine and busy, but I needed a phone call to feel really connected. Knowing it wouldn't happen that day, I banged away at the keyboard instead.

Around five, I stood up for a long stretch. Taking an apple, I walked outside to the fenced area just up the road where I surmised farmers sheered their sheep. Colder and cloudier than yesterday, today seemed like not such a good day for walking. Curious, I'd checked to see how many pages of draft I'd added since morning: four. Probably none of what I typed would survive in its current form to a second draft, but I considered this the foundation-laying for the future road. It leveled the surface and defined the final road's width and direction.

Unlike my students, I had done this before, so I knew how it worked. I thought of how much faith it took for them to trust that their drafts would show them where their essay or report would go. Part of my job included telling them such things, but telling them went only so far. They must write the draft and treasure it for what it gave them, even though they instinctively believed that once they pressed *Save* they had completed their job. Except for the odd genius, the first or second draft provides just a map, not the treasure itself, and mortal writers learn the difficult lesson that they often must part with words they had sweated over or even fallen in love with. As a teacher, I said things to students then created practical work opportunities for them, but their learning did not come from my telling. I had to encourage them to develop trust, to write, then to make sense of what they'd written. The tricky part involved how many other people—authors, researchers, theorists, peers, family members—became part of the process. And it all happened in around fifteen weeks. A semester's length was no less arbitrary than the 10,000 hours of Gladwell's formula.

Though part of me wanted to write every minute of my time at the cottage, I took a break to prepare a simple dinner that I ate while listening to Celtic music. Apart from the brief encounter with Michael, my only companions today had been on the other end of the radio. I could not recall such a day of productive isolation back home. Pecking out a journal of my month's experiences and knowing that I could send it to Kathleen whenever I had access to the internet helped, but it did not eliminate that twinge I felt every time some event or moment conjured her up.

The other people I'd met on this trip filtered into mind. I'd had more encounters with Deirdre away from the village than in it. The two women from Limerick I'd met the first night might have left or died, for all I knew. More likely the other artists were making good use of their time here.

I'd met red-haired Rona, the German video artist from Cottage 7, when I'd returned from hiking on Wednesday, our paths crossing just below Cottage 1. Here at Cill Rialaig for the next three weeks, she'd told me that her project involved shooting footage of the sea up at Bolus Head, near the place where engineers launched the first transatlantic cable. Later in the year, she would shoot the ocean from the cable's destination, a beach in Newfoundland. She'd arrived the same day I had, and since then she had made daily trips, sometimes more than one, to the ruins at the top of Bolus Head, well past what I called the "End of the World" sign.

When she asked, I said, "I'm doing a nonfiction writing project about my work—teaching and learning," a little surprised that I didn't hem and haw. While accurate, my response reflected my intention more than any measurable product.

"Have you had other residencies?" she asked.

I told her no and that crossing an ocean in order to write was a big deal for me.

She had spent time at a number of artist residencies, including one in Norway and two in Canada. "Newfoundland," she said. She told me how the terrain differed from Ireland's, how much she enjoyed her time there. "That's how I got the idea for this project. I did the other residency in a village in Quebec."

"Really? I go there almost every summer."

"A small town on the Saint Lawrence."

"Where?"

"Saint-Jean-Port-Joli," she said.

I spun in a circle, my mouth agape. "*Very* small!" I exclaimed. "My mother came from the village beside it. Yikes." On a road by an Irish cliff, I was comparing notes with a German woman about the best places to obtain fresh bread in Saint-Jean-Port-Joli.

Apart from my momentous meeting with Rona and my contact with Deirdre, I'd laid eyes on no other village residents, if, indeed, any existed. The solitude hadn't bothered me. It wasn't like missing Kathleen and the kids. In fact, the isolation made concentration on writing easy. Cooking meals and stoking fires provided all the activity I needed. If my previous experiences in Ireland offered any indication, I would meet people here soon enough.

The cottage felt warm that evening, so I didn't bother starting a fire. I settled at the computer again, thinking about my students meeting each other. They rarely had any idea how important those relationships might prove. As a young learner, I certainly hadn't either, whether I'd found myself in a classroom-learning situation or in a very different kind of place.

Rona's knock on the door at seven broke my concentration. She informed me that Noelle had invited all residents to an opening at the gallery tomorrow. She'd met a woman in another cottage who would happily drive us down and back if we turned out in the car park about 11:30 in the morning. Saturday had now turned social!

I drafted to the end of Day One of the semester then listed my questions about the day's writing. I typed a quick entry in the journal file and returned to my musings. Today I'd had the blessing of a work-day with a minimum of responsibilities or distractions. Tomorrow's schedule already had a big fat interruption right in the middle of it. Good students would kill for the wide-open spaces of time that made up my days in Cill Rialaig. I was tired but found that I could not go to bed without spending just a little more time on the computer.

So many of my students had to shoehorn their studies into an already jam-packed life. Prior to the beginning of a semester, most students' lives already seemed hectic. The comparatively low cost of community colleges tempted many prospective students, but their well-known scheduling flexibility must have clinched the deal for many busy people.

Many nontraditional students saw entering the uncharted waters of a college classroom as an interruption of their customary activities, which they had not reduced. Imagine West Point or Annapolis plebes suggesting to their superiors that they expected to continue all of their previous jobs, family responsibilities, and off-campus activities. Commuter students did not see themselves as in the same situation, yet once the semester started, they too began what should be a life-changing experience, and they faced time challenges from day one. Serious students wished they had more time.

I faced my computer screen and banged away, mindful of how lucky I was to have so much time in this cottage.

Fall Semester, Week One

Friday, September 9, 2011: Philadelphia

By the time I arrived for the second class of the semester, early arrivals had arranged the desks into a rough oval, as I had asked them to do at our first meeting. The black-garbed Bulgarian student who introduced herself as a restaurant server on Wednesday had dutifully taped her name sign so that it hung over the front edge of her desk: "Zhiv"—short for Zhivka. Flowers adorned the name sign of sweet and earnest Charisse, a forty-something black woman from West Philadelphia. After squinting at a sign in the rear of the room, I walked toward the student's desk, stopping a few feet short of him where I finally could make out the tiny lettering. "Just turn it over, Ryan, and make a version that we can read." I praised several students for their creativity.

"Mine is plain and simple," Zhiv complained. "Just like me." Her accent sounded like a cross between French and Russian, and her pouting was pure theater.

"No, no, no," I told her. "Big and clear printing is good."

Jim from Judge entered and took his place beside Zhiv. Smiling
hopefully, Lourdes occupied the same seat she had used on the first
day, having apparently eschewed my suggestion about relocating to a
different section. Afafa, a young woman from Senegal, sat beside her,
and I wondered if in time they would team up in some useful way for
the semester. Charisse informed me that she was seeking a degree in
human services. Douglas, a black man in his forties, explained in the
minutes before class that he had taught in the public school system.
I wondered if I would learn what brought him to Freshman English
and what he meant by "teaching." Like Charisse, he showed polite
deference to everyone during the pre-class chatter. I always learned
names slowly, despite employing various strategies, but already I knew
the names of several striking students.

One assignment for today involved selecting and paraphrasing a
key point from the introduction to *They Say / I Say*, Gerald Graff and
Cathy Birkenstein's decoding of academic writing. Freshmen arrived
at college with writing experience, but the kind of writing they did
in school bore little resemblance to that performed by workers in
academic fields. Yet they arrived with rhetorical experience that could
be applied to academic writing, another source of surprise for many of
them.[1] Anyone who'd tried to convince someone to go out on a date
knew something about rhetoric, though they might not have been
familiar with the term. Artists, athletes, musicians, and carpenters
knew plenty about improvisational use of their "tool kits."

On the board, I made a column of the chapter's page numbers.
Two small stacks of papers awaited me on the table at which I sat
during class. When I reminded them that they must place assignments
on the table at the beginning of class, several folks scrambled to the
front of the room with papers. At 11:15, with pen in hand, I looked
up from my class list and said in my outdoor voice, "On what page

is the passage that you paraphrased?" I called the first name on my alphabetized list.

"Bottom of page five," said Ella, a young black woman wearing a tracksuit. She'd been one of the chatters the other day but seemed completely tuned in today.

I wrote her name on the board beside the number five and moved on to the second name. When I reached the end of the list, I saw the names of all but one of Wednesday's attendees on the board. I posted the Do Not Enter sign on the outside doorknob and asked Jim, whose name appeared beside the lowest page number, to read his chosen passage then give us his paraphrase. To avoid using all of the hour on this exercise, we skipped through the list enough for me to see that most students prepared something other than a paraphrase, but with a little prompting, they started self-correcting.

"You're writing back to the other people who've already said something on the subject," offered Luther, a thirty-year-old black man.

I nodded. The discussion bounced through the points covered in the assigned text.

"I used to play bass," Luther added. "When I'd try to play a new tune, I'd use stuff that I already knew, like the book says basketball players and musicians do. 'Playing licks.' I never thought about 'making moves' in writing."

"Yes!" I said, trying not to gush over the fact this student had unearthed two essential points in the section: academic writing is, by nature, conversational, and it involves making *moves*.[2] The class seemed willing to accept the notion that the same might hold for activities like talking or even writing.

This constituted only our first pass at the Graff and Birkenstein book, so I resisted the temptation to rush as if I only had today's discussion to get these ideas across. All teachers believed that their work rested upon their students getting certain foundational ideas, so they must resist committing the instructional equivalent of announcing on a first date that you loved the relative stranger sitting across from you.

Class discussion shifted from the Graff and Birkenstein book to the online lecture given by Randy Pausch—not his well-known presentation as a faculty member at Carnegie Mellon University about making your childhood dreams come true, the text of which he subsequently transposed into the *New York Times* best-seller *The Last Lecture*—but his lecture on time management, delivered at the University of Virginia shortly after the more famous CMU talk. Who better to learn about time management from, I asked my students, than a man with terminal pancreatic cancer who still gets the most out of his time?

Most students spoke about how deeply moving they found the video, often the case with this lecture. That night, I would go through their renderings of what they considered three significant points made by Pausch. I did not identify this as a writing sample, but it would serve that function.

For the remainder of our class, we talked about time. Unless he was sitting quietly outside the door, one of Wednesday's attendees had landed in another zip code, as had two roster ghosts, who had not yet fathomed the classroom's location or contacted me. The nineteen students who made it to Day Two appeared attentive. Time issues also affected engaged students who rarely missed classes or due dates but who, for various reasons, did not or could not devote adequate time to the course's outside work.

Most classroom participation came from Charisse, former teacher Douglas, and Ian, a short black man whom I'd run into in the hallway before class. He had told me about his return to school after tours of duty as a Marine in Iraq and Afghanistan, though he hardly looked old enough. Their energy in class pleased me, but I was aware that I needed to gently steer the mostly seminar-based course by directing comments and questions to all students and by insisting that talkative students raise their hands and wait for recognition. Otherwise the hour would turn into a show for the stars, allowing the bulk of students to disappear into the woodwork. Most likely, both the stars and the silent partners had years of experience playing these roles.

We read aloud parts of "It's About Time," the article that presented two fictional case studies of students facing time issues, and I introduced another short writing assignment, asking students to anticipate the advice Pausch might give to the fictional characters in the syllabus article.

"And guess what we've just run out of?" I said, closing my book.

"Time!" someone shouted from the back. We all laughed, packing up our things.

"Those schedules you filled out the other day?" I called above the din.

"Yes?" Charisse said.

"Might be a good time to revisit them in the light of our reading and discussion." I rushed off to my next class, thinking about my students excitedly talking about the Pausch lecture and feeling energized about their enthusiasm.

Do I really want to walk away from this?

I knew I could do this work beyond the semester. The feeling of having been plunged into the middle of things rushed through me. Chasing the intruding thoughts about retirement from my brain, I instead focused on the living, breathing students around me.

Classrooms on Fridays always rang with talk about the weekend, and I heard it today before all four classes. Like four-year college students, community college students talked about going drinking, seeing a movie, or just chilling with their friends, but for my students, their weekend also represented precious time for earning money. Most of my classes consisted of full-time students, and most of them also held down jobs. More than a few of them tried to manage full-time work on top of their course load, a well-known recipe for academic disaster, but every semester I met students who had convinced themselves that if they could schedule it, they could do it.

Many of them worked in the service industry. The Honors students I shared with Vince flocked to jobs in bars and restaurants and knew more about food and the city's fast-growing restaurant scene than I did. "I was a vegetarian for six years," second-semester Honors student Nora confessed, "then I moved to Philadelphia." Other students worked in stores or nursing homes; some had computer-related jobs or worked in construction. Like people anywhere, they had roles as sons, daughters, fathers, mothers, grandparents, boyfriends, girlfriends, or spouses. They played sports, created art, danced, played music, cleaned and cooked, went to religious services, served in the community. Some of them or their family members had committed crimes or were crime victims.

We all deal with having to wear various adult-sized hats, but community college students must adapt to adult realties more quickly than typical residential students at four-year colleges. Some students literally wore those other hats to class on Friday. A soccer team member had brought his kit bag to class. Zhiv arrived for class dressed in the black outfit she would wear to the restaurant where she worked. Rashid wore his FedEx uniform. I imagined them all heading off from class, looking ahead to the weekend's tasks and adventures.

Residential college students also wore many hats, but dorm life provided them with a cocoon, risky but insulated and somewhat protective. In certain ways, doing a stint away from home at a four-year college provided nearly grown teenagers with a transitional period from typical American home life to at least the beginnings of actual independence. Behind the scenes, of course, someone else usually paid the bills, freeing up more potential study time for residential students.

Families also maintained a home base to which these students could safely return for holiday breaks, recovery from illness, or just laundry services. Dormitories provided safety nets absent from community college commuters' lives. Either they maintained their own place, shared an apartment with others, or lived at home with their families, if those families still welcomed them and if they could survive there. Those lucky enough to have such a safe port available to them would most likely take at least partial responsibility for their own expenses, including the costs of attending college.

I had never completed a semester without at least one or two students talking to me about their impending or actual homelessness, information that invariably involved fire, eviction, abandonment, or worse. These stories also might include violence or illness. Such realities also broke into the lives of residential college students, but it happened frequently enough at community college that I expected to run into it during the course of each term.

Driving home from campus, I thought about the past. Every year on my birthday, on my mother's birthday, and on the anniversary of her death, I imagined that Hélene Pellerin Bachus could observe life on Earth, could listen in on conversations, and basically got to visit and see how we were doing. I never pictured her zooming into the

Oval Office or the Pope's chambers, but I easily pictured her checking in on the people she'd left behind thirty-three years ago today.

We all had low points during the year that she was dying of esophageal cancer, but she beamed irrepressibly the day Kathleen and I told her that we were going to try to have a baby. No one had to say that it wouldn't happen while she was alive. She sat in her chair by the living room window of her second-floor apartment, above the rumble of the trolleys on Germantown Avenue's cobblestones, smiling and gazing off into the distance.

"She couldn't be happier if the doctors told her they found a cure," I whispered to Kathleen in the kitchen, pouring hot water into the teapot.

The shrinking little sixty-two-year-old woman spent the afternoon scribbling down baby names.

"*Gordon?*" I exclaimed, deciphering her scrawled list.

"It's a strong name," she replied, laughing at the fact that I was laughing.

Hélene had lived to see Kathleen and me move from an apartment to a row house on Durham Street in the Mount Airy neighborhood where she and I had lived for most of my childhood. Her pride for me defied rhyme or reason. Entering our little home for the first time, she paused at the front door, got the attention of the large man sitting on the adjoining porch who was sipping out of a brown paper bag, smiled, and said, "This is Ned Bachus." He just grunted, but his eyes seemed to say, *Yeah, and I'm B.B. King.* I smarted from that for years.

We'd talked with the kids about her as soon as we could. They knew her through stories, photos, and the reverent reaction people who'd known Hélene gave whenever her name was mentioned. They'd visited the gravesite at George Washington Memorial Park where her ashes were buried. I liked to think that Hélene knew

Stephan and Anna from her occasional "visits." Through our life without her, she'd watched my weight go up and down, and cheered Kathleen as she became a full-time mother, then a registered nurse, a career move largely prompted by the experience of caring for Hélène in those hard months. I imagined Hélène smiling as Stephan learned to play "La Bastringue" on the fiddle and lugged a hockey bag as big as he was down the stairs, and as Anna sang in the Henry School musicals and was accepted at Duquesne University.

Some years after her death and the birth of our children, we moved six blocks west to a larger twin near Carpenter's Woods, and I knew in my bones that she had studied its every nook from the basement to the third floor, that she loved the deck, smiled when she saw how we'd changed the kitchen, and probably boasted about the meals we'd concocted. More than anything, I knew that she'd savored her glimpses of Stephan and Anna. Driving home, I hoped that as she looked upon her son's family on this Friday in September, she was still smiling.

Thoughts of her and of everything else that had occupied my mind all day shifted to the back burner as soon as I arrived home. Like so many of my students, professors too changed hats, although I doubted that my students imagined me doing anything other than lecturing and reading student essays. Their old teacher would switch gears dramatically tonight. The Sacred CowBoys were playing at a small club on Friday and Saturday night.

Kathleen called a sixty-two-year-old full-time teacher playing in a band "hard fun," but unlike my students' work, I did it entirely because I loved it, scheduled it as sanely as possible, and did not rely on it for economic survival. Still, it gave me a taste of the kind of hectic schedule that many of my students constantly lived with. I packed up my hardware and percussion bags and brought them to the tiny but energy-filled Mermaid Inn.

In a way, the hardest band weekends were the one-nighters, when we set up, played, broke down, and loaded out all in one night. But this weekend, we were able to spread the work out over two nights. In between the grunting over heavy equipment, we got to play our music—a Louisiana-influenced blend of original tunes and odd covers, which someone once described as a cross between Little Richard, Pink Floyd, and The Grateful Dead—watch people dance, and, at the end, share a beer with friends.

The Mermaid drew an eclectic range of individuals, and over several decades, the Sacred CowBoys had developed several rather unrelated audience constituencies, including male rugby players, women who liked to dance with other women, college professors, swing-dancing Unitarians, a tree surgeon with a penchant for a good raccoon, lettuce, and tomato sandwich, and a staffer from the Bush I White House.

They paid their admission to Michael Napoletano, who sat at the door beside the band's CDs, hats, T-shirts, and e-mail sign-up list. With noise reducers packed into both ears and a phalanx of extra pens swelling his shirt's pocket protector, Mike interrupted reading his issues of *Smithsonian Magazine* and *Model Railroader* to make change and encourage newbies to add their names to the list.

At the beginning of sixth grade, Sister Paul Emmanuel had sat the new boy next to me at lunch. After observing me do rude and suggestive things with the shapely Bartlett pear I'd found in my lunch bag, he figured we were likely to become friends. He'd instantly assumed the identity of uncle to our children, and also had been dubbed the unofficial seventh member of the band, the only non-musician we dragged to band dinners.

During a pause between our songs on Friday night, someone from the rugby club bellowed, "John Ga-*lan-te!*" prompting half of the audience, including the band, to sing along. John, my old friend and one of the founders of the Blackthorn Rugby Football Club, stood in the rear, proudly taking it all in. "John Galante is a horse's ass!" the crowd roared with gusto. The ditty descended to coarser levels, all to John's apparent delight, offering as genteel a bow as one might expect from General Robert E. Lee. The song had legs. The fill-in-the-blank insult song had preceded John but became his song to the point that it had been published as such in the club's book of rugby songs. The band had learned it through me. And, of course, there was the oral tradition. An old teammate attending a post-rugby match party in Paris nearly spewed his beer when he heard ruggers from Racing Club de France and their opponents belting out John's name. Here, the eclectic crowd seemed to form a perfect choir.

All night, I swapped lead vocals with guitarist Michael Bailey and banged the Cajun triangle; shook tambourines and maracas; struck cymbals, bells, and wood blocks; and, using two metal bottle openers, scratched out rhythms on the *frottoir*, the galvanized steel zydeco rubboard vest that guaranteed a late-night cardio workout. *I'm floating down the crazy river, slow as I can be. Who got the dog? Who got the cat? And who goin' away with me?* Teacher friends had told me how lucky I was to have such a secret life. I didn't want to imagine life without band nights at the Mermaid and knew that wherever Kathleen and I ended up, it would have to include regular trips here to perform.

After Saturday's final set, a marathon load-out ended around 3:30 a.m., landing me home later than my students probably imagined me capable of. The CowBoys did not trail the Rolling Stones much in age, but I suspected that Keith, Mick, and the boys had not lugged their own gear home deep in the night for a long time. On this particular Saturday night, like many of my students, I had burned the candle at both ends. I hoped to continue playing with the band until so many of us had dropped that we no longer sounded like the band.

This first Sunday afternoon of the semester seemed pretty much pain-free until I'd put in fifteen minutes or so of grading. Five papers into the first stack of student work, I remembered what I always managed to forget between semesters: people who seemed so articulate while speaking in class could not write a comprehensible essay. I knew I was in for a long afternoon when, after commenting on just five papers, I had written more than the students had.

Commenting on student writing required equal parts art and science. Like most writing teachers, I strove to grade by balancing clear honesty in my comments with empowering guidance, but students tended to read them rather narrowly. I thought of the Gary Larson cartoon showing what a dog heard his human saying. "Blah, blah, blah, Rocky." I knew from experience that absent my required conference discussion of the paper and my scribbled comments, many students would register only the letter grade amongst the blah, blah, blah of written explanations, questions, exhortations, and suggestions.

The papers contained all of the expected grammatical originality, creative spelling, and mystifying organization. Though some papers seemed on task and effective, I found myself writing "clarity" beside many passages. On the students' data sheets, containing placement data and previous grades, I noted writing strengths and problem areas, mindful that for many students I still would use the exact same descriptive terms when I reviewed their work two months hence, which doused any overblown thoughts I harbored about my usefulness. Some of them had problems greater than what a student with the help of a teacher could solve in fewer than four months.

I looked up from my papers. I knew this kind of moment from years of experience. Rumination at this point was a distraction from whatever good I could do. At the end of every academic year, I focused upon what I could rework to increase the odds that I might help students. Come spring, I would focus on such thoughts again, but this time it would be to write a book about teaching. *You'd miss this work. But wouldn't writing about it be like doing it? Work for* these *students now.*

Despite their placement test scores and collegiate academic records that suggested that all of my students had adequate control over their written expression, perhaps half of them actually possessed such skill. I knew that part of this job included helping students alter long-established faulty writing patterns, but identifying these trigger points was just a first step: the elusive second step involved getting students to recognize them on their own. Surely I was not the first writing teacher to attempt to convey this to these students.

Probably what they wanted to say made perfect sense to them, so they believed that their writing conveyed exactly what they were thinking. Grades from previous writing teachers had never effectively countered this belief; in fact, because of grade inflation in secondary schools, they might have reinforced it. Perhaps because they had managed to travel this far in the educational process, they hoped that ultimately I too would just punch their ticket, allowing them to move on to the next station on the journey without having learned enough.

I finished all of Friday's collected papers before dark. Sitting at my desk, I extended and flexed my fingers to get rid of the first-batch-of-the-year stiffness. Not so bad. Some of the papers showed genuine thinking, real effort, even skill. I'd seen worse beginnings from students who went on to pass the course. We had fourteen more weeks. With two classes behind us, my students no longer felt like complete strangers to me. And I had a plan that had evolved through successes and failures. I could do another semester of this without becoming disillusioned or embittered. I felt like a coach that knew more about his players' potential than they did. Monday morning couldn't come soon enough. I went over Monday's activities in my head, made sure that I'd packed all the texts I would need, and went to bed, hoping that all of my students would show up on Monday.

8

Spring Sabbatical, Day Five

Saturday, April 7, 2012: Ireland

Avril, a painter who lived in Cottage 3, drove Deirdre, Rona, and me down to the gallery for the Saturday opening. We all had dressed a step up from the comfortable gear we worked in at the village. The gallery bustled with curious locals, Easter weekend visitors, and folks connected with Cill Rialaig Project. The opening featured work by Avril and other artists who had spent time in the village. At the gallery, I e-mailed Kathleen, asking her to call me at the gallery on Monday at 8 a.m. her time.

My fellow villagers and I munched on hors d'oeuvres, mingled with the crowd, and listened to opening comments from a celebrity guest. Her black skirt, high-heeled black boots, and heavily applied, equally black makeup suggested that at the end of the day she would not return to some nearby farm to attend to milking duties. I might have been the only person in the room who did not instantly recognize her as the weather reader from one of the national television stations.

I realized that I had not properly thanked Avril for driving us to the event, so when she approached the other side of a broad table of hors d'oeuvres I caught her attention and called out, "Thanks for the ride!" She and everyone within earshot stopped and stared at me. Was I too loud? Surely my expression was one of genuine gratitude. "Very nice of you!" I added, giving her a thumbs-up. Now they all acted as if I were not even there. I placed a couple of appetizers on a napkin and crossed the room. Chewing on the second canapé, I realized my faux pas: I had forgotten the critical linguistic distinction that I thought I had mastered on a previous trip to Ireland. I promised myself that I would never again ask an Irish person for "a ride," an expression that did not even remotely refer to anything automotive over here.

Later, Noelle Campbell-Sharp introduced each of the current villagers to the crowd. *Oh, that fool's American. Well, so.* The roll call revealed two painters I had not met, a man and a woman, but I did not spot the two women I had met on my first evening. Soon Deirdre mentioned to me that she and the others wanted to head back, even though the building still pulsed with energy. With the male painter now squeezed into the backseat, we rambled up the road, back to our posts. "Thank you so much for *the lift*," I said loudly, exiting the car. "*The lift, the lift, the lift.*" Finally they all laughed.

Avril lived in England but grew up in Northern Ireland. Her accent matched exactly that of my mother's old friend and coworker Greta Timoney. She invited all of us to join her when she drove to Caherciveen on Monday. Rona and I accepted.

I wondered if any of the others had felt just a bit like an imposter when their turn to smile in the spotlight had arrived. Here I wrote around the clock, but back home, as a summer writer, I had always defined myself to others as a teacher. I knew that writers weren't defined strictly by how much money their books earned, but I suspected that my fellow cottagers devoted more time to working in their artistic fields than I did. I went all out when I strapped on the *frottoir* vest or when I dove back into a word processing file, but those never became the only hats I wore. Back in the quiet of the cottage, I contemplated scaffolding, roles, and identities.

Others usually figured into the learning process, as I'd found this afternoon. Perhaps the next time I found myself at such a gathering, I would behave as if I belonged there, but the people around me had enabled me to skate through the occasion. Pioneering Russian sociocultural psychologist Lev Vygotsky brought the concept of scaffolding to learning theory: temporary help provided by skilled practitioners that, like a construction project's metal scaffolding, workers removed after they completed the job.[1]

Scaffolding, I explained to students in class and in syllabus articles, was social in nature.

"Like a teacher?"

"Yes," I'd say. "Or something used by a teacher or guide, like an activity or a book."

"Like what you're doing now?"

Such rare classroom moments forced me to suppress my urge to hug the insightful student or to drop to my knees and thank them for making my day, lest my wild energy frighten those in the class who were not experiencing the same epiphany. "That's the idea," I commented, aware that too little emotion from me could leave them cold but that too much of it could take attention away from the point. "But often it's not a professor or classroom teacher who helps the learner. The guide knows more than the learner but could be younger."

"Like kids showing adults how to use a computer or a phone."

"Exactly," I said. "Picture a grown-up watching the kid put a new number into her phone for her then doing it herself—with corrections and reminders from the kid. She tries it again and probably needs less help each time, right?"

Heads nodded.

"Eventually, even the adult can do it by herself. Although you might not want to trust me with your phone just yet."

Students readily recognized this phenomenon when they recalled moments when they had taught someone or when another person had taught them how to ride a bicycle or stir-fry chicken. It didn't much help if the teacher/guide made the learners do things that they already knew how to do.

I asked, "Were you ever force-fed worksheets in high school?"

Loud groans always greeted that question. Better to learn in that tricky range where you can't quite do something all alone but can stumble through with skilled assistance and guidance—what Vygotsky called the zone of proximal development.[2]

Scaffolding also came to mind when I recalled the semesters I spent teaching with colleagues like Vince, Gary, and Clint. College teachers do not regularly observe colleagues in action, let alone work with them in course design, teaching, and student evaluation. My growth as a teacher leaped ahead once I began working closely with colleagues, including professors from different disciplines. People in all fields had to write, so one's departmental identity mattered little—we all taught writing. Together, we planned a comprehensive curriculum, broke up the workload into chunks, and learned information and practices from each other that we might have thought ourselves incapable of doing. Our roles shifted from one day to the next. I'd experienced much the same in my years of playing rugby and performing with the band.

Last week, I would have found myself up to my ears in several other roles, but here at Cill Rialaig Project, where I had come to write, I defined myself as a writer. Many opportunities to change roles consumed my thoughts as I headed back to the computer.

Adventurous or desperate people, I thought, find ample opportunities for starting over, but less adventurous or more complacent folks fail to recognize when their lives call on them to take desperate measures. Such chances remain obscure and elusive to them. College remains one of those rare institutions that offers people socially approved opportunities to change—indeed, to reinvent themselves.

This offer holds true at all colleges, but community colleges—the only choice available for some people and the last choice available to others—offer people a relatively low-cost college mulligan in a couple of senses. Sure, they provide students with a second chance to succeed academically, but they also enable students to change and even reinvent the way they think of and present themselves to the world, particularly in the classroom.

Whatever role they played in a previous life—goth, jock, anti-intellectual, nerd—no longer matters when they register. Matriculate then re-create. From last year's bad haircut to a history of misbehavior, students can leave their baggage outside the admissions office door. College hands them a free pass to change whatever they want to change about themselves, including their approach to studentship. And when they try on the persona of a serious college student, do they feel like imposters? Experience with the work itself and with other people helps us feel legitimate about our new roles.

Such transformations happen even more at community colleges, where the mean age of students might be a good ten years older than students at four-year colleges. Individuals who failed, dropped out of, or never tried college often find their way to community colleges, bursting with readiness to try a different approach from the previous one that didn't work. Right now, Gary Mullen was teaching American government. Vince was teaching psychology. And in over 1,100 community colleges across the country, others were teaching physics, accounting, art. And students at those community colleges were learning independence.

I thought about my fellow artists at Cill Rialaig, some who were here only for a week. We knew so little about each other. They'd been as anxious to return to our cottages as I'd been though, so we shared a certain drive. The place invited us to attempt our own kind of change. For all of us, this was a limited, precious opportunity.

"I'm here to lie fallow," one of the painters in the car had said. She explained that she had just finished a major project that had consumed her days and nights for the better part of a year. She planned to do some printmaking at the studio, but otherwise was opening up her creative soul to whatever might seize her. For her, the rewards of this experience might not happen until months after she was far removed from this beautiful place. Most of them were returning after previous residencies here. I saw my sojourn as a once-in-a-lifetime opportunity, and I'd arrived with a clear agenda. Our reasons for being here differed, but whatever the others were up to in their cottages, we were all equally motivated.

Motivation drives students into college courses, and those driving forces vary as much in them as they did in the artists inhabiting the neighboring cottages. Students know all about motivation before arriving at campus. "Follow your dreams!" graduation speakers shouted at them. In many cases, they believe that motivation has magical powers—hardly a surprise, considering that they've grown up in America, where they receive constant reminders from pop-psychology TV talk show hosts, clergy, school leaders, graduation speakers, and well-intentioned family members that they can achieve anything that they put their minds to.

Many first-year students arrive at college trusting that through the sheer force of their own will they can maintain their high level of motivation, but no one can hold it at that level constantly. Motivation ebbs and flows in reaction to many factors, including health, family, and personal relationships, to name but a few. While first-year students lack experience with a college semester's reality, their teachers witness the challenges to student motivation every term. Students also remain unaware of contributing factors to its inconsistency; if they realized as much, they could compensate when their motivation dropped after that hard-charging first day, when the new book smell, fresh pens, and pristine notebooks combined to make freshmen feel like real students, boldly headed down "The Path To Possibilities," as the Community College of Philadelphia's slogan stated.

Some motivated students enter college possessing intelligence, skills, core knowledge, healthy intellectual curiosity, and familiarity with studentship's "rules of the game." They receive sane course selection advice, and they have physical and emotional health, sufficient financial backing, supportive families and friends, schedules reasonably balanced with other responsibilities, and social networks that include similarly engaged peers. In addition, challenging and fair teachers await them in the classroom. However, many such well-equipped students lose that first day's confidence within weeks, if not days.

Still, many of them survive and even thrive, if their lives contain enough stability. Only so many things can go wrong in students' lives before their chances for success become irreparably damaged. Both expected and unexpected problems impede students. When they reach the tipping point, their behavior changes, and their grades go down. Sitting alone in Cottage 8, I recalled students who had survived such collapses. Their accounts often pointed to people in their lives whose support proved critical.

Of course, they talked about motivation. Students tend to think of motivation as separate from the many other factors that affect and influence their academic performance; they believe they can rely on its steadiness, like the ease and precision of a car's cruise control. They see motivation as their magic sword and shield, both the protection against every obstacle standing in their path and the weapon they can wield to defy the odds. But only if students have enough supports in place will their odds for success not plummet when their motivation takes a downturn. Mistaken notions about how motivation works can harm engaged students at selective colleges, but for many of the poorly prepared at a community college, such misconceptions prove an unbearable burden.

I stopped in my typing, exhausted but fueled on the feeling or the illusion of progress. It was dark and quiet outside, except for the wind. My language gaffe, my feelings of being neither fish nor fowl among the artists, my joyful intake of hors d'oeuvres at the gallery all felt like events from days or even a week ago. Since returning to the cottage, I'd let my erratic ruminations move me like the gusts on the road outside. I'd gotten somewhere. I just wasn't sure where.

9

Fall Semester, Week Two

Monday, September 12, 2011: Philadelphia

A new face arrived in Monday's class. He approached my table at the front of the classroom and announced that he belonged there. I told Diego that luckily for him, I had brought the handouts from the first two class days but that he needed to read through the schedule to learn about all the work he'd missed. He looked at me blankly. "We started last week," I said. I caught Zhivka shaking her head and heard a low rumble starting up in the class, something between muffled laughter and a groan. It sounded like a sitcom audience reacting to one of the stupid characters outdoing himself.

"I was on vacation," Diego offered.

Ah, September makes a lovely month for vacation. Now the students had braced themselves, waiting for me to burst into flames or perhaps escort him out the door. Charisse and Douglas exchanged meaningful glances. Diego turned briefly, as if looking for a clue to what was going on.

"This is our third meeting," I said, confidentially, "so you have some catching up to do, if you decide that you want to stay in the class."

He nodded.

"Not having heard from you," I said, "I thought you either had decided not to attend or had found yourself in the middle of a drop and add."

Nothing.

"The syllabus has my e-mail address," I added. I could see the students calculating in their minds: this guy had already blown one-third of his allowed cuts. "Here," I said, doing my best to not sound sarcastic. I handed him his materials and announced his name to the class, which had gone quiet but adopted a genuinely welcoming look.

In the next class of the day, another roster ghost appeared, with just as feeble an excuse as Diego's. I reprised my neutral performance, reminding myself that teaching often closely resembled acting. I gained nothing by humiliating students in front of the class, but I could lose a lot. Getting started in college involved hard work. These guys had shown up at the starting line just as the rest of the runners had finished the first lap. To compete in the race with a passable performance, they needed to stride longer and harder than the others just to catch up. For their sakes, I hoped they possessed some personal resources that they had not displayed today.

To take the roll, I said, "Describe one change you made in your schedule." No one reported having added more study time. Some students promised that they would. I sensed the end of the honeymoon.

The behaviors of the roster ghosts had not come out of nowhere; their perspectives suggested no inclination to move toward more active engagement, not a particularly unusual attitude. Students bring much of themselves to the classroom, like the student I had passed earlier in the hallway. He was wearing a "Romo Is A Homo" T-shirt, most likely intended to express a deep and abiding hatred for the Dallas Cowboys and their quarterback and an indirect expression of support for his beloved Philadelphia Eagles. However, other people might interpret his slogan to mean that he intentionally wanted to insult the LGBTQ community or that he remained blissfully clueless or indifferent to the cringeworthiness of the message on his chest. Obviously, the shirt screamed more than "Fly, Iggles, Fly."

Some of this went with our fair city's territory. Rightly or wrongly, Philadelphians—who often began sentences with a sharp "Yo!" just in case you weren't listening—had earned a certain reputation. As Karen Heller once reported in her *Philadelphia Inquirer* column, traveling Philadelphians often feel struck by how darn nice the people in the rest of the country are—in contrast to a hometown norm that calls for directness and clarity, to put it in the most favorable terms. The T-shirt that best captured this *je ne sais quoi* read, "I'm not angry, I'm from Philly." Teachers new to the city would do well to assume that half of their students wore such a greeting as an undershirt. When worn on the outside, it displayed another bit of baggage they brought into the classroom.

In Monday's class, we discussed the task of the first major paper for about half of our hour. They'd already read the syllabus article that introduced and explained the assignment. Students would supply a story from their experience in which they functioned as either the learner or the skilled practitioner/teacher, as Vygotsky would put it. I reminded them, "Use your story, but Vygotsky's explanation for how the learning happened." Charisse related her experience of learning how to cook beans and rice with her aunt, and other students identified examples of scaffolding in her story. Nodding heads convinced me that I could move on to how they would use the next two weeks to develop the essay.

"We'll get the papers back?" Jim asked.

"I collect them next Monday, log them in as on time, then return them to you."

"You said you won't write anything on the papers," Ian said, "but you'll tell us what's wrong with them in the writing seminars."

"We'll talk about how each paper is doing or not doing the task."

Several faces showed something like distrust and fear.

"Each time we do an essay, you'll find the process more familiar and you'll need less help, or different kinds of it, so that you can do more complicated tasks—just like Vygotsky would suggest. Two weeks from today, you'll staple the revision on top of the draft and turn them both in. That way I can see what you changed."

By and large, they disliked all of this, but the process forced them to put *something* down on paper halfway to the final deadline. They didn't yet know that completing even a crappy draft before seeing work by other students had great value; it kick-started the whole writing process and gave them something to work on, a mercy for reluctant writers. I told them that at the draft stage, almost anything qualified as satisfactory material—an imprecise expression I'd come to regret a week later.

My teaching schedule had me teaching on Mondays, Wednesdays, and Fridays, leaving me Tuesdays and Thursdays to keep up with the paper chase involved in teaching four writing classes. The flexibility offered by working at home as much as I did allowed me to take care of the weekday cooking and a lot of the cleaning.

Sitting at the desk in my study, I heard Kathleen's voice downstairs. I was in the middle of a student paragraph and did not want to lose the thread.

"Please come down!" she called louder.

Putting down my pen, I clumped downstairs and followed her voice to the basement stairway.

"Look at this," she moaned.

I found her standing beside the long wall of our twin home that ran back from the street and parallel to the driveway. Platter-sized chunks of plaster from the wall lay at her feet. Drops of water splattered onto the debris-covered edge of the floor. Scallop-shaped sections of soggy plaster bowed out from the wall, defying gravity. "I was about to do the laundry," she wailed. I had not heard her voice this sad since the Phillies were eliminated in the National League Championship Series the previous year.

Before beginning to clean up the mess, I headed upstairs to find its source. Water streaked down the entranceway wall, making it wet to the touch. *How did we not see this until now?* More water soaked the bathroom wall on the second floor. Only the third floor had suffered no damage. We turned off the water, called the plumber, and started to clean up.

Our plumber Junior's abject fear of dogs required confinement of Roux and Jack, our "Mutt and Jeff" Border Collie mixes, which meant that I must do my grading on the deck with them. I knew something about obedience training, having dutifully learned how to employ a policy of appeasement. I admitted Junior to the house, then took my papers and joined the dogs outside, a stash of dog treats within reach of my well-trained hands.

No one would have thought that our dogs came from the same breed. Jack featured the classic black and white coloring of the Border Collie and a heft that suggested German Shepherd or Lab ancestry. Roux, all white except for rust-colored ears and weighing just fourteen pounds, carried more of her miniature American Eskimo dog heritage, although her snout and tail suggested a very small-scale sheep dog. Together, they provided our home security system. Jack barked more deeply and more menacingly, a trait that Roux employed when acting as his de facto handler. Confronted by invaders, such as dinner guests, Roux nipped at Jack's most vulnerable parts until he reached full fury.

Three essays later, I learned from Junior that he had found the source of our problems: a leak in the wastepipe. His son, also terrified of dogs, arrived to help. I had enough essays and dog treats to last most of the day.

My student work consisted of brief responses by the second-semester Honors class (generally our most experienced and talented students) to the first six chapters of *Identical Strangers*. They'd all successfully completed English 101 and Psychology 101, some of them in our linked Honors classes. Clarity issues troubled some of the papers, including the work of Sid, a young man from Indonesia, whom we worked with last semester. I was familiar with ESL expressions from my mother's writing and from the writing of foreign students. Hélene was mostly self-taught, and her English featured minor but regular verb errors. She tended to form her verbs and to construct her sentences the way she did in French, a pattern that one must labor long and hard to eliminate in a second or third language. I also was well aware of my own blunders in French and the reactions they produced in my cousins.

Determined to become as good in English as humanly possible, Sid had learned to start the revision process immediately. The assignment he turned in Monday called for no more than two pages, hardly a major paper. The class learned about the assignment last Wednesday. On Friday, Sid had been my only visitor during my unofficial office hour at 7 a.m. to discuss his draft. Over the weekend, he'd e-mailed to ask if he could see me Monday between 7 and 7:30 to talk about the changes he'd made to the paper that he would hand in at 9:05. This was the kind of guy that people wanted working on a cure for cancer. After teaching him for one full semester, I knew the drill. Each revision bore witness not only to his having listened to my questions and suggestions at our last conference but also to the fact that he might always need such persistence in crafting his written English. He approached exam preparation the same way, using all available time to make his work as good as possible.

Vince and I hoped that the experienced students would help orient the new folks, who lacked Honors curriculum experience. Donald, one of the link's new recruits, had already announced his intention to transfer to the University of Pennsylvania. Wearing a Penn T-shirt, the twenty-something black man from upstate New York asked for an appointment to discuss the transfer process. His first written assignment proved quite good; already he had a voice that I could count on in class. Nora joined him in the hot prospect category. A recent Hofstra University graduate, the young white woman sought to take prerequisites before applying for graduate school. Not surprisingly, her written work showed that she grasped the material, and like Donald, she added much to classroom discussions. As at other kinds of colleges and universities, many freshmen at community colleges were young, right out of high school; however, at community college, they shared the classroom with somewhat older students like Donald and Nora, who often provided models for effective student behavior.

In midafternoon, I took a break from grading to rebuild part of the once picture-perfect backyard woodpile that had collapsed overnight. As I redid the fallen end of the stack, my mind turned to our master plan for the future, and I wondered what the scheme would look like in a month. Quickly working up a sweat, I slowed down so I would not pant so much and told myself that I needed to spend more time on the exercise bike that sat in my study. By the end of the day, a nearly foot-wide opening ran down the length of the bathroom wall. The plumber had finished his work, but drywall and painting projects loomed ahead.

Wednesday's classes went well, and I left campus with only late papers and the handful of on-time papers that I hadn't gotten to on Tuesday. In the late afternoon, I powered through more grading before Kathleen and I went out to meet Vince and Joan Castronuovo for a quick dinner at the Lucky Dog Saloon in Lafayette Hill. They provided a much-needed sounding board for our wild scheme of moving to Maine.

As we pulled out of the restaurant's parking lot to drive home, Kathleen blurted out, "They don't think we're crazy!" I laughed because the same thought had struck me. In my head, I worked on a second e-mail to send to Lee, our Maine real estate agent and new best friend, to reassure her that we were seriously considering Unit 337, the beautiful condo we'd viewed on our visit. To move ahead with this plan, we needed to line up many ducks in a row, including getting the nod from our TIAA-CREF financial advisor. At any moment, somebody might buy this unit. We needed to move as if we already had decided that I would leave the college.

In bed, allowing myself to believe that we would accomplish this big change, I suddenly felt the full impact of moving away from our grown children. *They'll feel like they don't matter to us. We'll feel like selfish heels.* Kathleen had managed to fall asleep, but I kept mulling over the pros and cons of such a move. Although in the long run, I saw this move having good effects on them, I still winced at the thought of telling them about it—but of course, I told myself, we were still just exploring possibilities. Nothing would be decided tonight.

Thursday's breaks from grading included exchanging e-mails with a retired psychologist who'd recently moved into one of the Maine condos with his wife. His response did nothing to undermine my enthusiasm for the idea. They walked everywhere and enjoyed the people. The little town had undeniable beauty and felt removed from society's hustle and bustle but still hosted enough cultural events to stimulate them. All of that and it sat on the Maine coast.

"We don't want the kids to feel abandoned," I told Vince on the phone, finding words to express the lurking concern that troubled Kathleen and me.

"Anna's returned to the nest for grad school," Vince said. "But she'd been out of the house for years and probably wants to get her own apartment as soon as she gets a job. Stephan loves West Philly."

I reiterated how regularly we'd return. "And they'll visit us," I said, "once they forgive us for selling Tara."

By the end of the conversation, I saw more clearly the proposed move's advantages to the kids, as well as to us.

During the break between Friday's morning and afternoon classes, a former Honors student surprised me in my office. Now a secondary education major at Temple, he hoped to teach history in a city high school.

"Remember those abbreviations for common blunders that you put on our papers?" Kilgore asked, stretching out in the more comfortable of the two chairs I kept for students. I told visitors that the smaller rickety chair encouraged students to leave their sidekicks and distractions behind.

"Yeah," I said, wondering why reminders about run-ons or sentence fragments would stick in his mind.

"About crazy endings."

"Oh," I said, remembering one that I was sure I'd learned from fellow Honors warrior Ralph Faris. "DSE."

"Dopey Student Ending!" he exclaimed. "I thought I was hot shit."

I laughed. "Haven't used that for a while." So many otherwise solid essays concluded with the rhetorical equivalent of a forced smiley face, a *non sequitur* just tacked on.

"No more pretentious essays?"

I shook my head. "Yours showed real thinking," I said. "They just deserved a coherent ending."

Kilgore's classes at Temple were fine, but he missed the intimacy and intensity he'd known in CCP's Honors classes. He'd gone on from our part-time psych link to two semesters of full-time classes with Ralph and other CCP Honors professors before transferring with a scholarship. "I'm going to graduate," he said. "It's all good. But sometimes I just catch myself wondering if I'm going down the wrong path. Like, is what I'm doing, you know, me?"

"You're trying things out," I said. "Seeing how they work, how they fit. Whether it's in a classroom or on a job, work helps you know who you are. You may think you know. Then you take on some new task and end up surprised as hell at what you can do. You meet a new side of you."

"Becoming a teacher," he said, "was it like that for you?"

"Eventually!" I laughed. "I found out I was a slow learner. Slower than I ever realized at the time—speaking of being *pretentious*."

"Just hold onto your dreams, right?"

Right when I think you're one of my smartest former students, you hit me with a commencement speech line. I sank back into my chair.

"Uh-oh," he said. "You got that look on your face."

"What?"

"Was that a DSE?"

My explosion of laughter got him laughing too. I felt my face instantly redden, and hoped I hadn't hit him below the belt.

"It's not that simple," he went on, his expression that of a comedian in mid-pratfall, not entirely sure he'll survive intact.

"You and I will never play for the Sixers or the Philadelphia Orchestra," I said, "no matter how long and hard we practice. But that leaves a *lot* of opportunity."

"And you don't make it to your top level," he said, his poise now fully recovered, "unless you hold onto your dreams."

I nodded, appreciating the fact that he was not as slow a learner as his former teacher.

"Have ambitious but realistic goals, and work like a mother!" he concluded.

We howled together.

"Doesn't sound too dopey to me," I said, finally catching my breath.

As the next class hour came to an end, we still had a short but key paragraph in Laurence Steinberg's *Beyond the Classroom* that I wanted to go over, despite the time. Ryan, who had missed last Friday's class, still sat in his usual spot in the back of the room with no book in sight. The young white man probably already had stowed it in the backpack that rested atop his desk. I called on him to read.

He generated disapproving noises while shuffling around his possessions a bit. "You're killing me," he mumbled.

Almost everyone else in the class already either had read a passage or responded to a question. His complaint was his first utterance since he'd answered the attendance question.

"I have to get to work."

"Places to go, people to see," I said, evenly, "things to do."

"I got ten minutes to get to my job."

I asked the student two seats away to read, then said to Ryan and the rest of the class, "Let's finish up with these two sentences."

Grudgingly, he remained at his desk. When the young woman finished, I leaned over Ryan and told him that he could leave, then made a closing comment about the paragraph. As he moved toward the door, I told the whole class that I was sorry for running past the scheduled end time.

Some of my colleagues would have lit into Ryan; others never would have apologized for delaying the class. Still others would apologize profusely. Maybe the smart ones would have ignored the whole situation—or stopped before the bell rang. I considered that I might not be as good at this as I thought. I should not have stumbled so easily into the trap of making a comment that might exacerbate the situation, and I didn't even know what response would appropriately address the issue. I needed to tread a delicate line: I could not fault the guy for having to run to a job that he probably needed to keep; on the other hand, I felt the need to prod him into demonstrating some indication that he took responsibility for the course's demands. I ended up saying something that he probably heard as sarcastic, an approach better saved for a private conversation in my office.

Apart from this minor train wreck, I considered the four Friday classes successful. We had covered *Beyond the Classroom*'s first chapter and would double up on chapters, starting Monday. My second-semester Honors students seemed excited by the book about the identical twin sisters, raised separately, who learn about their twin's existence when they reach their thirties. They were amazed to learn how similar the twins were in terms of personal tastes, interests, and sense of humor, despite having been raised in totally different environments. Grasping Thomas Sowell's *A Conflict of Visions* would prove more difficult for them. For that text, pairs of students met with me before leading classroom discussion of a particular chapter. This forced them to read the text for a level of understanding that would enable them to explain it to their peers. We met again after their class to debrief. They usually surprised themselves with the depth of their understanding of the text.

My energy level held up through the day's teaching and the office hour afterward, but these days my body made me aware that teaching four classes approximated performing four sets with the band. By the time I reached home, the impact of the day's "performances" started to hit me. Not so much the performer of a one-man show, I was more a master of ceremonies who also must direct and manage the production. Shortly after helping Kathleen sort out some banking transactions, I crashed on the couch. I woke up around dinnertime with something like a hangover and little desire to prepare our meal. *Did my evenings feel like this ten years ago?* Age, wear and tear, and lack of fitness had taken their toll on me. I joked that nowadays teaching or performing with the band left me feeling the way I used to feel after a rugby game.

After dinner, I crafted an e-mail to Lee, asking for more specific information about the condos. Somehow, in the next week, I must find time to prepare questions for our financial advisor, with whom I would meet at the end of the month. Tomorrow I would try to finish all of the late papers that came in, prepare for Week Three, start the weekend's cooking projects, and, with a little luck, pop out to the rugby field to watch the Blackthorn game. I knew the weekend would fly by. But I felt like I was indeed experiencing my last semester. Too busy to spend more than a few moments considering the possibility, I focused on the thirteen weeks ahead of me, which, despite today's fatigue, seemed very doable. Completely changing our lives felt a lot less so.

I calculated some of the likely trade-offs, were I to retire this year. I knew the campus as intimately as I knew our home. I remembered bringing two-year-old Anna to campus to let her ride the escalators. I had been a full-time student here for two years. I had worked under every president in the college's history. It was my *jawn*, to use the Philly-ese. Students too should feel like they owned it, but unlike them with their two-year stints, I was a lifer. One semester followed another, and my history here went back practically to the beginning of the college's history. After working somewhere for over thirty years, it became a place "where everybody knows your name." I liked the feeling that I performed a useful function, in addition to knowing that my job provided for my family. I liked knowing that some students in my classroom learned things that made big differences in their lives.

Like astronauts setting off for Cape Canaveral, students brought their big plans to community colleges. My own educational trajectory had been nothing to rave about—I did my share of sputtering and fluttering before firing retrorockets and changing course—but I'd witnessed countless others *get started*. The Sids were easy to "sweat with," but the Kilgores had much the same effect on me. And even the Ryans evoked in me a gritty determination to pull something good out of them. Walking away from that rare job that provided meaning and efficacy pretty much every day you went to work would prove difficult.

Many of my colleagues continued teaching long after they reached Social Security age. Shaky hands spelled the end of a surgeon's time in the OR, but teachers with all sorts of age-related impediments lectured on. Whereas most people's jobs offered minimal opportunities for them to recover from fatigue, modify the way they approached their work, or recharge their creative batteries, the academic calendar offered all of those things, making the job manageable.

I didn't want to die with my teaching boots on, hovering over frayed dusty notes, forgetting appointments, and sounding to myself and to students like I'd said it all before and perhaps one time too many. It might be years before I lost my teaching ability; indeed, I might never reach that point. I realized that some teachers remained sharp into old age, but I wanted to leave the college at the top of my game, still possessing enough belief, sharpness, and energy to apply my skills to other pursuits, whether or not they earned money—and whether or not that life would be measured in semesters.

10

Spring Sabbatical, Day Six

Sunday, April 8, 2012: Ireland

The calendar assured me that it was Easter, though my activities that morning were much the same as on any other morning at Cill Rialaig. In between tea-related trips from the desk chair to the kitchen or the bathroom, I pounded away at my computer keyboard. My heaviest exercise consisted of standing at the stove and stirring my small pot of oatmeal, or porridge as the Irish insisted on calling it, hardly the workout entailed by hiding Easter eggs in our terraced backyard when the kids were young. Not a bar of chocolate in sight. No enticing aromas wafting from an oven's simmering roast. I recalled Vince's Italian grandmother's Easter greeting: Happy Yeast!

It was after one before I realized I had not stopped working for more than five minutes. Surely a break would do me good.

I ate some leftovers then took a slow walk up the hill, letting my eyes ease over everything around me. My eyes, strained from fixating on the little screen, relaxed in the cool air. The overcast day yielded no rain, so I noticed the quiet. About a hundred yards above the village, a bend in the road brought me past a wall of tall bushes, at the end of which I found an open field, where I startled a pair of pheasants. The sound of them fluttering off sent a charge up my spine, and I watched them hover before resettling about fifty yards away. Without a warning, they had launched themselves simultaneously, flown side by side, and landed at the same moment right beside each other, as if they'd planned their synchronized maneuver or talked each other through it, step by step. Yes, they had powerful instincts and had done it before, but had they not experienced a first time, when they did not quite know what they were doing?

The road climbed, and turning right and left I glimpsed other hillsides that had not been visible just a few steps downhill. Making sense of a new environment takes time, whether one finds oneself in a college classroom for the first time or the windswept nooks and crannies of the Kerry coastline. Sheep and pheasants seemed to have been built for life in this place—hardly the case with most community college students who discover themselves in a new land.

Freshman year marks a period of transition for all, but it's an enormous one for some. Prep school graduates headed off to Princeton or Amherst as a logical and fairly comfortable next step, and products of decent public high schools similarly move on to decent colleges or universities as a normal and expected transition towards adulthood. Educators created community colleges to serve a broad range of Americans, but one slice of the American population that they court consists of nontraditional students, usually the first of their families to attend college. Many of them arrive with interests in technical or non-bachelor's degree–level programs; however, others, like me in 1966, register for courses in the hope that they are taking the first steps toward at least a BA or BS degree. These were the students that I had kept in mind each time I revised my composition course and had been thinking about all morning in the cottage.

In important ways, traditional students at more selective universities do not differ terribly from their professors or from people with jobs in the fields to which they aspire. Nontraditional students, however, tend to differ greatly from faculty and also from their future workforce peers, mentors, and superiors, especially if they aspire to professional level work.

Some first-year students begin college with their feet already pointed towards independence and success; this does not describe most nontraditional students. Because teachers at some colleges see comparatively few such students, they may see college as a freshman's expected continuation of normal growth, not as an epic expedition through unknown parts in the hope of reaching a better but somewhat vaguely understood destination. The logic employed by people who expect such students to achieve the same graduation rates as traditional students at upper-tier universities would suggest that Central Mountain State Tech's football team had an even chance to beat Alabama's. In terms of key beliefs, practices, and experiences, traditional students differ more from their nontraditional counterparts than they do from their professors.

I thought about those pheasants again. Biology matters in human learning, as my second-semester Honors students came to understand, but human learning hinges less upon biological instinct than does pheasant learning. I'd come upon a pair of pheasants, not one, and my limited encounter pointed to their social nature. For our species, learning is far more complicated, but social influences matter greatly. Beliefs and values—distinctly human qualities—factor into our ability to learn and to change, and they come to us through the people around us. How we understand the purpose of education matters because it influences what we do.

Ask students why they enroll in college, and you will hear answers that have to do with the future. This makes perfect sense, and should cause no surprise or alarm; it parallels the view that many people hold about their jobs. Getting a degree and holding a job are seen as means to an end—dues to pay, hoops to go through on the way to a better life.

But we're not pheasants. Practically every student's view is that going to college is a step toward that life dream. For some, however, that is the limit of their expectation. Their professors are more likely to also see education as an invitation to make significant change in oneself. References to "conversion" may frighten some, but the term gets at the implicit nature of learning. Real education is not exclusively or even primarily about grades, academic credit, and the career possibilities that those things can enable—its goals are deeper and broader. Real education subversively calls on students for more than a quid pro quo task performance, so recipients of real education undergo change, like it or not. Because those goals concern the very make-up of the learner, they can pose a threat to students with strictly instrumental mindsets.

On the way back downhill, gravity helping with my descent, my classroom and students were still very much on my mind. When late-arrival Diego, Jim from Judge, job-conscious Ryan, and their classmates entered my life last fall, neither they nor I had any idea how much each might need to change in order to achieve their dreams. I was anxious to find where I'd left off in my writing file. Nearing the line of cottages, I was huffing, puffing, and sweating, but I felt better than I had all day.

I stopped working when I noticed that the sky was turning dark. I'd unraveled two more days of the semester, and although that effort hadn't added much to the manuscript, it felt like progress. For Easter dinner, I cut up potatoes, carrots, and turnips, boiled them, and served the vegetables with margarine, chopped scallions, and the two spices I'd found in the cupboard—garlic powder and ground black pepper. *How could this food taste so good?* I allowed myself to make all the satisfied noises one suppressed when eating with someone else. Before serving myself seconds, I opened the bottle of white wine I'd placed in the refrigerator on arrival day. My neck and back stiffness faded. "Happy Yeast!" I called, toasting Vince's nonna over the plinking of the rain on the glass roof.

Outside, the wind had returned with gusto, banging the outside half-door against the exterior wall for the first time since the first night's storm. I started a fire and tuned in a new radio station. Listening to Radiohead made me think of my artist/musician/writer son Stephan and how much he would love to hole up with his pencils, guitar, and computer in a place like this. I sat at the table and returned to writing until drooping eyelids finally made me give it up. It was 11 p.m. I had never written for so many hours in one day.

The rain continued into Monday and made for a soggy walk down to the Cill Rialaig gallery. Again, checking e-mail proved less of a chore than I'd expected. Apparently, the other parts of my world were making do just fine without me, with Kathleen being the exception. As planned, she called the gallery telephone at 8 a.m. her time, which was 1 p.m. in Ireland. We exchanged good reports, and I immediately recognized the enormous difference between absorbing news by e-mail and the sensation of a live conversation.

"You sound like you could use a hug," she said. More familiar with the use of projection from my own end, I laughed at the irony. *You really need a Guinness, Kathleen. A kiss. Tickets to see Pat Metheny.* Did she even realize she was doing it now? "Of course I need a hug," I said, and pictured the people and dogs that were the subjects of her reports.

"Tomorrow I should be able to get the damn phone thing straightened out," I assured her, explaining that Avril, the landscape painter, would drive me with her to Caherciveen.

The next morning, I climbed into Avril's VW, and off we went to the phone shop. As I'd found on the previous Thursday, the place again was locked up tight. After noting the "Open At Ten" sign, we headed up the narrow main street, seeking a pot of tea.

A half hour later, we returned to find the shop well lit and a young woman standing at the counter. "You sure are a sight for sore eyes!" I said.

Avril and I came away with phones, but my Northern Irish friend asked me why I'd said what I did to the clerk, who I'd noticed had seemed rather distant after I first addressed her. "You don't use that expression?" I asked.

She shook her head. "Where I come from, it means quite the opposite."

She's having a bit of fun with me. After publicly humiliating her on Saturday, who can blame her? She maintained complete sincerity. I felt myself caught in the trap of imperfect and incomplete enculturation. As I stumbled through adapting to this residency in a remote corner of Ireland, I thought about my students and wondered how many times they found their professors so alien, quirky, and inscrutable. However, I was hardly in their predicament. My experience would last a shorter time and put only my artistic expression at stake—my survival did not depend on it.

In the cottage, I thought about my adaptation to life in this remote corner of Ireland. Like entering students, I had changed my environment. The previous night, I'd been reminded that around Week Four of the semester, students had learned about Albert Bandura's concept of reciprocal determinism. Change, of course, was the subtext. I laughed, suddenly thinking about the pheasants on my recent walk and the mental tangents they'd led me on.

According to Bandura, change in environment often influences other things in one's life, and, of course, that can be one's intention in the first place, such as a prospective student registering for classes or an artist applying for a retreat. Your environment, behaviors, and personal cognitions, such as beliefs and values, influence one another. Sometimes one factor serves as the influencer, while at other times it is influenced by one of the other two factors.[1]

The syllabus article that my students read at this point in the semester tells the story of my third grade audition for the school choir. Asked to sing "do-re-me-fa-so-la-te-do," I did. The teacher asked me to sing it higher. Like a fool (or a concrete-thinking child unable to comprehend the abstract musical concept), I got up on my tiptoes and sang the same exact notes again. Sister Bernardo was not pleased. Unfortunately, she failed to explain to me that she meant something very different than what I, in my musical ignorance, had understood.

Years later, after singing countless songs in the shower and listening to all kinds of recorded and live singing, I started playing rugby and quickly found myself attending my first post-game party. Packed into a living room with thirty or so muddied and bloodied fellow combatants, teammates and opponents alike, I discovered the game's "third half," drinking beer and singing bawdy songs passed down over the years. By the end of the night, I had sung more songs publicly than I had in my entire life. By the end of the season, my club had selected me songmaster. Within a decade, I had performed and recorded as a solo act and as part of a band.

Bandura would certainly point to how a change in environment boosted my learning (or changing) experience. Joining the rugby club put me in a completely different physical and social environment. This new environment influenced my behavior: suddenly I found myself belting out everything from ditties about saucy wenches to solemn Welsh hymns. Singing and learning songs quickly (mistakes with lyrics brought on instant beer dousings) led me to develop a brand-new view both of myself and of singing. My new environment (the rugby culture) led me to new behaviors (public singing), which changed the personal factor of how I saw myself vis-à-vis singing, which prompted me to explore yet other environments for singing, including concert venues and recording sessions.

And so it goes, around and around. Learning implies change. People can become different when they learn something new.

I changed as a teacher after grasping concepts from learning theorists. I applied their ideas in my work. As Bandura might put it, my newfound cognitions prompted changed behavior. Of course students should study the subject of learning, so into the course curriculum the subject went. But the theorists' influence on me went further. Next I was reshaping my course's policies and practices and its sequence of activities: à la Vygotsky, each assignment made use of previous learning and introduced recently shared knowledge from the field. Students surprised themselves by making connections they wouldn't have made before the semester began.

Stepping outside the cottage, I attempted to make a different kind of connection that I had not yet been able to make from my aerie. I pulled out my newly purchased phone, carefully pressed the dialing code for the United States, then the familiar numbers for Kathleen's phone. Suddenly, Kathleen and I were talking about weather, children, and dogs. Later, I called Anna and Stephan. The rest of my world felt less distant.

Sprawling onto the loveseat beside Cottage 8's turf-burning stove, I tried to slow the rush of ideas vying for attention in my brain. We understand new things based on what we already understand. We make connections. Builders add one brick onto one already there, join one section of drywall to another, again and again, until they've made a house. Likewise, learners piece one bit of knowledge onto what they already know.

As a student, I did recognize connections, probably more than my less well-prepared students, but not with the efficiency of a quality student. And the connections I did make I took as informational in the way that a historical fact was informational to me—more as a curiosity or factoid that I should remember for one-time recall on a test, not as something that I would use. For instance, I studied Latin for several years, and though many teachers told me how Latin undergirded English and other languages, I did the work for courses but never made connections between the subjects or the texts until much later.

Trading the loveseat for the stove, I boiled water for pasta and fashioned a sauce with canned tomatoes, mushrooms, onion, garlic, and a splash of red wine. I made enough to have leftovers of what had become my favorite cottage meal, fusilli with a red sauce. At home, I'd rarely made pasta sauce or stew without meat, but in my cottage kitchen, years of experience were helping me cook with limited resources. For a change, the radio offered nothing of interest for dinner, so I listened to Miles Davis, playing my favorite album of his twice in a row. For the first time, I associated *Kind of Blue* with the beautiful but dangerous-looking waters that surged against the rocks below the cottages. In my journal, I wrote, "Living large."

Fall Semester, Week Three

Sunday, September 18, 2011: Philadelphia

Michael Napoletano would join us for dinner and the Eagles–Falcons game, a possible preview of the NFC Championship Game, according to the Sunday Night Football pundits. Having caught up on grading and planning, I looked forward to gathering around the TV with Kathleen, the kids, and Michael, who felt like family. By seventh or eighth grade he had made me realize that I could make someone laugh and that sometimes I might want to unleash my imagination. Truly funny himself, he was an adept enabler, or a "near occasion of sin," as the nuns might have put it. Once he cracked my shell, there was no going back. From the very start, Michael contributed to me becoming a teacher and performer.

By the end of the game's first quarter, there was still no sight of Michael, but by his standards we had not reached the point when someone would mention the L-word.

"I'm sorry I'm late," Michael moaned when he finally opened the unlocked door and stumbled into the living room, bearing a bottle of wine and a white cardboard box that held cannoli or some other highly caloric prize. Our normally riotous sentry dogs made no sound when Michael stepped inside the house but followed him, tails wagging, as he moved from the hallway to the living room. He collapsed on the sofa between Anna and Stephan, who greeted him warmly. Jack and Roux settled at his feet, and he patted them. The game was well into the second quarter. "They're losing. I know they're losing. I listened in the car. They always do this. They suck."

"It's good to see you too, Mike," Kathleen piped up from a rocking chair planted as close to the TV as she could arrange without blocking anyone's view.

"I'm sorry," he moaned again. "How are you, Kathleen?"

"I'm great," she said, leaning closer towards the TV.

"Him, I don't need to ask about," he said, as I planted a full plate on the coffee table in front of him—chili served on a bed of Fritos. "I'm kidding, I'm kidding. This looks great. What is it?"

"Frito pie," I said. We'd already eaten.

"And you remembered to garnish it with the tiny bits of scallions. Perfect."

"Hot tea? Or do you want me to open that wine?"

"No, tea would be great, but only if you're going to have some."

"The kettle's on, Mike."

Suddenly, Mike rose and screamed an obscenity. "Why did he drop the ball? We always do this."

"It's okay," Anna comforted him. "There's a penalty. It's coming back."

By the time she'd turned eight, Anna had grasped more about the nuances of football than Michael but, like Stephan, had never lorded it over him.

"Just watch, Mike," Kathleen called back, still hunched over and studying the quarterback's eyes for an indication of where he might throw the ball.

Michael's commentary—relentless, passionate, and ill informed—inevitably drifted into tangents of a non-football nature. Watching the Eagles without Michael practically guaranteed unmitigated anger and frustration. With him, we laughed more than we cried. "How are you *doing*, Stephan?" Michael asked in the middle of a pass play.

Stephan knew that he really wanted to know and was happy to talk about his music with Michael.

At halftime, we ate dessert in the kitchen. We also learned the reason for today's lateness. He'd been at his cousin's. Or his former coworker's. Or his train buddy's. He didn't leave them when he should have because, after all, he hadn't arrived there on time either.

We talked about the movie *Gettysburg*, which we'd watched again the last time he'd visited. He mused about what the filmmakers went through to hide the battlefield's monuments during the filming. We spoke about Joshua Lawrence Chamberlain, the young Maine professor whose leadership played a pivotal role in the second day of the battle.

"I read somewhere that Victorians believed that one's role in life determined their character," Michael offered. "Make them generals, and they acted like generals. Not me. I couldn't have done that."

"Me neither," I added.

"You don't know that," Kathleen mused. "Maybe we all could, but I'm with you guys. Chamberlain was incredible. We visited his home in Brunswick, Maine. You'd love it, Michael."

Kathleen and I had agreed to keep our Maine scheme to ourselves, and now it was hard. I knew that if we spoke a word of it to Michael or to the kids, so much would change for them. It still was an idea, a possibility. Better to let them deal with a reality—if such a thing were in the cards—when things were certain.

Michael-induced laughter had been part of my life since sixth grade, part of Kathleen's since she'd met me. She'd married me and immediately found herself related to this short Italian American man. The ultimate BOGO—buy one, get one free.

"I don't need a second cannoli," he said, flashing Kathleen a desperate look.

"Oh, Michael," she sighed. "Don't wait for anyone's permission."

"Would it help if I had one," I offered.

"You just love to help people, don't you?" he said, sliding the box toward me.

"Delicious," I garbled, savoring the chocolate filling, but I kept thinking about this evening as something I might be leaving behind. We'd surely spend significant time with Michael, whether or not we moved to Maine, but I didn't like the idea of fewer such connections with him. Moving meant that time with Stephan, Anna, and Michael would be different—limited, with a definite end time in sight.

The Eagles surged back in the third quarter, taking a ten-point lead into the fourth quarter. Michael uncharacteristically announced his departure with fourteen minutes left to play. "You guys gotta get up early," he said, rising. "They're going to lose anyway, the bastards."

I tucked the unopened bottle of wine under his arm when he headed to the door.

"He's probably late for dessert somewhere," Kathleen said.

In our pajamas, we watched the Falcons score two touchdowns to beat the Eagles.

Monday brought stacks of drafts and our first rounds of writing seminars, which meant that I must operate the document camera—one of the few contraptions of the modern classroom that didn't make me feel like a hopeless dinosaur. One plopped an essay page on the machine's glass, and presto, it appeared on the wall or on a screen large enough for the students to read it from across the room. No copying at the copy center by me; no copying by students of other people's work. A page showed up on the screen then disappeared. My two unlinked 101 classes met in "smart classrooms," which did not seem all that clever after all. Equipped with the gadgetry of an Air Force jet cockpit, these classrooms could perform approximately 113 feats of electronic technology. But I needed only one: the "doc cam," as I referred to it when I wanted to impress multimedia services staff. Unfortunately, the document camera function had gone kaput in these two expensively revamped classrooms, so even though the room had a document camera, I would need to have one brought in every time I wanted to use it.

The classroom looked full but probably wasn't. Regular attendance didn't guarantee success on the student's voyage, but irregular attendance was akin to charting an ocean-crossing through placid-looking but rocky straits. I went through the roll, asking if students remembered to include a references page in their paper. By the last student's answer, the usually prompt multimedia technician still had not shown up. Without the smart cart, I needed to tap dance. I pulled one of the drafts from the stack, read aloud the first paragraph, and started talking about its architecture. I filled the board, outlining the organization evident in the draft. Finally, the technician arrived, and after a scramble involving her, Ian the tech-savvy former Marine, and me, the first page of the essay popped up on the screen, and we started noting what each paragraph tried to do to the reader. For some reason, the temperature in the room had soared into the nineties, making everyone in class miserable, including me, still wrestling with the cold that had slowed my weekend.

Writing seminars involved working on previously unseen drafts, so the entire class became an improvisational routine. Students tended to focus on writing errors and, if left to their own devices, would contentedly tinker a bit on sentence construction. Few drafts contained actual organization. For the first writing seminar of the semester, I could pretty much count on finding at least one essay in each class that consisted of one gigantic paragraph. Picking randomly from the pile, we read through two such offerings, spending most of the hour talking about task and organization.

When class ended, I rushed the smart cart to the second classroom, mindful that without the assistance of the tech, I was on my own. The classroom felt even hotter than the first room. Ian, who had hopped up from his seat to secure the uncooperative projection screen in S2-12B, trailed me, connected the smart cart in the 12:20 classroom, then disappeared before I could thank him. Please, I thought, let his writing match his citizenship.

We read aloud the first draft that appeared on the screen: one rambling paragraph that ended in the middle of page two and never mentioned Vygotsky's concepts.

I made no effort to hide writers' identities on papers used during writing seminars. Sometimes I picked blindly from the stack; other times, I scanned the possibilities and selected one that promised an interesting discussion. From the start of the semester, my students knew that I might well project any ill-conceived, poorly thought out, unedited mess onto the classroom's big screen, an inducement for them to do more than the bare minimum. However, the first assignment's drafts looked as if the writers had written with no fear of embarrassment. Many students missed the task's point, doing something entirely different. More than one paper told the story of a learning experience with absolutely no mention of Vygotsky, let alone any application of his concepts to the story. By the end of the hour, we had read one paper that attempted to complete the task in a logical way, although not with control over the writing.

A frowning woman across the room stared at me. "You won't write anything on these papers to help us see what to fix?" she asked. Others appeared to share her irritation and disappointment. They expected that as the way a teacher should conduct the course. I reminded them that I would gladly go over their work with them, one on one, in my office but that such review would not happen in class. At this point, I was sure that some class members had written me off as a teacher who did not go out of his way to help. A few students followed me to my office after the writing seminar.

"How will I know what to do?" Charisse asked, desperation in her voice.

"That's the reason we do writing seminars," I said.

"But what if we don't look at my paper in class?" Afafa asked.

"You can come here during office hours, if you want."

Disgusted facial expressions suggested that they had just determined the particular nature of my cruelty.

"Did looking at Rashid's essay today help?" I asked.

"Yeah, but we don't have time to go over every essay in class," another whined.

"That's what makes those sessions so important," I answered. "And students can get together for study groups or extra writing seminars."

"Without you?"

I nodded. "It happens. Sometimes students organize little groups to do things like that, usually to go over difficult texts but also to help each other figure out writing assignments."

They looked at each other, not sure if they wanted to pursue that novel possibility.

"You can e-mail me drafts with questions," I said. This seemed to calm them a little bit.

"Just don't do it at the last minute," I warned them. "I need time to get back to you, and you'll need time to deal with my response."

The little group stood around, taking in the photographs and posters on my office walls, the books on my shelves—signs that I belonged to this alien world of academics and a measure of their distance from it and from me. Sometimes with such first-time visitors, I saw a glimmer in their eyes that made me think they might want to join this world, or at least want to give it a chance; other times, I saw only distrust.

We went through one of their drafts, noting what each paragraph tried to do to the reader, and how that related to the task. I sensed that they might feel like someone wanted to force them to learn chess, a game that they had no intention of learning. One of them thanked me, and the others smiled and said they would see me in class. They still talked to each other as they walked down the hallway, and I wondered if the nucleus of a little crew might have formed, a group that I'd see next month in the study lounge at the end of the hallway or in the cafeteria or the library.

I could not know how many students in this class would founder. Most of them did not follow me back from the classroom. Jim from Judge and most of his classmates had shuffled off to other classes or to their jobs, keeping the level of their engagement to themselves for now, except for the ones who could not hide or did not bother to try to hide their disapproval or disinterest. And, as always, some of them already had started missing class, smashing my hopes for a class with perfect attendance.

On Wednesday, Ryan, who'd told me I was killing him last Friday and who had missed Monday's class, showed up, but he said nothing and produced no paper. Halfway through Week Three, he had just about flat-lined. Diego, who had his class debut delayed by vacation, had turned in no work to date but had told me all about his background at prestigious Central High School, and had mentioned his plans to transfer to a good school.

Meanwhile, in the first-semester Honors class, lack of attendance already threatened to decimate the class. One student seemed barely present even when he *did* attend. After taking roll, I brought the Do Not Enter sign to the door. Looking down the hall, I saw LeSean and a classmate sauntering toward the room. I let them enter, telling each of them that they had made it by the hair on their chinny chin chins. Had I not let LeSean in, he would have received his third straight absence. I mentioned him and the worrisome writers in the other Honors class to Vince, and we agreed to have a little chat with them on Monday.

Friday also brought another wrangling session with the multimedia equipment and one more writing seminar on student drafts before the revisions would be due next Monday. Douglas, the fortyish black man with over a hundred credits at a local university, maintained a straight face while asking me if he could resubmit his untouched first draft as the revision. I paused, hoping that Douglas was joking, since I had repeatedly detailed the revision process to the class since the semester's first day. The syllabus article fairly pounded them with the idea. "It looks that good to you?" I said.

"I think it's done," Douglas said innocently.

I did my best to explain that although I appreciated that he apparently put in a great deal of work on the *draft*, his official final copy must reflect whatever he had learned from the revision process done during the week since he wrote the draft. The most sobering aspect of this exchange came from my sense that no one in the class saw that this polite, sincere student had missed the whole point. Others would submit a revision that differed from their original draft in only the most trivial ways. Apart from correcting the odd spelling error, these writers made no revisions to organization or content.

To a lesser degree, the same held with the Honors class students' versions of the same assignment. The Honors students uniformly possessed talent, so I was convinced that the method's newness had frozen many of them into an unsure state, leaving them prone to missteps, a state that I hoped they would pass out of quickly.

Most of my students considered word count academic writing's most essential requirement. Once they produced a relatively clean-looking document that dealt with the correct topic and approached the minimum required length, many students believed that they had finished the process, save for perhaps catching a few misspellings or typos. This common student approach to writing an academic essay matched the way they viewed their workforce jobs, an instrumental perspective. They worked a shift and got paid for it. So when they wrote a paper, they expected to get a grade and credit for it. Most jobs that students held did not require redoing work unless the boss complained about quality, and at the end of the day, workers received pay for hours worked, regardless of mistakes or how long acceptably performing a task had taken. They clung tenaciously to this view, no matter how many times an instructor explained the revision concept to them.

Revision constituted one of the most essential parts of the writing process. I told them that it held just as much importance for authors who had produced a long shelf of books as it did for English 101 freshmen. Shock and disbelief appeared on Douglas's face when I told the class how many times I revised stories I had written, how many years I had labored over fiction pieces, seeing new issues, concerns, possibilities every time I returned to a story.

An engaged student who wanted to become good at this, Douglas suddenly seemed unsure if he really wanted to take on all that this writing thing seemed to demand. "Years?" he asked.

On other faces, I saw something else. *What kind of fool wastes his time like that?*

We had completed eight days of classes. We had reached the end of Week Three, and I realized that all of the familiar old issues already had presented themselves.

Our financial advisor agreed with us that if I retired the following year, it would require us to downsize, though desirable possibilities that we could afford existed in Maine, not nearby. Since our fact-finding mission, we had devoted several weeks to online property research, e-mail correspondence with our Maine real estate agent, and to our own soul searching. Crunching numbers had become my nightly routine. Three or four times each week, alone in the car or in bed before sleep, Kathleen and I grappled with unquantifiable elements in this decision-making process. By Week Four of the semester, we had clarified three things: we loved our home on McCallum Street; we believed we would love the condo in Maine just as much; and we could not have both things at the same time.

After I'd graded Sunday night's last paper, I crunched financial numbers, bringing the same urgency to weighing the pros and cons of our scheme as I did to returning students' papers on time, but with a difference. The semester went on for a fixed length of time. I knew exactly how long I could give due diligence to teaching and grading, but in an instant, someone else might buy the condo out from under us. Yet we could not move rashly. I realized that some of the truisms that applied to our real estate deliberations also applied to my students. A missed class or an hour meeting with a teacher or tutor meant something, but at certain times, it meant more because more rode on it. Successful life transitions required a certain amount of time and effort, and always timing was everything.

Shifting from weekend mode on Monday required more time and effort than normal. When road closures directed me away from my customary route, I found myself driving down Broad Street past Temple University, where Laurence Steinberg worked as a professor in the psychology department. By this point, I assumed that my students had seriously taken on Steinberg's *Beyond the Classroom* and had started to read about factors that led to American youth's rampant disengagement, which Steinberg characterizes as a "deliberate disenchantment," a state that many of my students should have recognized when they read about it.[1] Also, Steinberg rates peers as a huge adolescent influence.[2] Peers remained a key to understanding college freshmen, even those much older than traditional student age.

The idea that Ryan belonged to a circle of friends who shared serious commitments to college would have surprised me. Likewise, Will, Ryan's baseball-capped white classmate and a recent high school graduate, sat in class displaying a demeanor that screamed, "I will perch here quietly when I do make it to class, but don't expect me to speak: I'm not that kind of student." With a revision due in three days, he still had not turned in his first draft. I was fairly sure that Will did not rush directly to the library or to the computer lab right after class, and I suspected that his student friends did not either. For him, trying college constituted a rite of passage, as it did for most low-achieving students with vague future plans. Most likely, he had minimal interest in college; family members probably urged him to give it a shot, or he had no better options, so fall arrived, and in the fall people went back to school. He did not possess a successful student's behavioral profile. Exposure to college might change his attitude, but a whole string of changes would have to occur before the odds of that happening improved. If a young man with his profile experienced some success in college, he might start to spend more and more time with other students, and his social network might broaden to include more engaged peers.

Stuck in traffic, I pondered Steinberg's findings about peer influence. The first time I'd read his book, I'd been surprised to learn that peer influence did not require intimate friendships. Besides friends and acquaintances, the category of influential peers included strangers with whom individuals shared likes and dislikes. [3] A good chance existed that these strangers presented themselves similarly in terms of dress, hairstyle, and manner of speech. Fashion in its varied forms might be created by the clothing and fashion industries, but this kind of indirect peer influence surely helped its proliferation. How else could one account for those little hipster hats so popular with baristas? Ways of dressing or grooming enabled members of the same subculture to recognize peers as *their people*. Of course, like the rest of us, they did not limit themselves to just one group, perhaps identifying with and thus exposing themselves to various crews of influence at different times.

My classes presented the picture of diversity. No doubt, when my students left class they returned to social circles that in many cases reflected their particular ethnicity. Steinberg's book talks about the indirect but telling influence that ethnicity had on students via their peers, and often that influence did not benefit nontraditional students. The story did not end there, though, because students who persisted in college experienced more relationships with more people, broadening a student's previously uniform social network and exposing them to peers who modeled effective learning practices.

I'd seen that happen over and over again in the Honors curriculum and in other support programs that entailed more than the usual social immersion one finds in taking classes à la carte. I thought about once-disengaged Trevor, who, when nearly thirty, had enrolled in courses in the College's Transfer Opportunity Program, one of the programs that subsequently evolved into the Honors curriculum. This Norristown carpenter and son of a carpenter had connected with classmates and faculty as if his soul had been starved for such contact, achieved high grades in every CCP course he took, transferred to Temple University, and now was teaching in one of the city's public high schools. "The program changed me," he told me years later. He probably would have succeeded in just about any kind of academic situation, but he pointed to his relationships with his classmates and teachers in the program as having locked him into successful behaviors. He was right about the influence of classmates. It was different from the experience students have in unlinked classes, where classmates barely knew each other. Students entered TOP or Honors expecting that the teachers had something to offer them, but they had no idea that we considered their peer relationships to be among our best tools.

In conversations with Trevor and other former students whom I'd taught in collaborative programs, I often felt embarrassed by how much they credited the faculty. From the start, their dedication had been apparent. *What did we do that was so special?* We offered them a safe yet challenging environment in which formerly weak students could reinvent themselves. And timing mattered on both ends. *They* were ready. We told them how much we enjoyed watching them grow into active learners, but I doubt they understood how much their progress fueled us. We taught them about psychology, political science, academic writing, literature, and sociology, but most importantly, we tried to teach them about learning. They in turn taught us about teaching.

I had been one of those disengaged community college students, but because I'd attended good schools, I had a solid knowledge and experience base, and I traveled in a peer network whose members all enrolled in college. My students' initial peer networks might see college as a potentially useful experience, but not as a gateway to change. Some members of their original peer groups considered taboo the idea that education might alter or threaten one's essential self.

Family members and partners also could exert pressure that undermined a student's efforts. Two semesters ago, Cassie broke down in my office, telling me that her boyfriend had demanded that she stop school. "He says it is disrupting our life. According to him, I am always at school or have my head in my books. At first, he was okay with it, but now he says, 'What good is this?'"

Sliding my box of tissues towards her, I wrote down the name and number of a counselor that I thought might be a good fit for her. We talked a bit more about her situation and went over an essay, but after another week she disappeared. I e-mailed her but got no response. She left having never turned in anything below a B paper. Vince, Gary, and I heard at least one such story per year.

Teachers only sometimes learned the details that led to a student's departure. The flash of disappointment and frustration that hit me after such disappearances yielded to the grim recognition, familiar to all community college teachers, that I'd be better off focusing on the students who remained. Still, I hoped that in some future semester I might see that familiar face in the hallway.

Traffic continued to edge forward on Broad Street, allowing me to search for familiar buildings amidst the campus construction that had been taking place since my student days. Temple students swarmed the sidewalks. This was their normal. They belonged here. When I'd transferred from CCP to Temple for my junior year of college, I felt like someone leaving a small town for the big city.

When I turned onto Spring Garden Street, I saw CCP students emerging from the subway exits and bearing down on the campus, three blocks west. I thought about the distance I'd traveled from freshman year to a college teacher's position. By and large, professors were individuals who had been changed by education and who sought to facilitate such change in their students. They lived for ideas.

Engagement with ideas was but one of the qualities that beginning community college students did not necessarily share with their teachers. Many things separated one group from the other: skills, particular kinds of knowledge, experience, and, perhaps most significantly, engagement with and participation in academic culture. In so many important ways, faculty and students simply did not think alike, act alike, or believe the same things. This student/faculty divide had always existed, and continued to exist, but the gap never grew wider than the one that existed between nontraditional students and college instructors.

Community college teachers must never forget how alien, intimidating, and unwelcoming their students found this experience, despite their best efforts. I was a CCP alumnus and the son of a working-class single mother whose native language was not English. As a result, I never had difficulty seeing myself in my students and them in me. Every semester, my students reminded me of their dignity, decency, integrity, and intelligence. But I knew that, like me back in the fall of 1966, they needed more than new skills and knowledge. They needed their teachers to do what teachers did for me: welcome them into academic culture. As my Honors colleagues Dennis McGrath and Martin Spear posited in *The Academic Crisis of the Community College*, these students' teachers and counselors, along with college administrators and staff, "should be trying to bridge the gulf of disarticulation, to make academics inviting and engaging."[4]

Vince and I had thought about enculturation a great deal when we developed our Honors link for introductory English and psychology, and I had major concerns about it when I organized my most recent unlinked English 101 course. He and I hardly invented the wheel when we tried to create a semester experience that would assist the students' academic enculturation. For years, many educators had considered the College's full-time Honors curriculum—equivalent to five courses—a model for how to bring community college students into academic culture and for how to help them build skills and broaden and deepen their content knowledge. Working with Honors colleagues and others who had taught in collaborative ventures at the College greatly influenced and benefited my collaborative work with Vince and my solo teaching experiences.

That week, my non-Honors 101 students read another article from the syllabus that shone a light on the differences between students and faculty and that introduced students to Bandura's ideas. The article lays out the idea that ways of thinking, ways of acting, and kinds of environments impact one another.

While students usually found Vygotsky's theory a useful explanation of how they or another family member learned something like how to drive a stick shift or how to bake an apple pie, this part of the semester's reading usually helped them to see connections between ideas in the various texts we read, to view the different ways that the lives of literary characters and real people changed, and, on certain blessed occasions, to see connections between different influences in their own lives.

By this point in the semester, I should have seen several pieces of writing from all of my 101 students, but several individuals resembled actors playing roles as students rather than being real students who did the course's work. Others had revealed more to me than they intended to about themselves either in class, during office hours, or through e-mail, a communication method that exposed students more than they thought. For instance, I received the following message from one of the young women whose chatty passive-aggressiveness toward Chelsea had provided Day One's only bad note:

> hey I haven't gotton an email.from you yet I sent my paper in
> a email and asked you to email me back to say you got it and
> that I would bring a printed copy in on wenesday

Checking my records, I saw that Ella, a member of the track team, had turned in the draft but no revision, which had been due yesterday. Neither of her two previous e-mails requested a reply. I noted this in my response and reminded her that turning it in immediately would avoid any further grade reductions. After the next class, I approached her privately about the late paper. Reading tone in any e-mail presents difficulties, but I braced myself, expecting an encounter with a hostile student.

"I messed up," she said, flustered. "Coach wants us to start strong, and school's no different." Her pleasant enough demeanor came as a relief, but it betrayed her ignorance about how her e-mail's language represented her.

If my mind had worked more quickly, I could have made it a teaching moment. The next time I saw Ella I would say that I appreciated her effort to address a question, and I would stress the importance of representing herself well in any professional communication.

Her indiscretion betrayed a different set of social boundaries. Like changing shorelines, sensibilities about what one ought to say or could get away with saying to one's professor reminded me of how old I was, and of how long I had been in this occupation. Once, when I entered the building wearing a striped pullover and something that must have looked like a beret, an Honors student mused aloud: "Hey, you going all mime on us now?"

At home, I marked up essay revisions, noting errors and offering questions and comments. For years, I had watched students grab the marked-up papers and ignore the comments, flipping to the essay's last page looking for their grade. My practice of meeting individually with students, reading through their paper and my comments, and telling them the grade after they had offered their best guess at it irked them. I considered the hours I spent studying each paper's expression more helpful for them when I used this method. It forced them not only to reread their paper but also to read my comments and to try to make sense of them. The grades mattered to them—as they should have—but the route to earning better grades depended on them understanding and addressing the comments. Lines formed at the end of classes when I returned papers and trade improved during office hours, to the point that I had to apologize for eating my sandwich while I talked with a student in the minutes before my next class.

On Friday, I returned Monday's on-time revisions, sparking lines of anxious students after class and later at my office door. Jim was standing outside the office when I arrived after my last class of the day. He nodded as we went through my comments, mostly pleas for elaboration. "The writing is under control, Jim. And your paper is on the right track."

"So, that's good, right?"

"Definitely," I said. "Were you in a hurry?"

"Yeah, I got stuff to do."

"I mean when you wrote it?"

He laughed. "Sure."

I looked at him, waiting to hear about a job or a sick family member, but he just frowned.

I showed him places in the essay where a bit more explanation or support would have cleared things up or fleshed out the points he had made.

"It's probably something in the neighborhood of a C," he said, businesslike.

I nodded, divining no further reaction from his demeanor, and wondering what grade might elicit a noticeable response. "C+," I said. "Follow through a bit more, and your next paper should be more satisfying."

"I'll do that, Mr. Ned," he said, and packed up his papers. He flashed a smile and was gone.

He hadn't taken enough steps to "up his game" yet, but I saw that such steps were within his reach. I let myself savor the thought that this young man might be headed to a successful semester.

When tall, lanky Luther finished going over his barely passing first assignment, he told me about his life as a full-time parent, caring for his severely mentally disabled daughter. He also had two younger children. After fifteen years away from school, his wife, a paralegal, talked her high school–dropout husband into preparing for and taking the GED test. Having passed remedial courses during the summer, he fully appreciated all the help that he had received and continued to receive. He talked about his future with words of hope and determination, but I saw anxiety and fear in his eyes.

I found helping this type of student easy. After hearing such stories of hardship and courage, I concluded that only Dickensian villains would do less than everything they could to assist these people, but I knew that I couldn't carry the earnest, hard-working students on their uphill journey toward the finish line. I could try to serve as Vygotsky's scaffolding; à la reciprocal determinism, I could become an active part of an environment that encouraged useful behaviors and cognitions, then hope that students did their parts without encountering more obstacles than they could handle.

Bill, a quiet Polish American student who was perhaps in his forties, e-mailed me his four-day-late first assignment. In a private moment, he already had reported that since the semester had started he had lost his house and moved into a friend's dining room, lost his unemployment benefits, and had an intruder steal his computer. He had missed two straight classes, and when he returned that day without the revision of the first paper, I had to tell him that continuing without submitting the work made no sense. The e-mail had arrived when I got home. "I understand that excuses are just that and I hope that this indicates my willingness to move forward in class and shows my engagement.... I continue to adjust to my new environment and wrestle with getting my personal factors under control in order to change my behaviors. But I'll be going into depth on that for my next paper. I really appreciate the collateral learning that you've built into this composition class and I'll do my best to keep up with the work from this point forward. See you in class on Monday."

Obviously, Bill had kept up with the reading. And, as promised, he would show up on Monday with completed work, settling in as a strong student.

Matt, an Honors student, e-mailed about what he called his second chance to get an education. "Not to get all deep and personal, but a lot of what Steinberg has said in *Beyond the Classroom* has resonated on a very personal level, and brought back all sorts of intense emotions/feelings related to my time spent in high school/my late teens, and how chaotic that time period was for me. Painful as those times are to recall, I'm glad to be in this place now—(mostly) intact, and embracing whatever may come with hope and humility."

I might go an entire semester without receiving one such indication of efficacy, and I'd come home to find two of them waiting for me. At least a few students appeared to be learning. Doing so against the odds they faced firmed up my resolve to leave everything on the field, as athletes put it. Yes, I thought, the course was working for these two. I couldn't live with myself if I did not give as much effort to my part in their story as they were giving. This was the kind of fiery moment that I would summon up when facing a fresh batch of essays in the middle of a semester's darkest night—a student's Saint Crispin's Day speech to their teacher.

I might have died on the vine had I been confined to a corporate cubicle, but at CCP I'd found work that roused me on a regular basis. The cause of my students had taken over part of me. It wasn't entirely rational. Not so many months ago, that something inside me had led me to risk injury to preserve the peace on the third floor of the Mint Building when the fight had erupted during exams. Even knuckleheads like the one I had been as a student deserved this incredible shot at redemption. I got to play a role in that struggle.

But that didn't mean that I should go on doing this work indefinitely. This opportunity to retire had to happen now and was not something I could postpone. All of the reasons that had convinced me that this was the time to retire still held. Yet, as I started the semester's fourth weekend, part of me wondered if leaving this job would indicate that I had gone crazy.

Spring Sabbatical, Day Nine

Wednesday, April 11, 2012: Ireland

I'd quickly learned that radio operated by different rules in Ireland. I got a variety of programming without moving the dial, a good thing considering how few stations I could find. RTÉ Lyric FM kept me company when I gave the computer screen a rest and tempted me to delay my return to work. In the morning, they played the Rolling Stones, plaintively singing about failure to make a connection, which until yesterday could have been my theme song. But I now had a phone that worked from the top of Bally Nowhere, so I was flaunting it—two calls from my rocky aerie to Kathleen and the kids yesterday and two more today.

After getting caught up in a spoken segment about myth in the African American community, I puzzled over a Schubert piece until the host announced that it had been used in the movie *Au Revoir Les Enfants*. Van Morrison wailed "Ballerina." Finally, I made myself turn the thing off and return to my laptop.

I had entered the second week of my month at Cill Rialaig. At the equivalent point in the semester, my students had just about finished reading the Steinberg book. Jobs and extracurricular activities caught Steinberg's attention in one of his final chapters, enticingly titled "Making Jack a Dumb Boy." Americans love the idea of individuals paying their own way, and according to Steinberg's view, high school parents make a great mistake when they allow their children to overdo the nonacademic activities, be they extracurricular or income producing. Football and basketball are major offenders because of the great amounts of weekly time involved and the length of the training and playing season, but any involvement that required more than twenty hours a week became a threat to adequate engagement in school.[1]

High school students often rush into after-school activities, both because they wish to round out their profile for college admissions offices and also because jobs offer students a chance to earn spending money, an activity that tends to please rather than alarm parents. Well over half of high school students work jobs, and this prevalent distraction tends to further encourage disengagement from school. Work in excess of that twenty-hour-per-week mark generally leads to lower interest in academics and to lower achievement.[2] If doing so in high school alarmed Steinberg, one can only imagine his concern for college students doing the same.

While relatively few of my students became involved in student government or intercollegiate athletics, most of them held jobs, many of them full time or close to it. I learned this when they showed me their filled-out schedules in the first week. In class, Vince had cited the research, and their assigned reading informed them about the standard formula that called for at least two hours outside of class work for every hour spent in class if they expected to earn at least a C grade in a course. Four courses usually equated to at least twelve credits, which meant that a typical student needed to devote twenty-four hours each week in order to achieve the lowest grade that would transfer to another college. Of course, a transcript of all C grades hardly impressed a university's admissions department, so this figure set the bar about as low as possible.

"Write JOB in every hour block on your weekly schedule that you must work or commute to your job," I'd directed them on Day One. Invariably, not enough blank hours remained in their schedules to meet the calculated minimum for study time. They frowned and hoped for the best, but when we reached this part of Steinberg's text, I pointed out his claim that students could reverse disengagement when they reduced or eliminated their job hours, an option that caused their academic interest to rise.[3]

But my students rarely felt that they had such an option. Instead, they would make the most of a bad situation. For most of them, job hours were an economic reality, and once the semester began, their heavy schedules were subject to only minor tweaking. "Before you know it," I told them, "you will be registering for next semester. If you can't reduce your job hours, take a lighter academic load. Do the arithmetic *before* you pick your next classes."

The rain had let up, so I popped outside the cottage with a cup of tea and took in the rainbow that rose from the white-capped waters below and reached to the mountains behind the next neck of land down the coast. Rona stepped outside too, commenting that it wasn't quite as dramatic as the one she'd seen the night of her arrival. I laughed at the thought that one might ever grow jaded about rainbows in such a setting.

Suddenly, the din of the ancient green truck that I'd seen once but heard often enough from my cottage interrupted our conversation. We stopped talking and watched it rattle down the hill toward us. Rona waved to the driver, who nodded. The same galloping dog trailed the truck by only a few feet.

"Have you met the farmer?" she asked.

Truck, dog, and dust disappeared down the hill's curves. "Sheep farmer?" I asked.

"He has flocks he tends up and down the hill."

"Why doesn't he let the dog hop into the truck?"

"It's a work dog. He told me the dog likes to run."

Finally the hurly-burly commutes throughout the day made sense. I just hadn't seen enough to put two and two together. "I think my head's been in the computer too long," I said.

"Apparently."

I learned that she'd been a physicist before abandoning science for art. She also told me she'd been to Cable O'Leary's pub, drawn by the pub's artifacts from the laying of the original transatlantic cable in the middle of the nineteenth century, the historical event behind her current project. This O'Leary fellow, a worker on the ship beginning to lay the cable, had jumped into the water when the cable had been accidentally dropped into the deep and presumably lost. The rescuer was dubbed Cable O'Leary for his efforts.

After Rona had left, a Welsh mother and her adult son paused in their hike to ask about the village. They were just back from ascending to Bolus Head. We connected, talking about their hometown of Swansea and about Dylan Thomas. They were taking their Irish holiday, as everyone here called vacation, and their superb good humor convinced me that they indeed made a holiday out of every vacation day. Tonight they were headed to Tig Rosie, the second-nearest pub, located just across the line in Dungeagan. "Beside the church," they chorused. The pub just might host some traditional music. How had I spent a week in fiddle-rich Kerry and not heard a note of live music? But I'd been as happy as a clam in deep mud.

I returned to the cottage, amazed at how much I'd learned in so little conversation and about how learning built on previous learning. I supposed that Rona's studies and her work background had touched on the science of rainbows, and that she had more useful background than I did when it came to grasping the intricacies of connecting people who were separated by thousands of ocean miles by means of an underwater cable.

Students arrived with different kinds of foundational knowledge, but theirs might not constitute the proper basis from which to learn what we needed them to learn. I thought of my students who had the weakest skills. The greatest lecture or laboratory demonstration meant little or nothing to them if they lacked the base upon which the teacher built the presentation. Attempts to read James Joyce after I had learned something about Irish history and culture proved more successful and rewarding than earlier efforts.

Save for speaking with Kathleen, the only other voices I heard that day were the ones in my head when I was staring at the light of the computer screen. When the rain let up around five, I stepped outside with a bag of laundry to try my luck with the coin-operated washing machine next door. Despite the cold wind, birds sang and the sky had turned blue again. Michael, the village caretaker, stood just inside the laundry, its red door propped open. When he saw me, he stepped outside. "Oh er oo?" he trilled, as I climbed the winding stone steps toward him.

"Great," I said, after a painful moment of translation. My answer mostly referred to how much work I had managed to do. He was well too. Somehow tufts of grass managed to grow on this stony patch, and I stood shivering between green clumps. Michael commented on the fineness of the day, to which I agreed, despite the ominous clouds already gathering in the distance.

He showed me how the washing machine worked, mostly gesturing between utterances in a brogue that sounded even more extreme than the previous time I'd spoken with him. Thanking him, I smiled and headed back to my computer.

At five before nine, I put on a few more layers and headed out for a short, slow walk. Darkness had not yet fallen. I found this one of my favorite times of the day here. I walked down past the other cottages and a bit further east, to a spot where I could see the Waterville lights twinkling across the bay. Out on the water's expanse, a small boat's light gave off the only hint of human life. On an island to the west, a lighthouse lamp rotated, illuminating my vantage every ten seconds or so.

Hours of writing had turned into days, and now I was well into a second week of it. The work might leave me with little more than recovered memories and a string of questions, yet still I felt rewarded. Whether we write all day in a cottage or enroll in college, we do so in order to gain something, whether it be extrinsic, intrinsic, or both. My feeling of satisfaction brought to mind former Reed College president Colin S. Reed's piece about the purpose of education. In it, he wrote that we all share an instrumental perspective—that practical, purposed approach—but for some of us, it sums up our motivation. Diver contrasts the instrumental view as the limited alternative to an intrinsic-rewards view built around the concept that education and, indeed, life, are about "inquiry and discovery... [and] pursuing knowledge for its own sake."[4]

Diver acknowledges that students holding an intrinsic-reward approach surely also want and expect financial reward and advancement in their chosen fields. A prospective student reading the piece reasonably draws the conclusion that going for meaning instead of just for moolah suggests that you can end up with both.

The night I read Diver's essay, I knew I would include its thinking in the next article I wrote for the syllabus. It may seem hard to sell nontraditional students on intrinsic rewards when they're looking for extrinsic ones, but Diver's view is not impractical or elitist at all. Pitting extrinsic against intrinsic rewards presents a false choice, because the one need not rule out the other.

The artists in the darkened cottages behind me knew something about intrinsic and extrinsic rewards. But apparently, like me, they were far too consumed with their work to have time to sit around and chat about such notions. Only a few weeks into the story of the fall semester, so much ground loomed ahead, but my progress, never purely linear, felt real.

In the gathering dark, no lights twinkled on the mountains across from me. The original cottages' last residents, back in the time of the Famine, had glimpsed this exact same view. In the thirteenth century, when the monks left Skellig Michael, eighteen miles out to sea, they settled in the abbey on the beach near where the café now sat. They might have walked up here and taken in the same view that I now drank in like a fine port. From this vantage point, I could hear the waves smashing into unseen rocks far below. Lined up above me, the cottages looked like ruins I might have discovered on some centuries-forgotten island. A few clouds scudded across the sky above them, as they had all day, harmless enough on an evening predicted to produce many showers. To the east, the sky appeared darker, thicker, with different kinds of clouds. My ten days in Ireland had taught me that people here needed only one forecast: cloudy with wind and rain. Every day, except this one, the same conditions had prevailed. When I heard the same exact forecast on RTÉ Lyric FM for the fifth straight night, I laughed. I walked back to the cottage, hoping that my memory would return the images of this night always.

Five minutes later, rain drummed on the glass ceiling. The radio weatherman had nailed it again. Gratefully sheltered, I found where I'd left off and resumed typing.

Fall Semester, Week Five

Monday, October 3, 2011: Philadelphia

Already I had heard many students speaking of their jobs, and a number of them arrived for class dressed for work. Except for the second-semester Honors section, each of the other classes included two or more students who already had reached at least halfway to the semester's absence limit by Week Five. I wondered how much their employment factored into these dangerous attendance patterns.

Of course, students did not always toil away at coursework, run off to first and second jobs, change diapers at home, or volunteer at the city homeless shelter. Only the rarest of students did not use Facebook or some other social networking system. They hardly restricted cell phone conversations to work or emergency use. Television remained a daily temptation. When romantic relationships did not loom in the background, they occupied the foreground. Most students considered free-range hanging out an essential right of life. Consumption of alcohol was known to occur in their midst, and they texted as often as most creatures breathed. The young of the species have always participated in some version of distraction; however, society had never before provided so many distractions.

Classroom discussion had put time management on the table since Day One, and at least two students from each class already had spoken with me privately about their struggles in this area. With midterm conferences around the corner, unless this semester turned out differently from every other one I had taught, soon I would hear plenty more about problems that either directly traced to schedule issues or that they could remedy with radical surgery to their weekly regimens.

E-mail messages at the beginning of Week Five alerted me to different problems from two very different students. Nora, the Honors student who was taking prerequisite courses for her planned MA in art therapy, wrote to inform me that her grandmother had just entered hospice care an hour away and she was needed. She asked for an extension on the current paper. I e-mailed back, telling her to e-mail the work she had done as soon as she could and to keep in touch.

A terse e-mail had brought Jim's draft for the second assignment on time, but he had missed back-to-back days of class. Was Jim from Judge calculating the least amount of work he needed to do in order to manage getting a C in the course? He also might be caught up in a world of interferences. At least his paper had arrived. I thought about the student whose hallway brawl had interrupted my midterm exam the previous semester. I had not seen or heard from him after that day, and I hoped that neither Nora nor Jim would vanish as he had.

Having to set up then dismantle and repack audio-visual equipment in different rooms with only a short break between the two afternoon classes made my teaching on Monday another physical and mental workout, but the students stayed involved in both 101 classes. Since I ran the same curriculum in both classes, I had told students in each class that they could attend during the other hour. Several chronically late 11:15 class members had used this fail-safe mechanism, spending almost as much time in the 12:20 section as in their assigned class.

Chelsea from my 11:15 class showed up at my office after attending the 12:20 for the second time in a row. The young black woman explained that a doctor's appointment had kept her from attending at her normal time. Visibly pregnant, she informed me that she was expecting twins in November. Her boyfriend joined her for appointments, and she anticipated that he and her mother would help when the babies came. The semester ran deep into December. "I don't know much about what you're going through," I said, "but I know that they come when they want to, not when you do."

Chelsea laughed. She told me that she planned to return within a week of their birth.

"Wow," I said.

She smiled confidently. "You'll see," she said. "I'm serious about school. I am *engaged*," she added, playfully stressing Steinberg's term.

She told me about her experience at two high schools. After a Catholic school kicked her out for "some problem with a teacher," she transferred to a public city high school, where she claimed the lack of structure and discipline undermined her studies. She told me that "as long as you said that you were on the way to the cheerleader director" you could walk the halls and do anything besides go to class. In time, she feared she would never do anything in the lax atmosphere and asked her mother to transfer her back into the Catholic school. She eventually returned and earned a scholarship to a small college in the area. Telling the story, she stopped to point out how Bandura would cite environment changes as influential in her life. My eyes widened.

"See," she said. "I have been listening. And reading."

"You want to change things in your life."

"Yes. I'm hungry for that."

I could see this young woman taking on challenge after challenge, growing in ways she might not expect. I felt a rush run through me. I might have been sitting beside a professional athlete or musician, primed to go off and perform at a high level.

"I'm not afraid of those changes," she continued. "It's just going to add to me, make me stronger, fuller." She patted her middle and laughed. "Although I can't imagine feeling any fuller than I do right now."

Well-intentioned students often used the M-word—motivation—in conferences, which in many cases proved to be wishful thinking, unless that motivation translated into behavioral changes. Chelsea hadn't used the term. Her story, however, suggested genuine engagement. Engagement is a fundamental step towards real learning, and success in difficult tasks requires persistent engagement. As a student, my engagement came mostly in fits; however, as a teacher, musician, and writer, I experienced persistent engagement and its rewards and witnessed the same thing in my students. This student, I told myself, would be one to watch.

I knew that Vince and I both were taking home the semester's first waves of major papers from each class, inevitably the weakest work we'd see all fall. Leaving my office at the end of the day, I paused in his doorway to say goodbye.

He eyed the bulging briefcase in my hand. "Oh, boy," he said knowingly. He sniffed sharply as if he were trying to discern the nature of a particular odor. "Fresh?"

I nodded, patting the leather bag. "Great steaming stacks of scholarship," I intoned.

"Yes!" he boomed in his best Ed McMahon, not missing a beat in the old routine.

At home the next day, I read and groaned. The two stacks on the desk before me included only a handful of passing papers. Basic writing problems plagued some of them. Rarely did a paper display organization and development. The third essay in the pile consisted of one paragraph that ran on for a page and a half. Even the papers from the Honors classes included grammar-challenged efforts.

At Wednesday's Honors class, we used the document camera to look at a randomly selected draft. Details about Jenny's pre-college life revealed an environment that the case study's fictional character would recognize. Like the fictional Lee, she attended college at her mother's insistence.

> Many of my peers became addicted to drugs. At the age of fourteen, I was exposed to cocaine, crack, and heroin (among other things). It wasn't considered "cool" to my friends or crowd to go to school unless I was going to party. That being said, it seemed almost automatic that I didn't take my courses seriously …. And, after eighteen years of abuse, my father was finally gone from the house that my mother, sister and I lived in. I adopted the attitude that it was my time to do what I wanted to do and that no matter what I did; it didn't matter because I would get by somehow …. Now, at twenty-six, my way of seeing is completely different …. It took me a long time to get here, but I did. My new environment is CCP, and I'm already attempting to make friends here. Before I even knew about Vygotsky or Bandura, I knew that I wanted to let the school influence me in positive ways. Everything from class, to fellow students, to how I thought of myself became extremely important to me. After learning of Bandura, I realized how much personal factors, behavior, and environment really all effect each other, and how they play into one's overall success.

Though falling short of the focus and organization expected in the assignment, the piece as a whole showed a grasp of the theoretical concepts and some skill in applying them. While the young white woman's story deeply moved the parent in me—a reaction I masked by doggedly asking students to identify the relationship between sentences and between sections in the essay—I noticed that no one in the class appeared at all surprised by the tale recounted. Scattered casual nods suggested acknowledgment that, yes, this sounded like an accurate description of life. My classroom was not a counseling office; neither her classmates nor I served as her counselor, but I brightened upon reading about her attempts to connect with her classmates, probably the most important revelation in the draft. This determined, thoughtful young woman could not possibly know that her motivation would fluctuate as much as it would. Nor could she know how valuable her peers could prove in helping her succeed even when circumstances conspired to interrupt or discourage her.

In my unlinked 101 class, Rashid's essay presented his torturous journey just to reach this semester. The same age as Jenny, the FedEx driver had packed much into his twenty-six years. His essay spoke of what he shared with Lee. He had been shot three times and had gone to prison for murder. A single father of a six-year-old girl, he believed he had found a different path now. His writing skills and grasp of the academic content of the course fell well below Jenny's, but he had made it through a round of remedial courses and wrote with passion about his determination to succeed, no matter the obstacles.

Students in my unlinked classes clamored around me at the end of class when I returned ungraded but annotated revisions. With another class in ten minutes, I only had time to speak with a few of them. Zhivka found me in my office after my last class of the day, and we went over her paper. Dressed for her evening shift at a restaurant, the usually bubbly woman frowned over my scribbled comments in the margins. "I thought it was so good," she murmured.

"It's a strong paper," I said, "especially at this point in the semester."

"It can't be better than a B," she groaned. "With all the things you wrote on it."

"Is that what you think it deserves?" The paper showed organization, but she could have more fully developed it with specifics. She wrote clearly and effectively. Like every other paper, it needed work on APA formatting, something I had not yet stressed.

"I don't know," she lamented. "I don't know anything anymore."

"It's a B+."

She gasped. "It's awful."

"No."

"*You* think it's awful."

I repeated what I had said about the paper's numerous strengths and its few weaknesses.

She aimed her pen at me. "I want to stab you in the eyes!"

I took a deep breath. "I won't be much help to you if you do," I said, thinking how complete her Philadelphia enculturation had been.

She emitted a noise halfway between a laugh and a cry.

"You're a perfectionist," I said. "Let that help you, not hurt you."

She grabbed her paper and stood to leave. "We will see," she promised, exiting with a flourish.

At my next class, Ryan showed up after missing a couple of days. We had started working on the second major paper, but I still did not have his first assignment, meaning that when—or if—he did it, it automatically would earn an F. He told me before class that he had attended another college. For some reason, they would not give him credit for the courses he had taken, and his mother was making him take them over. I doubted neither the story nor the great possibility that this was not the first time he'd found himself explaining his failure to do an assigned task.

As I elaborated to the class on Steinberg's examples of student disengagement, I noticed him studying his cell phone screen. Weaving behavior such as texting during class into my comments, I noticed him look up, an expression of something like embarrassment momentarily replacing his blank expression as he tucked his phone away. If past experience held, Ryan would not last very long around here. At a certain point, even he would recognize the impossibility of the hole he had dug himself. But for the moment he sat there, dutifully present in a strictly physical way.

They got to me, these space eaters. I knew they had their own stories, and I knew that like the rest of us they held within themselves the germs of possibility that, unless activated, would remain still and lifeless. They did not realize that they would get only so many opportunities. They resembled the frowning back row of a comedian's audience, a challenge that, for many reasons, probably was beyond my very best material.

With the constant tacking back and forth between the fall's issues and responsibilities—which also included editorial revisions to a short story collection Fleur-de-Lis Press would publish the following fall—I had little time for exercise, except an infrequent stint on the exercise bicycle that sat in my home office, usually done while listening to music and reading something related to an aspect of the envisioned move. Quick exhaustion during a snowy walk the previous December had led to a visit to the doctor and ultimately to a series of tests with a pulmonary specialist. He had gotten good results in his own case by taking Flonase and suggested that I give it a try. "Don't back off the exercise," he cautioned.

So, through one of the hottest summers in Philadelphia history, I'd biked, scraped and painted walls at home, walked the dogs, and split firewood—my favorite exercise. The resulting stacks in the yard became my pride and glory, enough wood for the next two winters for sure. Heeding my nurse-wife's advice, I took frequent breaks and drank copious amounts of water. Losing a bit of weight had given a sense of progress to a summer somewhat bogged down by endless real estate searches and shifting degrees of certainty about retirement.

Like my involvement with fiction writing, my exercise regime dropped away with the first waves of essays. With envy, I noticed the casual fitness of many of my young students. As had happened every previous September, more and more hours went into grading and less and less into writing or exercising. I reddened, realizing that like my students dealing with their compromised schedules, I was robbing Peter to pay Paul. The familiar twinge of guilt quickly passed. I had other things that had to be done.

In ten days, Human Resources would send department heads the list of employees in their department that had signed on for early retirement, allowing them adequate time to hire new faculty. Kathleen and I remained on a path that, unless altered, would make this my last semester. I scheduled a meeting for the following Friday with Cindy Giddle, my department head, when I would tell her that I had signed on for early retirement and would ask her to keep it under her hat for the time being until Kathleen and I had made a firm decision.

Surrounded by shelves of books in my home office that I had acquired over nearly three decades, I read the rest of Thursday's to-do list. It looked long and imposing. The books lining the walls seemed to stare at me. We were halfway through *Black Ice*, a book I never tired of teaching. Was this my last round with that pleasant task? Soon

I might be bidding adieu to *No Earthly Notion*, another favorite. But retirement and moving meant opening the door to other possibilities.

I stood and walked over to the back window, watching leaves blowing across the deck. The basketball backboard creaked in the wind, its screws in need of tightening. Now, only Hannah from next door occasionally shot baskets, but the familiar thumpings against the backboard always triggered images of Stephan and Anna as much younger children. I admired my two woodpiles on the concrete slab below the deck's steps.

Sitting where our kids' swings used to hang was our two-bench wooden glider. In all my time in Philadelphia, I'd seen only one of these swings, which were as common in Quebec as spoken French. As much as any addition to the property, this *balançoire* stamped it as mine, a daily reminder of our place in my mother's family. Selling a house required a certain emotional neutrality, but every blemished inch of this place evoked history, none of it neutral. Kathleen and I had developed strong roots and branches here, but moving to Maine would open unique doors that might close for us if we waited five or ten years.

The previous evening, Kathleen and I had gone to the supermarket together, our version of date night. In the produce aisle, we ran into Marco, a former Honors student.

"I'm in Honors classes at Temple," he told us.

We listened to his story about graduating from CCP, keeping his job, transferring with a scholarship. Kathleen beamed at the young man.

"Tell Mr. Vince that I'm majoring in psych."

"Awesome!"

"I got to run. My girlfriend is waiting for me."

"Don't mess that up," I warned him.

He shook my hand. "Thanks," he said.

Driving home, Kathleen remarked on how impressed she'd been with Marco.

"Great student," I said. "Didn't have it easy." I'd been surprised at the rush of memories that seeing him ushered into my mind.

"You hated grading his essays, right?" Kathleen asked, breaking into my reverie.

On the ride over, I'd complained that after the afternoon's grading session, I wasn't sure I could ever grade another paper. "No," I laughed.

I thought I heard her say "Honey." It seemed like an afterthought. I turned onto Henry Avenue and passed a pedestrian waiting at the traffic light.

"That guy on the corner," she said, pointing. "Didn't he play for Blackthorn?"

I craned a look back. "Oh, yeah. Remember Weed from Roxborough? He played in the late '70s then moved to Florida? That guy was one of his buddies."

Honey. Interplanetary visitors to earth, I thought, might conclude that human couples in America fell into two groups, the Babes and the Honeys or Hons. "Babe" users were ever youthful or had a bit of the hippie in them, it seemed. I didn't know why, but we were among the Hons, and had been since the wedding. I certainly hadn't played a role in the Hon decision. It was one of those things that wives seemed to determine.

"Are you listening, hon?" she said.

"Yes."

"I said, how can you leave that?"

"What?" I said.

"Your *people.* I didn't grow up here. I love my friends, our friends, but this would be a big deal for you. Do you realize how big?"

"Well, yeah," I mumbled.

"And we haven't even talked about Michael or Vince."

I drove in silence the rest of the way home. Unlike the Hon thing, this was a joint decision. I appreciated her concern that I not rip myself apart by leaving Philly. I might change addresses, but this place, these people would remain an anchor, a magnet. I felt sure of it.

Pulling the car to a stop in the driveway, I looked over at her. "We wouldn't leave the kids high and dry," I said. "We'll be back for gigs too. We'll see Mike and Vince. It's our *next* step. It might not be the last one."

"We don't have to do this."

"I know," I said. "We didn't have to get married or try to have kids."

She squeezed my hand. We grabbed our shopping bags and headed inside.

Several hours later, we were in bed, ready to turn the lights out. "Are you excited about Maine?" Kathleen asked.

"You know I am," I said.

She was too. We agreed that it felt right. "Even if it's complicated," she said.

"But it's good complicated."

I looked lovingly at the best stacks of firewood I'd ever made then returned to my desk. I graded several papers, recorded my notes on them, then tinkered with the language of my e-mail to Lee. I hit Send. The short message was clear: We wanted to buy the condo. Now it felt real, almost as if the purchase had already happened.

I rose and stood at the window again. I shuddered and welled up, felt like I might break into tears. My composure returned almost as suddenly as it had vanished. I caught my breath, grateful that I was alone.

Several weeks had passed since Nora, one of our strongest second-semester Honors students, left to care for her grandmother. Her seriousness had been apparent to Vince and me, and we hoped she was keeping up with the work, though an e-mail of reassurance would have helped. We would deviate from our absence policy for good reason, but we had started to become concerned.

Students in the first-semester Honors class worked their way through *Black Ice*, Lorene Cary's memoir about her years at a New England prep school. The book chronicled the Philly-area teenager's immersion into an alien world, radically different from her black community, yet offering her opportunity for self-development. The movingly told story of her often-painful experience ultimately yielded hard-earned insights about the writer and about her identity. Socially, culturally, academically, and intellectually, she grew and learned at Saint Paul's School in New Hampshire.

This beautifully written book provided students with a rich case study of someone also embarking on a journey fraught with emotional and cultural obstacles. Armed with the perspectives of all of the psychological theorists they had studied thus far, students wrote an essay in which they explained the learning and change experienced by the young Lorene Cary.

By this time of the semester, I was unlikely to receive a personal opinion paper. Instead students wrote papers in which they unleashed their understanding of several respected thinkers whose explanations and analysis would not always be in agreement. They found examples of Vygotsky's scaffolding in the experiences and structures in place at Saint Paul's. Clearly, Cary's cognitions about both academic and personal matters changed as a result of her behaviors there and as a result of aspects of the unique environment, as Bandura would anticipate.

Occasionally when I led students through writing seminars, one of them would provide an analysis that no other student had written about before, and sometimes it was an analysis I'd never thought about either, as Nick did during that day's Honors discussion. The short man from Trinidad had already completed two semesters in the full-time Honors links with other professors and from Day One had been a solid contributor to class discussion.

"Learned helplessness actually fits here too," he offered. They had heard about this concept only in Vince's class. I jumped from my seat and furiously sketched out Nick's points on the board. Students seeing my delight might have realized that what we were doing was not unlike the work of people in the field. Yes, they consciously made use of certain writing templates from Graff and Birkenstein, and employed the big ideas of established thinkers, but they used *their* minds, *their* voices, and they interacted both orally and on paper with their classmates, launching themselves into academic conversations that, until recently, had been alien to them.

That, of course, was how it should go. But not everyone got it. Some papers came in woefully constructed, barely developed. One or two papers had not even arrived yet. So many of our students, regardless of talent or placement level, started either already disengaged or with interfering circumstances locked and loaded.

Numerous forces undoubtedly contributed to the preponderance of disengaged students in our classes who likely would perform poorly. Having already read three syllabus articles that included case studies, students in our Honors link should not have felt surprised when the fourth article they read started right in with two apparent examples of disengaged students.

An eighth grader, smart enough to attend a college prep school across town, believes along with the majority of his classmates that real men don't go to such schools, and so he opts instead to enroll at the nearby Catholic high school with his neighborhood pals. Throughout freshman year, he sits in front of the funniest person in the class, getting into trouble for laughing. For four years of high school, he never studies but passes his courses, spending most of his time thinking about girls and watching illegal drag races on Front Street.

A young man enrolls as a full-time college student, confident that his abilities will see him through. He attends most of his classes and takes notes but spends more time stocking shelves at the local supermarket, listening to the latest music, following college basketball, and shooting hoops late into the night at the playground than he does going over notes or reading assigned texts. His grades reflect this distribution of time, and he nearly flunks out after his first semester. He manages to play catch-up by repeating courses and taking summer classes, but when he graduates, he does so with a humble grade point average and without a single professor on whom he can rely for a recommendation. His level of confidence is low.

The article acknowledges that Vince and I had faced such students during decades of teaching at an urban community college and that at times we had been perplexed and chagrined. We had studied the problem of student engagement, and we had worked individually and together with other faculty help such students. At earlier points in our lives, we also had attended school as disengaged students. The article goes on to identify Vince as the girl-crazy guy and me as the basketball aficionado.

At this point in the semester, from what the students had learned about me in over a month's work together and from what I had told them about my colleague, they should have realized that something happened to both of us that altered the directions we had chosen and improved our odds for success. Clearly, theorists like Vygotsky and Bandura and a researcher like Steinberg would have had plenty to say about how our approaches changed. Multiple factors raised or lowered our odds for success. We hoped that our stories offered some encouragement to students but were wary of holding ourselves up as models; after all, our circumstances were hardly the same as those of our students. Multiple forces impacted their lives. We could provide them with tools, but they must make sense of their choices, learn what the best minds of psychology could offer them, and chart their own path.

By Sunday, October 9, the workmen had finished repairing our house's second-floor bathroom wall, ripped open when the plumber repaired the drainpipe leak, and I was painting the refinished wall, beaming with intrinsic satisfaction. If this work helped us to sell the house down the line, could I consider that extrinsic reward, I wondered.

I e-mailed Agent Lee in Maine to pose the viability of a spring closing. She called back immediately, telling me how quickly people had gobbled up units in the development, a reclaimed mill by the Megunticook River. "Apparently, quite a few people have been going through the unit you liked," she said. "Some for the second or third time."

Our unit. We'd immediately loved it during our visit.

I called our family friend Bob Elfant, who owned an area real estate business and whose advice always steadied me. I brought up the idea of due diligence. "Sometimes in a situation like yours," he said, "you reach a point when all of a sudden you must move with great speed." *Sure.* Could we really pull the trigger on such a thing immediately? We'd collected enough stuff among the four of us to ensure that no room in the house lacked a stack of loaded storage bins or boxes. The attic and the basement had reached full capacity long ago. No matter what timetable we might end up on, we must start the great purge immediately.

One way or the other, I would spend the spring semester on sabbatical, a benefit of the teaching life that I planned to put to good use by writing. Depending on the fruits of our scheming, I might also spend part of it moving. Teaching the Honors links offered Vince and me the great advantage of working with students who might return the following semester to catch our second act, so to speak. I looked forward to sabbatical, secure in the knowledge that I would leave both Honors links in the capable hands of my younger colleague Mark Hughes, whom I had spent years recruiting for this one-semester replacement role. He did not know yet that the opportunity might extend well beyond the spring term.

On Wednesday morning, checking e-mail at home before charging off to the College, I found a message from one of our H1 students, titled "Petition To Teach Next Semester."

> I suppose there's no way to convince you to teach next semester ...? I plan on continuing these two classes ... I know it's a selfish request ... and I'm positive you have legitimate reasons for the break ... but would it be wrong of me to tell you that you've been very inspiring to me, and that I've really enjoyed the class? Would 20 signatures agreeing with this convince you? (joke ...sort of ...)

> OK, I'll lay off with the guilt now ...lol ... :)

> —Matt

I laughed out loud but felt the gravitational pull. *He has no idea.*

Recent telephone conversations with Bob and e-mails with Lee had added urgency to my real estate research that only a few weeks ago seemed calm and measured. My appointment with my department head loomed two days away. And that night I would drive Kathleen first to 30th Street Station to meet her college roommate, Jill, then bring them to the airport. They would fly to New Mexico for a reunion of college friends planned over a year ago. I could not remember when we had last spent time apart.

Kathleen and I did not see ourselves as capable of selling our home and moving for a good seven months. She had started making lists of everything that would need to happen, showing me charts indicating a full schedule for each of those seven months. It was daunting. I felt something akin to what many students had to feel on Day One when they looked through my syllabus. *Can we do this?* I wasn't sure.

Bob was due to come over in ten days to look at our house and talk about both ends of our possible move, but now on the phone he suggested moving that up. We needed to do much work before the house could go on the market; that would be true, even if our house's rooms had sparse furnishings and fresh paint. "The sooner we get the house ready, the better," he said.

"I'll be on sabbatical in January," I reassured him.

"Good," he said, "but you still won't have time to do all the work. You know some contractors, right?"

I told him how much we trusted our plumber and electrician.

"If your people can't do the work in a flash, I've got a list of people who can."

I agreed that we would not show the place to anyone until we had made it ready for all to see, and Bob announced that he would come over tomorrow.

Later, as I drove home from taking Kathleen and Jill to the airport, my cell phone rang.

"Yo," I answered, steering onto Lincoln Drive.

"You don't lose your friends," Kathleen said.

"No?" I said, keeping an eye out for cops that might be looking for a cell phone user on the twisty turns along Wissahickon Creek.

"If they're really your friends, you keep them. You just don't see them as often, no matter where you are. I had to tell you that before we board the plane."

I drove on, wondering which friends we might lose, but feeling more assured that we would keep connected with most of them somehow. By the time I reached home, I was thinking ahead to my next class.

During Bob's Thursday visit, we called Lee, who told us that other buyers continued to look at the place we wanted. I didn't like the look that crossed Bob's face when he heard that. Due diligence, while essential, came with a risk. He walked through the whole house, offering suggestions and caveats. His team would follow up in a much more thorough way.

Back in the kitchen, he made lists and ran numbers, nodding every once in a while. Looking up from a table full of notes and calculations, he gave me an Eyes Of God look. "How bad do you want this place? Because I think you need to move, now."

Kathleen and I spoke on the phone that afternoon. Before the end of the day, I had called Lee and bid on the unit with a proposed closing date in February. If this all worked, I would retire. That much I had decided. A sudden rush of anticipation surprised me. And I felt relief. We would do this.

When Jim from Judge missed his fifth straight class, I e-mailed him, explaining that if he wanted to continue in the course, I needed to see him and his work in two days. I did not. Sitting in my office a couple of weeks later, I electronically withdrew Jim and several others who had long since run past the course's limit of absences. Their semester had ended some time ago, but now I had made it official. The little that I'd seen of Jim's work had shown skill and intelligence. I would never know what caused his departure, as with most student disappearances, but it always felt worse when you saw hints of talent and energy. Before tearing up Jim's draft, I reread its two largely error-free and thoughtful pages. Perhaps he would return to college some day under better circumstances, or maybe he'd already turned his attention to useful work. The College would be there for him if he ever wanted to return. Knowing that helped me close the book on Jim, but the commute from campus felt the same as the ride from a Phillies loss—familiar and miserable.

Friday morning, I broached the retirement issue with my department head. Because I would not know the resolution of the condo bid for some time, I asked Cindy to keep my tentative decision confidential. Even though I'd mailed earnest money to the Maine real estate office, we had not yet reached a point of no return.

After class, I saw that I had two messages from Lee on my cell phone. Her office staff could not find the fax I had sent. I needed to resend it. *Crazy.* The second message indicated that they had found it. "And they want to move up the closing date." *Okay.*

At 6:25, Lee called, saying that the developers had received another bid that day and that they still had a problem with the timing of our closing. I wondered if price was the real issue. We had offered the asking price, as Bob had suggested after studying the previous sales data.

"I didn't hear anything about price," she offered. She surmised that the other offer involved cash, with no mortgage contingency.

How do you compete with cash? "Sounds like we've lost," I said.

"Let's go for a closing in thirty days," she said.

"Thirty?" I said. "Three-zero?"

"If your mortgage app is approved, you can do this."

"Push has come to shovel," as my old friend from Puerto Rico said. By the end of the conversation, I had directed Lee to offer a thirty-day settlement. Lee's suggestion that if worse came to worst, other units in the building remained available stuck in my mind, but not in a good way. "This is the only one we were serious about," I'd told her.

I related all of this to Kathleen in a brief phone conversation. The call from Maine might come at any moment—if not that night, then by the end of the weekend. I planned to keep in touch, but our situation soon would become further complicated. On Saturday morning, I would fly to Providence to see my godson play rugby, an equally rare overnight trip booked months ago. What once seemed like wonderful once-in-a-lifetime getaways had become exercises in dreadful timing. Through the evening's furious grading, I steadily moved papers from the to-do pile to the done folder.

When the phone rang at 10 p.m., I jumped. Bob wanted an update. I knew that he had gone to a neighborhood affair to receive an award, which made more sense to me every time I spoke with the man. He and his wife would fly abroad Saturday night to visit their daughter, but he would take calls until his plane left. I accepted that I probably would learn the news when I was in Providence.

Waiting in the airport Saturday morning, I continued grading. My cell phone rang with the Maine area code at 8:25, just as I stepped onto the aircraft. "Lee," I answered as quietly as I could as I walked down the aisle. I was sure that every pair of eyes on the plane focused on me. The passengers chattered away to one another, which forced me to ask Lee to repeat herself.

"The developers took the other offer, a thirty-day cash deal."

It was over. I thanked Lee for calling. "I'm just boarding the plane," I whispered, five rows from my seat and amazed that I hadn't blurted out something that would get me tossed off. The seated passengers were all watching the red-faced man fumble with his cell phone. If I'd gotten this call at home, I'd be shouting profanities, maybe punching something. I found my seat, stowed my backpack, and buckled my seatbelt. I was sure I must look like I was having a stroke.

The plane took off smoothly and climbed above the clouds. Kathleen still slept in New Mexico. *Over.* I told myself that even if we had submitted our bid a day earlier, the developers knew that two bids would arrive, so they still would have waited. The soul-searching, number-crunching, scheme-hatching weeks had come to nothing more than repressed angst and a now-throbbing head. I gritted my teeth, keeping my grimacing face to the little window. I left the essays in the backpack and studied the banks of fluffy clouds shifting below, as if their movements might suddenly reveal a glimpse of next semester or even next week.

While waiting for my friend Jim Brady at the airport, I called Bob and Vince with the news—it was too early in New Mexico to call Kathleen. When I saw Jim, I felt relief that I could think about rugby, and at first we talked about his son, my namesake and godson, and his Saint Anselm team. I had taken a bus to Boston a year ago to watch him play, only to have the game cancelled at the last minute, but finally I could get to see him play. When Jim asked how Kathleen and I were doing, I could not stifle a dark laugh. He did not know about our retirement scheme, and I told him all of it as we drove to his home.

Pacing in their backyard, I pressed Kathleen's number on my cell phone. She and her friends had gone out for brunch somewhere, but she took the call. She didn't want me to beat around the bush. I winced, realizing that now it was her turn to receive the news in a public setting. Sounding philosophical, she urged me to enjoy the game. I suspected that she felt worse than she let on. She had confided about our plan to her friends the night before and now had some explaining to do.

After the game, we ate at Chili's and in no time started laughing, despite losing efforts on the field and in real estate. I was grateful for the distraction of conversation with friends and then canine antics back at Jim and Ellen's home. At the airport and on the flight back, I nearly completed the weekend's grading. Sunday night, when I finished reading the Honors papers, I turned my attention to searching online for information on the remaining condos, also tracking down similarly priced homes in the area.

Still numb, I climbed into the empty bed with folders of printed real estate information and renewed energy. I pored over fact sheets for non-condo properties in the area, but I reached the end of the pile without finding anything that fit our needs and budget. I paged through floor designs for the remaining condo units. Our price range eliminated the two larger units from consideration, so I puzzled over the three smaller ones that still were on the market.

When I turned out the light, I remembered when I'd had the same surreal feeling about everything around me, almost as if I'd suddenly found myself on stage without a script. On the December day ten years ago that I turned in final grades, Vince insisted on stopping in to say hi to Kathleen on his way home. Kathleen and the kids were waiting in the kitchen, their awkward half-smiles almost a parody of concern. "What?" I said.

"I have bad news about Eddie Roth," she said. "Honey, he had a heart attack and died in his sleep. I didn't want to tell you until you were done with your work, and I wanted Vince to be here, and the kids." Then too, I'd stifled my reaction, the strangeness of the telling almost as jarring as the news. They must have expected me to burst into tears, but maybe because of the way I'd learned the news mostly I felt aware of being watched and worried over.

Eddie, Paul Muessig, Michael, and I had been an unholy quartet of friends since high school. He was one of those friends who'd moved away but kept close. He might have called me the day before to talk about the imminent holidays, and now he was dead? The news stiffened me, as if I were watching myself with the others in the kitchen from a distance.

It was the week before Christmas. That started a long walk through a surreal haze. With Eddie, we'd attended his mother's funeral a month earlier. Ed hadn't been sick, nothing. For Kathleen, seeing Eddie in the coffin made it real, finally. But to me, it still felt like a strange and unwelcome dream that I might be able to wake myself from if I tried hard enough.

Driving back from the Boston funeral, Kathleen got a call from fifteen-year-old Anna. Hearing Kathleen's half of the conversation, I put together the impossible news. Alone at home that afternoon, she'd been playing fetch beside the house with our young Border Collie Teddy, when he dropped to the ground, dead. It all felt like it was part of the same bad, bad dream. Eddie. Our dog. Our Anna, hours away, now in the care of a kind neighbor. We couldn't help any of them. They couldn't help us. We just drove towards home through that haze.

Now Kathleen was out in New Mexico on her long-awaited reunion. I was dazed in Philadelphia and remembering that wretched

December. The dreamlike confusion yielded to deep frustration, and all I wanted was to be with Kathleen. I wanted to step over all those miles between us but felt as helpless as when we'd gotten the call from Anna.

On Monday morning of Week Seven, Nora, the missing second-semester Honors student, returned after the death of her grandmother. She would need to take Wednesday's midterm with very little preparation time. We'd soon see whether or not we'd misplaced our trust in her, but she'd returned with every bit of work done, suggesting that we might be dealing with a special student.

As I completed Monday evening's grading, I returned to the question of moving, narrowing my focus to the remaining condos in Camden, three houses there and two other condo possibilities up the coast. When Kathleen called, I could hear that she had become ill. Neither of us said anything about Maine.

After spending most of Tuesday grading, I picked Kathleen up at the airport. On the ride home, we talked about the kids, the dogs, her trip, my trip, and the weather in Philadelphia. After a late dinner of leftovers, we propped ourselves up in bed, and I brought out everything I'd printed and studied for the last couple of days. The ache of disappointment at having our bid rejected did not surprise me, but its intensity stunned me. The disappointment in her eyes matched mine. A "values clarification," Kathleen called it—unpleasant but useful. In very little time, we determined that we could take another stab at the condo development in Camden. I e-mailed Lee that we would bid on the first unit we had visited in the building, a slightly smaller spot on the second floor.

Matt arrived for Wednesday's Honors 101 midterm exam in a panic. He had known exactly where he'd parked his car last night, but this morning it had disappeared. He had reported it to the police, but he had been training for a job out in the suburbs, and he did not have theft insurance. He had gotten his father to pick him up and rush him to the exam, but he didn't know how he would get to his job now. He had done outstanding schoolwork thus far, but he feared that he would write gibberish today. Both instructors would read the two-hour essay exam, which would count toward both courses. We encouraged Matt to take the exam and do the best he could. We lost serious, fully engaged students to the hazards of their complicated lives every semester. Sometimes they brought to mind a squadron of World War II RAF fighter pilots, going out on sorties from which not all would return. Still, they must go out day after day, month after month.

Before the exam started, an e-mail from Lee informed me that the unit we wanted to bid on was now under contract to someone already in the building who wanted a larger unit. Four units remained, two of which we could not possibly afford. While proctoring the exam, I ran more numbers on a piece of scrap paper. I prepared questions for Lee about the two remaining smaller units and sent them off after the exam.

These latest events forced us, finally, to have the dreaded conversation with our daughter. Our leaving Philadelphia was not what Anna, now twenty-six and independent, was expecting or hoping for. We could see that she wanted to feel happy for us, but she could not hide her disappointment.

That night, she joined us as we compared the two available units. She liked the one farther from the common entrance because it looked like it might have better light and because the layout appealed to her. We marveled at her ability to step out of her own shoes to try to help us. We would tell Stephan next.

On Thursday, having digested Lee's answers to our questions, we bid on the unit that the three of us had preferred.

On Friday, before my 11:15 class, I heard from Lee that the developers had signed our offer. I called Kathleen, happy to finally have an opportunity to deliver good news. Only getting mortgage approval stood in our way, unless we suddenly developed cold feet.

At home, I read through the Honors students' exams. Nora, the long-absent Honors student, had written a comprehensive and brilliant exam. She had kept up with the work and had applied concepts accurately and thoughtfully. Despite the horrific start to his morning, Matt had produced a thoughtful and insightful essay. Reading their literate and thoughtful work buoyed my spirits. I graded late into the evening with renewed energy.

14

Spring Sabbatical, Day Eleven

Friday, April 13, 2012: Ireland

My work on the eastern side of the Atlantic had taken over my life the way cramming for midterms could take over a student's life. Having phone contact with Kathleen extinguished any desire to hike down to the café to check e-mail—I could wait to touch base with the rest of the world. Sitting from morning until eleven or so at night every day in front of my MacBook Air's computer screen, I willed my mind and fingers along, taking only occasional breaks to relieve neck stiffness. Pasta or rice concoctions from earlier in the week now provided me with a string of leftover dinners, giving me even more time to work. I thought of the Beatles in Hamburg. *Five more years of this ought to do the trick.*

During food breaks, the radio provided company that I could say a sharp goodbye to without causing offense. RTÉ Lyric FM played classical music most of the time, but I found myself listening to their morning drive time let-down-your-hair show. Similar impulses by American stations on which one's hair never got put up, usually resulted in several loud voices talking over each other or in spirited efforts to plumb new depths of crude humor. This Irish broadcast aired Pavarotti, Dusty Springfield, and a Spike Milligan comedy sketch within the same half hour. The show catered to listener requests, which further broadened the already eclectic play list. Silly but not dumb, Someone In The Morning provokingly commented about the smelly, dirty attraction of meerkats to a child caller on a holiday zoo trip, then offered warm encouragement when the little guy mentioned that he played a musical instrument at school. He was at his best in his rapid-fire reading of daily dispatches from an alter ego named Hugo, allegedly originating this holiday week from the Mouth of the Shannon, where somebody or something was skinny-dipping. Without self-consciousness, mockery, or irony, the radio host smoothly segued into "Clair de Lune."

In slightly loopy fashion, the show went somewhere in an interesting enough way that people wanted to tag along through traffic updates and forecasts for rain. A show tune followed a blues song. Sinatra led into a piece of Russian choral music without a trace of elitism. Listening while I ate a bowl of oatmeal, I learned something about Hollywood dancers one day and something about the activities of the Irish on bank holidays another.

I recognized connections between various topics that I previously had known little or nothing about, not so different from what I hoped my students did—recognize connections between ideas. Exposure to ideas that pulled people even just a tad beyond their usual activity range enabled them to see such connections, to build on top of what they already knew. Irish listeners might neither have realized nor cared, but their radios regularly provided potential scaffolding activities, which lightly exercised and might even have helped develop certain nonessential mental muscle groups.

I had no idea what my fellow villagers did. When I'd stood outside to drink a cup of tea, I had seen no signs of artist life. I knew I was not alone because a few cars had appeared and disappeared from the car park. Several cottages had remained lightless and presumably lifeless since I'd arrived, but for all I knew they might host obsessive artists who worked only during the day in the glass-roofed studio built into each cottage.

Returning to my cottage after a lunchtime sandwich enjoyed while sitting on a boulder below the village, I met a couple who had decided to explore the area while on holiday. They expressed curiosity about the village, so we chatted, eventually joined by a gaggle of five red-haired girls, sisters and cousins between the ages of six and thirteen, who had been snooping on us from behind the ruins of an as-yet unreconstructed cottage. The girls, innocent and open, were a delight to talk with. An hour later, I returned to my computer, having excused myself from the most fun I'd had in my whole time here, as I told the dissolving assembly.

The only such *craic* I'd shared in days sent me back to work with a smile on my face. Maybe it was the banter or the French music on the radio, but I was sure that my mother had followed me into the cottage that afternoon. I had become accustomed to spending days in the little studio surrounded by students and colleagues, but this time I could not get my mind off Hélene Pellerin Bachus.

I was raised by an English-as-a-second-language working-class single mother whose childhood education ended at fourth grade, and who, perhaps partly because she spent so much time as a young woman working for educated people, wanted a different life for her only son. Hélene was born to Joseph and Rose Anna Pellerin in 1916 and was followed by her sister Gracia in 1917. When Rose Anna died from complications following Gracia's birth, Joseph had to send the sisters to opposite sets of grandparents in their Quebec village. Several years later, after Joseph remarried, the sisters rejoined him, and he and his second wife provided for them and, in time, seven more siblings.

At fourteen, Hélene left to work full time in Quebec City and later in Montreal, never having heard a word of English. Like the parents of some of my students, she cleaned the houses of wealthy people and also served tables in restaurants, always sending home weekly contributions. In time, she found seasonal work as a servant on cruise ships that brought rich people to the majestic fjords on the north side of the widening Saint Lawrence River, miles east of Quebec City and across from her hometown on the lower shore. Surely those ships must have fostered temporary little communities far different from those like the one in small, isolated, French-speaking Saint-Aubert.

One day, after presenting herself to the ship's officer who doled out bed linens to staff, my mother, in her best English, asked for "Two shits, please," prompting an explosion of laughter from the man. That experience broadened her grasp of English pronunciation and Old English derivations. In cosmopolitan Montreal, she worked for English speakers and fell in love with English-language films. She continued to send money home but learned the life of the city, gaining an informal education not available to people in the village.

After the war, she and a Francophone friend from Prince Edward Island took jobs working at a hotel in far-off Bermuda, where the US Air Force maintained a base. One day, a military police jeep pulled over in front of Hélene and Eleanor as they walked down a Bermuda road. The driver, Sergeant Bachus, and another MP offered them a lift. Hélene sat beside Ned, the twin brother of Ted and the son of Oklahoma farmers Gomer and Bertha Bachus. Eleanor climbed in next to Sergeant John Pye. Both couples began seeing each other, and one pair stayed together as husband and wife until they died of old age. Hélene fell head over heels in love with Ned, but the relationship had brought together two people with extremely different views.

My parents' union had already turned rocky during her pregnancy, to the point that Hélene traveled to Montreal for my birth. Putting her best foot forward, she brought her baby to Oklahoma on a series of train and bus rides that culminated at Gomer and Bertha's farm. Hélene had arranged for Bertha to meet her and her baby at the Wetumka bus stop. The sight of her daughter-in-law and grandson in the back of the bus with the black passengers made Bertha laugh and shake her head at Hélene's lack of familiarity with local—and indeed American—customs. Taking her baby to the large back seat had seemed perfectly natural to Hélene, but in Wetumka at the time, housing and education generally segregated whites, blacks, and Native Americans. The young woman from the homogeneous village life of Quebec found this accepted discrimination mystifying.

She spent months living there, caring for me in the farmhouse, to which Bertha and Gomer welcomed her. She soon came to love them. There, she waited for her husband, stationed at an Oklahoma Air Force base, to make the little family complete, but his interests already had moved on. The marriage dissolved at his behest when I was around two, so she moved away, an ersatz French-speaking Okie traveling a dusty path farther west, armed only with her pluck and her determination to care for her child.

The court ordered Ned, as father, to provide child support, but my mother raised me without the contribution of a dime from my father. Aside from holiday gifts, from then until his death in 1970, when I had reached twenty-one, he contributed nothing to our welfare, a breach of contract that never surprised my mother but also did nothing to dampen her drive to fulfill the role of both parents for me. She feared that as an immigrant who was not yet a citizen and as a woman, seeking legal redress might open the door to losing me to him, who, having remarried and fathered another son, the courts might see as more capable of providing a stable environment than she. He was, after all, a man, a citizen, and a veteran of two wars. So, she took on single parenthood in an era that viewed it as shameful and suspicious, the word "divorcee" packing different connotations in that era, and she did so long before services for single parents existed.

Qualified for few kinds of work, Hélene found child-caring positions that allowed her to care for me at the same time. Nothing equivalent to contemporary daycare existed in those days, not that she ever would have entertained thoughts of leaving me with someone else for great lengths of time.

For a while, she worked for a family in Phoenix, where the people allowed the two of us to live in the house. She cleaned and cooked with me on her hip, a position captured in several of the photos from those wandering days. When that job ended, she made her way to Los Angeles, where she attempted to find housekeeping work. By the time I had turned three, she had taken me on the train to the Gary, Indiana, home of another of her Canadian girlfriends from her Bermuda days. Photos of us there, me in cowboy hat and boots, sparked one of my earliest memories—placing a cat in the washing machine. According to Hélene, I wanted to remove the dirt from the animal, so this might have been an early sign of my desire to assist others—but it might just as well indicate impatience and a safety-last approach to life.

From there, she left for New York City, home at that time to several of her father's emigrated siblings. Although too independent to expect to live with them, she did appreciate having family around with whom she could speak French. Except for one, Aunt Fabienne, they hardly found themselves in any position to help, and my mother's assistance from Aunt Fabienne came in the form of hand-me-down clothes and occasional small but valued gifts. Up the Hudson, in the town of New City, she found a live-in job, caring for a little girl, who was a bit younger than me and named Liza or Lisa, with the family name of Maisel or Maesel.

Her memory and to some extent her accent and expressions aided and shaped my recollection of these months before our move to Philadelphia. The Maisels treated her kindly, and Hélene held onto a couple of washed-out color photos of Liza and me on rocking horses in a grand living room, as if we were brother and sister or cousins, and as if my mother's peregrinations had miraculously led us to a rosy, settled suburban life.

I recalled a story she told, without self-pity, about us spending a Christmas day in the New York City bus station because she had decided that we should allow the Maisels privacy on that day and because for some reason, she felt that she should not or could not foist the two of us on her aunts. When, as a young adult visiting New York, I heard "Port Authority Terminal" announced on the station's public address system, I realized our Christmas layover long ago had taken place at this site. She had mispronounced the station's name all of her life. I had only ever heard about a Por-da-tar-a-dee Terminal.

The ability to pronounce the TH sound eluded her, as it does many French speakers, no matter how hard she worked at it, and I grew up hearing D's and T's galore from my mother but only the barest hint of a TH.

In those years, the unique working and living situation she needed was hard to find and lasted only as long as her service proved beneficial and sustainable to the host family. Knowing that the arrangement with the Maisel family would not last, she kept her ears open for possibilities. Around the time I turned five, Hélene's pregnant friend

Eleanor invited her to join her and her first son in Philadelphia while her husband, my father's one-time buddy, served a two-year tour of duty in Iceland. Hélene paid a New York cabbie to drive us and all of our possessions 100 miles to North Philadelphia. Her friend's Philadelphia-born spouse had become a solid husband and father. His family lived nearby, but Eleanor Pye, far from her people in Canada, felt happy to share her home and her life with her old friend. After traveling for so much of her first five years of motherhood, Hélene surely did not expect to live the rest of her life in a new city, far from family. Because of her friendship with this woman who also had met a man in a jeep in Burmuda, I grew up in Philadelphia.

Hélene found work at a downtown Philadelphia coffee shop, one of two local branches of the New York–based Schrafft's Restaurants chain, a job she would hold onto through leg and back surgeries until a heart attack finally disabled her out of the workforce. At first, Eleanor could watch after me, but soon I had to start school, and that changed my life dramatically. In those days, children attended their local public or parochial school, walking home at lunchtime and again at the end of the day. Laboring city dwellers lived their lives almost entirely in their neighborhoods, with husbands leaving to go to work. Working mothers had to rely on family help, and Eleanor could do only so much—and soon her husband would return from Iceland.

Orienting herself in a new city, Hélene found a private Catholic school where I could board during the week. Middle-class families might afford the school's tuition and board but not someone in Hélene's position. She knew nothing about learning theory but knew enough about her past life's limitations and about her future prospects to realize that she needed to put her son in the best possible position to avoid that kind of life. She calculated that with me in school, she could work even more hours, so she became determined to find and provide the most beneficial scaffolding possible for her only son.

In September of 1954, I was not yet six years old when I began my formal education at Norwood Academy in then-posh Chestnut Hill. She handed my little suitcase to my first-grade teacher, Sister Ancilla, and left me at the dormitory in The Big House. Thus began our first separation of more than a few hours since she had brought me into this world.

Before walking to the trolley to start her journey back to North Philadelphia, she helped me unpack, doing her best to appear calm, even happy. My mother set up a framed photograph of her on my nightstand. She had sewn white nametags on all of my clothing, which she now organized in my drawers. Maybe a dozen other boys had arrived and started settling in for their first night, and I observed one of them, a polio victim—to use the language of the time—moving to his bed and fiddling with the leather straps that attached his metal braces to his legs. He walked haltingly, and I immediately realized all that he had to do just to move from one place to another.

The time arrived for the parents to leave. I wasn't sure about this living arrangement, let alone about school, having never set foot in a preschool or kindergarten. The boy with polio seemed upset as well. My mother leaned over me and whispered words that confirmed my unspoken thoughts about the other boy's difficulties. I agreed with her that he must find this moment very tough. She suggested that I go over and say hello, that maybe I could cheer him up a little bit. It seemed like a good idea, and I stepped away from her and toward the boy. Engaging with him, I unwittingly avoided dwelling on my own sadness. My mother, who would go home to an empty apartment for the first time since my birth, had made a brilliant move.

On a visit to Vermont, years after Hélene's death in 1979, I recognized my eighth-grade teacher, Sister James Anthony, across a public room. I learned that my mother had received some financial assistance from the school once I reached fifth grade but that she had paid for my tuition and room and board for grades one through four without any help at all. Over the years of my schooling, the now-aged nun had grown to know my mother. She recalled Hélene's weekly trips to bring me to and from school: "She cried every step of the way back to the end of the trolley line, every Sunday for four years."

Living back home in our Meehan Avenue apartment for fifth grade, to my great relief, I could wake myself after my mother had left for work and take the trolley in the opposite direction to school. I remembered my mother buying my school uniform at Jacob Reed's, but I did not remember my mother ever buying anything for herself. Hand-me-downs arrived in packages from the New York aunts. She rarely went out except to walk to and from Mass, to pull a shopping cart back from the supermarket, or maybe once a year to attend a group dinner, if one of the other waitresses would drive her.

Because she never stopped loving my father, she refused all invitations to go out with male customers, who found her accent and reddish hair difficult to resist, despite her standoffishness. Often reminding people of Rita Hayworth, her good looks must have made other mothers nervous. She respected the fact that my remarried father had a family and never would have rocked that boat; in fact, she never harbored wishes to reunite under any circumstances. She knew that staying away from the hard-drinking charmer who had left her benefited both of us, but she never removed her wedding band. She just loved him, without needing or wanting his company.

Numerous personal strengths had enabled Hélene to survive with so little help from others. I could not think about her life without being reminded of a topic that loomed large in my course's curriculum, psychologist Julian Rotter's concept of locus of control, or the roughly equivalent one of attributional style, which my students would have recognized by midterm as one of Steinberg's major points. Steinberg's team of researchers had observed that some of the high school students in their sampling tended to attribute their successes or failures to external factors, to other people, and to circumstances beyond their control ("The teacher/test/assignment was unfair")—an attributional style the researchers considered "unhealthy," or what Rotter would identify as an external locus of control.[1] On the other hand, students who looked within for outcome explanations ("I should have studied more/gotten tutoring/reduced my job hours") were more likely to self-correct and become prepared to do something useful.

In his book, Steinberg makes the striking point that Americans tend to place great weight on one's perceived ability, discounting how much effort one devotes to the work. In contrast, people in other parts of the world more typically use the language of effort to explain success: "I need to work harder and longer," versus "I am not an A student." Because external factors sometimes prove determinant, especially for nontraditional students, possession of a healthy attributional style/ internal locus of control does not guarantee success, but at the very least it orients students in a useful direction.[2] Hélene Pellerin Bachus could have been the poster child for healthy attributional style. Had she not held such a perspective, my childhood would have been poorer in every way.

Ability provides an upper limit for all of us, but people's effort enables them to achieve as close as possible to that upper limit. Not all A grades go to A students who never break a sweat.

All that finally became clear to me by the time I registered for folklore classes at Penn. In my mid-thirties then, I'd gained background so that new knowledge had something on which to adhere.

I'd also acquired a taste for reading, writing, and folklore. And I was hungry to do the work that made learning happen.

I had been in Cill Rialaig for nearly two weeks but had experienced few social interactions with fellow villagers. Pausing in my reflections about students, I decided that my own locus of control could use a shift toward the internal and acted on my need to take a more significant break and to enjoy some of the other pleasures of this place. I left little scraps of paper under a rock at each cottage door, proposing a night out—a trip to the pub that the Welsh mother and son had told me about. We could take a taxi back so that nobody would have to drive up the winding road in the dark after imbibing.

The next day, around two in the afternoon, a knock at the door yielded one of the two Sineads from the first night. "We're up for it," she told me. "And Rona wants to join."

Vera, an artist recently arrived from Dublin, offered to drive. She did not plan to drink and would happily shuttle the bunch of us.

When Saturday night arrived, the week's working binge ended. I was amazed at how paltry distances seemed when traveling by car instead of by foot. Dungeagan, a village with no discernable border between it and Ballinskelligs, featured a laundry, church, and Rosie's. Five women and I entered to find six men sitting on one side of the L-shaped bar and three on the other. Under any circumstances, our entrance probably would have elicited a good long stare from the bar's jeff-capped crew, but led by Lesley, a pierced and carrot-haired painter from Limerick, our procession had no chance of arriving unnoticed.

The six of us, still strangers to each other, clustered around two tables so short that one might have mistaken them for children's furniture. We toasted Rona's Dortmund football team on their victory that afternoon. I listened to the redheaded art teacher's stories about trips to Skellig Michael and to the chocolate factory in the hills between Ballinskelligs and Portmagee, a middle-of-nowhere surprise that Kathleen and I had stumbled into on a trip six years ago. It became clear to me that some artists had come here to breathe deeply and open themselves to whatever inspiration might blow in from the northwest. As much as I understood and would have loved such an experience, I had been anticipating this obsessive indulgence since I'd learned of my Cill Rialaig acceptance almost a year prior. When Deirdre showed me the door the first night, I fully understood.

We went through two more rounds, finally engaging in the kind of camaraderie around the peat fire that I had imagined work-weary artists in Ireland would crave. When the conversation returned to Skellig Michael, Vera announced that tomorrow's weather forecast was for a clear and dry day. "I live in this country," she moaned, "and I've never been there." All conversation and drinking stopped.

"This shall not stand!" I bellowed, breaking the silence.

In short fashion, the redheaded woman produced the telephone number for the boatman who had brought her and her companion to the Skelligs. We learned that *The Flying Horse* would sail for the Skelligs tomorrow at eleven, but not again for at least a week. We ordered another round. My work break would continue at least through tomorrow afternoon.

Fall Semester, Week Seven

Saturday, October 22, 2011: Philadelphia

Grading midterm exams took up Friday evening and most of Saturday. Midway through Saturday afternoon, I reached the bottom of the last pile of blue books and shifted my attention to the cluttered bookshelves in my home office. For three hours, I dusted and triaged books into keep, toss, and donate boxes that lined the room's back wall. My hands had acquired a gray cast and a spongy feeling.

Three hours of playing and laughing with the Sacred CowBoys on Saturday provided a roaring contrast to everything I'd done for the past month. If our grand scheme became reality, as it now appeared it would, I would not quit the band—that much I knew. More brothers than simply bandmates, they had offered me no early retirement incentive. As long as the kids lived in Philadelphia, we would visit regularly, and those trips could coincide with band dates at the Mermaid. I rose Sunday morning from the sleep of the dead, shared Saturday night's highlights with Kathleen, and stretched every sore part of me before tackling Sunday's to-do list.

Sent to the basement to begin sorting through several decades of family memorabilia, I squeezed down the narrow space between the towering shelving units that formed a maze. Cheek by jowl on the rear wall's shelf sat ice skates, cans of primer paint, and a 16mm film projector. A shelf labeled "Seasonal" held enough ornaments to fill two trees and several strings of lights in various states of function— from wholly intact to wholly dead. There was organization behind this system, just not the kind that kept a house clutter-free.

I unearthed a milk crate filled with old notebooks from Temple University, my summer teacher's classes at Smith College, and graduate school at Gallaudet College, reminders of an undistinguished academic career. In a margin, I saw a girl's name and a telephone number. *Was she a lab partner? Did I ever call that number?*

Some of the content in the notes amazed me, as I realized how little I brought to those courses. If I took them now, I would bring so much more of a base to build upon, and the course information would make sense from the start and tend to stick, unlike during my original experiences with those courses long ago. Some of the information in these musty notebooks seemed brand new to me now; other more familiar concepts and facts made me wonder if the moment I scribbled these notes corresponded with the moment I first grasped points that I now took for granted. I had hoarded these mostly indecipherable relics for decades knowing that some day I must decide their fate. I stretched open the top of a trash bag and dropped in several notebooks.

On the other side of a shelf stuffed with boxes of painting equipment and LP records, Kathleen busied herself with the same process. If we anticipated staying in this house for ten or twenty more years, these tasks surely would remain on our list of things to do until we felt some equally cosmic push. "You can take a break," she called out, holding one of her mother's polka records, "but you can't stop."

I laughed and trashed a notebook from junior year at Temple without even looking at it.

Student comments in Monday's eight o'clock writing seminar focused largely on task and audience. "The fourth paragraph explains what the third one introduces," Eagles jersey–clad Jenny offered, "but ..." A pained look stole across her face.

"But the fifth paragraph has nothing to do with any of that," Matt cut in.

"Exactly!" Jenny thundered. "It's clean and clear," she said almost apologetically, "but the reader expects that paragraph to keep moving the ball down the field."

Stern-faced Nick, sitting across from them, made the referee's gesture for first down.

We all laughed. I had learned to trust the improvisational nature of these discussions, and this one could not have arrived in a more timely fashion if I had planned it.

I watched as two once-quiet Honors students repeated moves they had seen made by more experienced classmates during previous writing seminars. Going public, as Matt and Jenny did today, was something I could not do in class until my second go-around in graduate school. Even then, I did not find it comfortable. At some point, my desire outweighed my fear. Suddenly, the baggage of underachievement that I had carried around for years felt less heavy. Many of my students preferred to save their voices for after class, but some of them had no fear of making fools of themselves. Every class had its jailhouse lawyers, people with more confidence than judgment, and I could botch handling them as easily as when I tried to prompt the terminally reluctant.

Fortunately, a critical mass of students in this class, possessing maturity and what psychologists called emotional intelligence, respectfully and effectively moved the conversation forward. Nick already had completed two semesters in the full-time Honors links, and he performed with distinction, so in seminars, we counted on such students to play a leadership role—not as opining experts but as learners who understood and valued the nature of academic conversation. Only in a perfect world would the entire class fit this description, but it took only a couple of such students to make a difference.

No doubt I had sat in the midst of such students during my own undergraduate career but had not responded the way Jenny and Matt did in this seminar. I could not know the extent to which observing and interacting with Honors veteran Nick contributed to Jenny and Matt's behavior, but I suspected that such peer influence matched or exceeded that of their teachers. Not everyone in class could do this, but I held onto hope that as the weeks rolled on, more students might venture into uncharted territory.

A good deal of cross-pollination was going on in this class, but most community college students went it alone, even the good ones. Those I saw at a single study carrel in the library or at the end of a lounge couch. As an undergrad, I'd done the same. Though not a stranger to the library, at seventeen I had less engagement than the solitary students I saw in there. I planned the courses I taught with a less than fully engaged student in mind, who, nonetheless, would attempt the work and might be amenable to a certain amount of introspection. I wondered how my seventeen-year-old self would have reacted to a semester with Vince and me. Would I have been any more engaged?

The nurture-heavy reading of my first-semester courses (including the unlinked 101s) became countered by readings in our second-semester link of courses that demanded that students give nature, especially in the form of DNA influence, its due: biology provided the imposing setting against which the forces of nurture did their best.

Our second-semester students also read *Habits of the Heart* and Thomas Sowell's *A Conflict of Visions*, which acquainted them with social and cultural influences that might or might not impact individuals at different developmental stages. Today, using the document camera, they shared their first drafts of a writing assignment in which they wrestled with questions that prior to the semester would have made little sense to them, or would have mattered much.

"So far, my essay is drawing from the conversation about social influences," Donald observed. "Bellah and them, mostly. Strains that run through American history."

"I keep going back to Sowell," Sid added.

Others jumped in, and by the time the bell rang, two students had announced their intentions to completely change their plans, having now found an angle that caught their passion.

The first of the afternoon writing seminars took a similar focus on task. Charisse took notes on every part of the conversation. In class, she provided a model of engagement and decorum, but her grades had hovered in the low C range, despite her efforts.

Halfway through the hour, I noticed Ryan looking at his beloved cell phone, which sat on his desk. Last Friday, after missing his scheduled class, he had showed up for the one I had the next hour. Though he had remained as silent in that class as he usually did in his scheduled hour, I felt encouraged by his initiative. I directed a question to him, eliciting little more than a shrug as he continued to glance at his phone. Other students had enough to say to keep the discussion moving. Recognizing that our time had run out, I complimented the class on their efforts. While they noisily packed up, I walked over to Ryan's desk. He was slipping the phone into his pocket. I whispered, "You're killing yourself." He left the room without comment.

On the phone that night, Vince and I discussed the Honors exams. Our assessments of the exams corresponded. Only one or two students received different grades for psychology and English.

When our tentative grades for a student's exam differed, we listened to the other's reasoning, which sometimes swayed one of us in the direction of the other person's evaluation. Other times it became clear to us that the student's work in one subject warranted a different grade than it did in the other. We always left these deliberations feeling more secure about our fairness and accuracy, one of the great advantages of collaborative teaching. Hearing the reasoning of your teaching partner sometimes helped you pick up something in the exam or writing assignment that you had overlooked or misjudged. Overall, collaborative grading provided us with a certain level of quality control.

The next night, we reconvened on the phone to determine midterm course grades for both sections of Honors students. This longer conversation touched on all aspects of student performance to date.

In Wednesday's 8:00 a.m. Honors class, LeSean, who had received a pair of D grades at the midterm, dozed off in class, prompting me to deliver my comments while standing beside his desk, which brought him to; however, I suspected that he had awakened temporarily and merely in the literal sense. I spoke with him privately after class, explaining that if I saw him sleeping in class again, I would ask him to leave the room.

"I think my learning style needs a more stimulating approach in the classroom," he offered.

I noted that the classroom discussion had been rather spirited and that pretty much all of his classmates had actively participated. We both had to run to other classes, but he agreed to return later in the day, at which time he repeated his concern about the approach of the class.

"Just sitting there in a seat," he said, grimacing. "It's so easy to fall asleep."

It might not be too late to get into a dance class. I restrained myself.

"My job hours changed," he said, "and I don't get to sleep until late."

I got that. If I didn't routinely collapse into bed around nine every non-performing night, facing an 8:00 a.m. class would give me trouble. "Would a blast of caffeine help you?" I asked.

"I barely get to class in time," he shrugged. "The bus, you know."

"When is the earlier bus?"

From his part of the city, he'd have to leave two hours earlier.

I raised the possibility that he could stock up on those little energy drinks or prepay a classmate to bring him coffee. He liked the latter idea.

"You're not going to sleep in class," I concluded. I told him that if he felt himself starting to slip off into slumber, he should stand up and stretch, even run down to the men's room to throw some water in his face. I would waive the normal restriction about leaving the room, let alone leaving his desk. "Speaking up in class might be a great way to keep yourself awake and involved." Under ideal circumstances, he would face a steep climb to handle the demands of the course, but pushed to the limit by his work schedule, he found himself in dire straits. Focusing on the notion that the course approach did not fit him—an external locus of control—didn't help him at all.

Midterm brought an eye-of-the-hurricane calm before the next wave of assignments, and I spent hours these nights in my home office, determining the fate of the hundreds of books that I had accumulated over the years, the room filling with more boxes. I had had time to let myself act and feel as if our passage to Maine would continue unabated, but even if our scheme imploded, this purging would benefit us. The little office had become a black hole into which I poured hours of each night. I worked as efficiently as I could, but the shelves still looked like I had just started. In the past week, I had found myself going to bed later than normal and later than I liked.

With the next two class days reserved for one-on-one conferences, I would have to wait before I saw how LeSean did with his sleep management. He arrived on time for his Friday morning conference, which he'd wisely scheduled for the last part of the hour.

He sounded more on top of his game when we met. When we finished talking, I hustled to class. My late-night rummaging caught up to me midway through my 9:05 writing seminar. Running on about five hours of sleep, I found myself word-searching during the slowest hour of the semester and perhaps of my career. *Who slipped sleeping pills into my morning cup of tea?* I walked around the classroom, willing myself through the last minutes.

When the class ended, I slipped into the men's room, where I doused my face with tap water. Looking at my gaunt face in the mirror, I thought of LeSean and turned crimson. Even with nearly forty years of experience, I still had nearly crumbled under sleep deprivation. It was easy to see the danger of students' ways, but less easy to grasp that their lives rendered them vulnerable. Still, I had to push LeSean, just as I swore that tonight I would practice what I'd preached to him and get to bed early. I pulled a fistful of paper towels from the dispenser, dried my face, and marched back to my office.

The worst of the sleepiness passed, and I felt almost like myself again during the conferences. At 11:15, when Vince arrived after his 10:10 class and I had a break between appointments, we shared a dark laugh about my pedagogical near-death experience. "I'm as bad as the ones I complain most about," I moaned, relieved that I had someone to whom I could confess before my next student arrived.

The College's grading system did not allow for plus or minus grades on midterm or final postings. Charisse's C– must be translated into either a D or a C. My nervous student's attendance and citizenship had been outstanding. I decided that receiving a D at this point (even though midterm grades vanished from the computer after midterm) might damage the confidence of this hard-working woman. In conference, I would explain all of this to her, but I marked C on the grade list. In her case, I trusted that this glass-half-filled assessment would encourage her.

My songwriter friend Tom Gala referred to the city block–sized Family Court building as the Hall of Tears. I thought of Tom's quote as I readied my college office for conferences. Today, like Monday and Wednesday, would include a mixture of conferences and classes. Next Monday, I would devote my entire day to these one-on-one meetings.

Alphabetized student data forms that listed contact information, placement test results, previous final grades, and current roster—now annotated with my scribbled notes about strengths, weaknesses, and patterns in their recent work—sat in four piles on my desk beside folders holding blue books and essays. On each attendance sheet, I already had crossed out the names of several officially departed students; other de facto withdrawn students had reached the brink, but I still held a glimmer of hope that they would appear for their conferences and return to the fray. There were fewer of them now, and we all knew each other. I'd moved the box of tissues to within easy reach of the chair that students used, and thought of a former student, currently a high school teacher, who'd reminded me of my observation that the wise teacher keeps both a tissue box and a fully charged bullshit detector in his office.

Midterm conferences always left me brain-fried, even though I knew ahead of time what would happen. I started each conference by asking students how they thought their semester had gone so far. In the environment of my office, which many students apparently considered a confessional, both of us could say things we would not say in class, and I heard explanations that sprawled into decidedly nonacademic areas. It mattered to many of them that I understood what they must deal with, but as much as I recognized the immensity of the forces that precluded a short, easy campaign for them, and as much as I might feel shocked and disturbed by incidents they recounted, I tried to stay focused on the options that remained under our shared control. We talked about what they could do and how I might help them. We also talked about connections they had made in the class, as well as possible sources of help or support outside the class.

Zhivka, Charisse's classmate, had a grade somewhere between an A and a B. Our midterm conference proved less eventful than her first one. She focused on the ideas in her paper instead of on her grade. Despite working many hours in a restaurant, she had perfect attendance and had done a fine job on every assignment. Her class comments always hit the mark. She found herself on a path that might well lead to an A in the course. "You have a B for the midterm grade," I told her. "But you're headed up, aren't you?" Her eyes lit up. She smiled and thanked me.

Plucky Sid from the second-semester Honors class revised and edited his way to an A- on a major paper. His B- on his midterm exam left him frustrated, but he probably always would have problems dealing with on-the-spot performances. He left my office looking ever the warrior.

Nora, whose absences while she cared for her dying grandmother could have disqualified her, had not missed a class since returning in Week Seven, had kept up with the reading, and had completed nothing but high-quality work—an example of why rules should have their exceptions. A few students knew that their work had earned no worse than a high B grade at this stage, including Ian, the young Marine from my 11:15 class, and Jenny and Matt from the 8:00.

Twenty-four of the forty-three students in my two unlinked classes had earned a midterm grade of D or F, including Lourdes and Afafa. In some cases, progress came quickly, as with Ian, who followed his initial C+ paper with nothing but A work. I reminded students that improvement in skill courses, though often slow, was common, a reality generally reflected in higher final grades.

They had heard me speak in class about social aspects of learning; they also had read what respected thinkers in the field of learning theory had to offer, and they had used those concepts in analytical papers. In a sense, the course had headed towards this conference all along. By midsemester, more than a few students sounded as if they looked at life through new lenses. They explained twists and turns in their lives, making accurate use of the psychology we had studied. Such insight did not automatically change their lives, but it reinforced the idea that they were acquiring tools that they might put to good use. But this did not describe the majority of students.

We went over their most recent work, and they usually overestimated its quality, not an uncommon trait among writers. I made referrals and suggested strategies. We told stories and shared dreams. And before the day ended, tears fell. The stories and tears related to student explanations and analyses, often accurate though incomplete. External factors figured prominently in these stories. Like LeSean, many students cited other people and outside forces when they tried to explain their problems. Like him, they might be correct about these situations and their seriousness, but focusing on factors beyond themselves often turned out to be a well-worn circular path.

Some students, clearly headed for undesirable grades, stood in the middle of a minefield, refusing all radio messages offering directions about where to step. Had Ryan turned in his second paper on time, it would have earned a C-, but lateness reduced the grade to F. Diego, who had joined the semester in progress, scored similarly on the second essay. Neither student had turned in the revision of their first writing assignment. When reminded of this omission during our *tête-à-tête* in my office, each remained mum, as if, given enough time, the old man might forget about this requirement.

During their little break from my classes (but not from Vince's), my first-semester Honors students wrote an essay in which they applied learning concepts to Lorene Cary, author of *Black Ice,* her memoir about her New England boarding school experience. In classroom discussion, students had touched on the book's scene in which a self-pitying Cary visits a residence hall staff member to tell the woman her tale of calculus woe. The scene provided students with a palpable example of attributional style or locus of control in action. Rather than merely consoling Cary over her plight as a young woman in Mr. So And So's class, the staff member accurately and concisely characterizes Cary's troubles and acknowledges her hurt feelings about dealing with a male teacher who may not have quite acclimated himself to the school's recent conversion to coeducation. She shifts the conversation to a perspective for which Cary is not prepared, asking the young woman what *she* was going to do about her problem.[1]

Cary's attributional style would soon undergo change. Not every student with an unhealthy attributional style experienced a moment of truth that led to such a healthy reversal of cognitions, but the Honors students' reading assignment put a huge example right in front of them.

Acquainted now with Steinberg et al., they hardly could read *Black Ice* without seeing how the concept applied to the narrator. Unlike the students in my unlinked English 101 classes, first-semester Honors students had read a smorgasbord of psychology content courtesy of Vince, so they brought a broader range of resources to the task. The writing assignment unleashed the theory-wielding student writer on a case full of interesting angles. I saw the task as an appropriate and useful exercise in academic writing, but I also used it for its somewhat more subversive subtext.

This assignment served as a set-up for the following one, unannounced until they completed this paper, which called for students to turn their analytical sights on a new case subject: the face in the mirror. After the midterm, they and the students in my unlinked 101 classes would apply the theoretical lenses now in their repertoire to explain their own learning and change.

Because this paper called for a certain amount of personal revelation, we did not consider it a public document, and we did not subject it to a writing seminar. Due a week after the midterm conferences, this assignment often prompted students to introduce the reader (me) to various previously unrevealed aspects of their lives. Though not required to raise the curtain on their lives beyond the classroom, many students did so at this point. I hoped to do something akin to what Ms. Deane had done for Lorene Cary, to get into their heads, to get the students to consider how they viewed things, and to do it in the light of research and respected thought.

On the way home, I stopped at my favorite used bookstore and lugged five boxes of books from my car trunk to the store counter and let the owner paw through them, which she did like a Yosemite Park bear grown jaded and picky around campsites. I caught her frowning over treasures that hadn't quite made the cut in my purges at home. *These books are in good shape. They're valuable.*

"I can give you eight dollars," she said, pointing to a small pile of paperbacks. I schlepped the five boxes back to the car. They felt just as heavy as they had felt on the way into the store. I detoured my trip home to stop at two other bookstores and a library to no avail, then headed to the recycling center.

At last pointed home with my eight dollars and empty boxes, I thought about the ways my students thought and the ways teachers thought.

I recalled hearing about a friend's conversation with another colleague who had chided her about wanting to change her students. "Do you want to make them into little versions of you?" he asked. The idea of trying to make one's students into mini-me's *was* creepy. However, helping students learn to think critically, even if it meant they disagreed with their teacher, should not creep anyone out. I wanted students to know what respected voices in psychology said about learning. I also wanted them to know how established thinkers handled disagreements, and to see that even they sometimes changed their own thinking during the process. Welcoming newcomers and showing them the ropes in academia hardly amounted to fostering groupthink.

In that day's conferences, I'd heard the names of brothers who'd been shot, partners who'd walked out, and children whose daycare arrangements had fallen apart. I'd scribbled down the terms for medical conditions and the dates of surgical procedures. Hearing about the extraordinary challenges that my students faced reminded me of the courage and strength that they needed to find every day. Most of them could have used what healthcare workers called respite care. But who would supply it? They led complicated lives, to say the least. One student after another expressed the kind of determination that coaches hoped to hear from their athletes. They had heart. Their tales did not merely entail woe; they made defiant gestures against unseen but mighty gods.

Hearing single-parent Rashid's terse and matter-of-fact tale about driving drugs and firearms across state lines in his teens and about being shot brought to mind Daravann Yi, one of the College's counselors, whose memoir *Salt Seeker* tells his story of surviving the horrors of life in Pol Pot's Cambodia. Despite the traumas of his young life, Daravann met every day with optimism and without bitterness. I'd observed it. Before ending our conversation, I wrote down Daravann's contact information, should Rashid need to talk with a counselor.

I didn't know if speaking with me did anything to raise my students' level of engagement, but listening to them always firmed up my backbone for the work ahead. Long ago, these people had ceased to be strangers to me. Dozens of them had just brought their anxieties, insecurities, and courage into my office. They had become the equivalent of my favorite team in every sport. But unlike the Phillies, I got to coach them, to prepare them for the challenges ahead. I liked a lot of what I saw in them.

However, having been privy to student thinking all day, I suffered no delusions that they could play for the World Series that day. They *saw* things so differently. Always, but especially in community colleges, differences in thinking, both large and small, abounded between faculty and students. In *The Academic Crisis of the Community College*, my colleagues Dennis McGrath and Martin Spear point out that faculty and students "appear to disagree about the most basic, most mundane features of the classroom, as well as the larger vision of the nature and purpose of education—whether being on time is important, for instance, or what counts as participation, what kinds of thinking are valued and whether any of it matters."[2]

The course's readings and activities had forced students to identify and grapple with some of those significant differences between students and faculty. A year ago, I'd had students rank-order items on a list of sixteen essential ingredients for college success, which I had adapted from an original list created by Vince and Max Eirich. Not surprisingly, students viewed *teacher's ability to communicate* as far more important than did faculty. More telling was the disagreement on *student's view of how the educational process works and what a student needs to do to function effectively in the educational system.* Students rated it in the bottom half of the list, while faculty consistently rated this at or near the top.

Faculty also highly rated environmental issues that often didn't rate even a nod from many students. Fortunately, the very aspect of students' lives that often had impaired or restricted their progress—namely, the people in it—had changed this semester, and the degree to which they took advantage of that change would make a difference in their odds for success. A new dance had begun, and students were not alone on the dance floor.

Teaching—difficult under any circumstances—was risky business because it was a dance that teachers did with unskilled partners who often had little interest in following their lead. Even students who possessed an instrumental view of education—a drive to amass credits, get credentialed, and become marketable—might never get the swing of the rhumba or grasp the synergy of moving with a partner and creating the uniqueness of that dance, that moment. I had greater concern for students who, lacking an instrumental, extrinsic reward–based view of education, had a hard time learning the basic steps.

As Cedric Jennings found out at Brown, well-prepared traditional students knew how the game was played, and teachers could take this familiarity for granted. So much of our work in education, whether we taught the cha-cha or Boolean equations, depended on the students' view of the educational process.

In addition to the ability to listen and to speak in appropriate and effective ways, they would have to read and write in their field, meaning that the ideas of other people would have to matter to them. Students rarely realized how entry into a college major and subsequently into a career in that field involved more than studying, writing exams and papers, and finally passing enough courses to graduate. Students might see college as a chance to add new friends to their existing circles, or perhaps as providing a new and exciting pool from which to seek romantic partners, but most of them did not see it as a social doorway through which they might return as a somewhat changed individual.

In his rich 1982 memoir, *Hunger of Memory*, Richard Rodriguez characterizes education as a transformative experience, risky and powerful but deemed worth it, one that people must bring on themselves, sort of like opting for Marine Corps boot camp.[3] This applied to all of us, but nontraditional students brought with them no history of dinner table conversations in which family members or friends spoke the language of or told stories about college-trained fields or about the college experience itself. Relatives and acquaintances provided bits of scaffolding in the lives of traditional students, but such figures did not appear much in the stories I heard so often at midterm conference time. Until I'd reached a certain age, the same applied for me.

Even students who had some or most of the motivational traits might not succeed if they did not know what college expected and required of them. They needed the enculturation, and we needed them to have it. Whether we realized it or not, in addition to teaching academic skill and content, professors also taught academic life. This was nothing short of guiding and welcoming students into the academic world of study and discourse of which we were a part. If they ever wanted more than a passing familiarity with a few of our dance steps, students needed to know what we chemists, accountants, designers, and sociologists did when we performed the work we loved—how and why we read, calculated, analyzed, and how and why we acted a certain way toward each other and toward them. We owed them nothing less.

Changed into my clothes at home, I descended the basement stairs to resume my triaging project, thinking about my students, teachers, and—as my eyes fell on a battered metal trunk—my mother.

The trunk's corners had been dented and dinged in countless baggage cars, moving vans, and basement stairways, as it had figured in every move of my life and had provided storage at every address I'd had in Canada and the United States. Clutching the dry, brittle leather grip at one of its ends, I dragged the heavy container across the cement floor from its dark corner to the middle of the basement and set it under the ceiling's lone light bulb, ready to plunge into the practical work of purging, only partially realizing that opening the trunk meant walking through an emotional minefield.

From inside, I pulled out two toy Greyhound busses (miniatures of what served as our family car for trips), one of Hélene's scarves, replicas of my father's military service medals, and a fold-out triptych photograph frame, with five-year-old Ned flanked by a shot of my father in Air Force uniform and one of my mother looking glamorous. I also found stacks of tax-related papers, school records, and family correspondence, much of which came in envelopes within envelopes.

A stuffed manila envelope contained a cache of Mass cards and sympathy notes. For weeks after my mother died, letters arrived every day, in French and English, from family and old friends from Quebec, Hélene's coworkers and neighbors, Eleanor and John—by then retired in Florida—a Bermuda coworker from the Midwest, whom I knew only by name and from inscriptions on frayed black and white photographs. Glancing at two other manila envelopes, I put them aside without opening them, sensing that I would do better if I postponed inspecting some of these relics.

From the trunk full of memories, I pulled out the faded little white gown that Hélene had dressed me in for my baptism in Quebec. I found a note in her handwriting on a jagged piece of paper attached to it with a tiny safety pin. No doubt she'd written this note during her last summer while she was sorting her things, all on her own. An English-born friend named MacDonald had given the gown to her in Montreal, and it had been forty years old at that time. I inspected the note. "I am so sorry, dear son, that I was not able to get you something real beautyful and new for your baptismal. So if you ever get rich someday, no one would hardly have started poorer, but I love you more then anyone or anything in the whole world. Love always, ta Maman."

I choked while reading it, but when I imagined her saying the words, I heard her laughing, not crying. My life as her son, both during her life and since her passing, had offered me a single, clear view of the woman: enduring strength and boundless love. She loved greatly and widely, but was no one else's mother, a reality that granted me a blessing like no one else's. This I would take with me wherever I went.

"I'm sorry I could not have given you more," she had said during the year when she was dying. Her own tears never lasted very long;

she refused to pity herself or to be broken. With a room to clean, or a pork loin or apple pie to cook, she had no time for such nonsense. While many of my non-Italian friends ate their bland, overcooked food, I grew large on hearty ragouts and roasts. My friends refused no dinner invitations to join my mother and me.

I assumed that everyone lived in a perfectly cleaned, neat as-a-pin apartment. Household tasks brought her joy, which I knew because I could hear her singing when she did them. Saturdays not devoted to putting in extra shifts at Schrafft's became deep-cleaning days, often resulting in furniture rearrangements of epic proportions. Once during high school, I returned to our row house, momentarily confused as to why my key had worked on the Magees' front door. She laughed at this, refastened the babushka around her auburn hair, and started in on another room. She would watch a little television at night, but she woke up early on any non-work day, ready to start scrubbing and singing.

At home, and by proxy through the nuns at school, she constructed great amounts of scaffolding in my school-age life. At home, I learned that some of her customers earned themselves a good life and didn't have to strain and sweat like my mother and her coworkers. She knew that these lawyers and accountants who worked on the floors above Schrafft's in the Robinson Building had college educations and worked with their minds more than with their bodies. Though she came home with stories about lawyers who stole the tips that their luncheon companions had left, and about traffic cops and construction workers who routinely and with no fanfare tipped better than any businessman, her hopes for me involved something more like the work of the people upstairs. And it was not primarily about money. Without her ever saying a word about it, I knew she believed that educated people had a desirable life of the mind that eluded people like her.

She helped me with my homework, learning with me and expressing delight at what we learned, and I saw that learning new things made her happy. She beamed and commented on the interesting and sometimes even entertaining nature of the things that we studied, and I saw the satisfied adult. I saw that it mattered. Bandura would say that I experienced observational learning or vicarious reinforcement, that in addition to picking up information about history or geography, I was learning something about the joys of learning, and thus I became more likely to imitate the behavior.

For a long time, residing in the company of an unschooled woman who derived rewards from learning contributed to my good work habits and to my success in school, but as an adolescent I would learn the hard way what we also see in Steinberg's research analysis: other factors influenced a student's engagement. Finding myself too old to sit with Mom over books must have felt like maturity to me at the time, but I wondered how much such "growth" might have contributed to my subsequent academic slide into mediocrity. She'd done her best to help me, and like many youths I reached a point when I mistook my wish to be independent for actual independence, subsequently turning away from the most helpful of helping hands.

Hélene admired the nuns who taught me, and they made their respect for Hélene apparent to me. With one exception, they remained on the same page. From Hélene, I learned that one fought for the vulnerable in your keep, even when dealing with revered and mighty authorities. I was neither outlaw nor angel in grade school, but I remembered spending hours at my desk after dismissal, filling both sides of page after page of lined yellow loose-leaf paper with the sentence that Sister had written on the chalkboard, some variation of contrite commitment appropriate to the offense. *I must not speak in line. I will never push others at recess. I must obey Sister at all times.* Each sentence had to be numbered in the left margin.

As the hours crawled by, Sister occasionally allowed those of us on punishment to stretch our cramped fingers, brief breaks when I would glance enviously at classmates playing out in the schoolyard. *How could Scotty or Rob already be up to 153?* Perhaps I could find a way to avoid finishing last. After numbering the lines on a sheet, I dashed down a second column with each sentence's *I.* Then I raced down the page making an adjacent column of *must* then *obey* and so on, unwittingly rendering Sister's dubious re-education program meaningless. Like most mothers of the era, Hélène saw this as appropriate punishment, though she enacted no such policies at home.

Friday was pick-up day for those of us who had to board during the week. Late on one such afternoon, I hunkered over piles of yellow paper alone with my second-grade teacher, Sister Terrance Joseph. One by one, the other punished boys had left when their parents arrived. I didn't know that my mother had called to announce that she would be late. By five, I'd had it. "S'ter," I said, putting my hand up. Asking about my mother must have pushed some button. She bristled and let me have it. "Your mother is not coming for you. You've been very bad, and she-is-not-coming!"

I dropped my head and scratched away. Last year's nun had been so kind. This couldn't be, could it?

Eventually, Sister's classroom phone rang, which prompted her to tell me to pack up my things and scurry off to the main building, The Big House. There I found my mother, who must have been surprised at the enthusiasm of my greeting. Walking toward the trolley stop, I explained the reason for my surprise. She stopped and made me tell her the whole story, then about-faced, leaving me outside the school with my little suitcase, while she visited Mother Michael Thomas.

When we resumed our walk to the trolley, she assured me that no one at the school would ever say such a thing to me again. And no one did.

Another time, a new friend's policeman father, wearing his uniform, pounded at our door to complain that I'd bullied the friend's younger brother. If he'd taken the time to talk to the older brother, he'd have learned that no one had been bullied. When she caught her breath, Hélène stormed to their house around the block and told the man that he had no right to use his uniform to try to intimidate her. The other mother was embarrassed by her husband's rashness. It served as quite an introduction, but by the conversation's end, all of the parents were smiling and never again shared anything but kind words and deeds in their long friendship. "Speaking up doesn't mean hurting people," she told me.

I felt fortunate to have one parent on whom I could always count, and I know Hélène had suffered tremendously from her divorce, but she never poisoned me toward my father. From his mother's and his sister's letters and calls, we gathered that he was a good husband and father to his other family. When he had to retire from the military and go on disability, thus qualifying me for a monthly share of his benefits, he made sure that I got it, support that helped during my college years.

My mother always made it clear that no matter what, he was my father and he loved me. Bandura might say that Hélène was showing me something about forgiveness.

16

Spring Sabbatical, Day Thirteen

Sunday, April 15, 2012: Ireland

The previous night's pub outing had provided a much-appreciated break after nearly two weeks of steady work in the cottage. In the morning, I wrote for about an hour before I joined Vera and Rona to drive down to the dock where two fishing boats had moored in Ballinskelligs. I knew from a previous visit to Skellig Michael with Kathleen that one did not eat or drink much before departing because the island had no toilet facilities.

She and I had talked about Skellig Michael ever since that day, hoping to return. For six hundred years, communities of about a dozen monks had lived in beehive stone huts atop the island, some six hundred stone steps above the water and the narrow slip of relatively flat land that sits at one side of the great rock's base. The monks set their sights on the summit of the skyscraping rock and there built living quarters and a chapel. The buildings remained remarkably intact. Each time Vikings invaded, scaled the heights, and slaughtered the residents, the mainland monks sent others to replace them. These men lived out their lives, working and praying, in sight of the mountains along the coast, eighteen miles away.

Skellig Michael's remoteness made my mountainside cottage seem like an apartment in Center City Philadelphia. One could drive from our cottages down to the café at the water's edge in minutes, to downtown Dublin in five hours. Skellig Michael had no room for a road and nowhere for it to go. You moved up or down in Skellig Michael, and you did it on foot. The thought of monks keeping the vigil atop that lonely rock for a period of time more than twice as long as the history of the United States of America gave one pause.

Sean, the unshaven skipper of *The Flying Horse*, was in his fifties and had a facial expression that alternated between smiles and smirks. He had the boat tied to his other boat, *The Naughty Lady*, which he had fastened to the pier, so six of us—a man maybe ten years younger than me, his daughter and her boyfriend, and we three villagers—had to climb down iron rungs that jutted out from the concrete pier and step gingerly across the other boat before jumping onto the open rear deck of *The Flying Horse*.

Under an immense cloudless sky, Sean collected our cash and warned us that we needed to mind our steps on the island. "It's a good thing you're here for this weather," he said. "Today's the only day I go out for about a week."

He backed the boat into the harbor slowly, giving us our first look back at the land from the water, before heading out, skirting the cliffs along the water's edge. When he reached a spot just opposite Cill Rialaig, he cut the engines to give us a good view of the row of cottages atop the towering cliffs. From out in the water, one could see that the village sat just midway between the sea and the sky. The several-story-high wall of rocks that we looked up at through our studio glass roofs formed but the foothills of a series of heights that continued away in the distance behind our cottages. I had lived on that ledge for nearly half of my month-long stay before I could get such an awe-inspiring perspective, and I felt a bit like a student struck with a midsemester epiphany.

We all snapped photographs, and Sean, between pulls on a bent cigarette, asked that we put any good shots on his website. The boyfriend from the midlands told me that his grandmother had grown up in Cill Rialaig, leaving in the early 1940s, along with almost any other holdouts whose families had withstood the previous century's famines. He pointed to the yellow building up the road from the cottages, which had served as his grandmother's schoolhouse. In her nineties, she had talked about the schoolhouse, one clear remaining image in the mists of dementia. An elder cousin, a successful American-born son of one of the emigrant sisters, once met an Irish girl working for the summer on the Boston Harbor holiday ship that he had boarded as a day passenger. She came from Balinskelligs. They married, and the couple now had a house here, where this vacationing young cousin stayed. Three generations later, a Cill Rialaig McCarthy had come full circle, back to this scenic spot. Remarkable stories, coincidences, and fateful turns filled the air in Ireland, so much so that nothing he said surprised me.

As the boat chugged past Bolus Head, I spotted what seemed like a tower at its top. We rounded the headland and moved into more robust sea swells, vast numbers of birds flocking just above us. I saw no other boats on the horizon and few buildings on the distant coastal hills. Still miles ahead, the two towering rocks of Little Skellig and Skellig Michael rose out of the ocean against the clear sky. What else could *skellig* mean but rocky?

Sean stopped the engines again, and I heard someone shout, "Sharks!" Two basking sharks swept back and forth, only yards from the boat, their movements precise and effortless. The boat had attracted them. When one of them rolled over slightly, I glimpsed most of its length just beneath the surface. "Oh my God," burst from my mouth. The skipper stayed until we'd taken our fill of photos, then steered on toward Little Skellig.

He circled the island slowly, and he again stopped the engine, this time to let us photograph the gannets perched on ledges that ran the length of Little Skellig's sheer cliffs. The mostly white birds sported black-tipped wings and a yellow cap. We could barely hear ourselves talk over the birds' racket. One grotto, white with their excrement like all of the surfaces on this pure rock of an island, sounded like a children's playground at recess. The skipper told us that what we saw made up only 20 to 40 percent of the island's population. More were flocking on the island's other side, but "the men are out at work," he said. Where would the guys sit when they returned, I wondered.

When we reached Skellig Michael's landing, we saw maybe twenty people, dropped off by other small boats from Portmagee on the other side of Bolus Head. "I'll be back in two hours," Sean told us.

We could move no direction but up. We stopped to catch our breath on the landings between sections of rock stairs. Each stop brought with it a more expansive view than the one at the previous level. "As good a summer's day as you get in Ireland," Vera said, as the sun beat down upon us. Irish born and raised, this grandmother and artist had never visited Skellig Michael. When we reached a small meadow, far up the mountain, we could see all the way around the island, practically the same view monks had from here a thousand years ago. "Like something out of a David Attenborough program," Vera said. "It doesn't seem like we're in Ireland."

"This is Ireland for me," I replied, explaining that Kathleen and I still marveled about our visit here eleven years ago, a place that had struck us as one of the defining things about Ireland. We had visited Skellig Michael at the urging of a friend, a former nun who had just visited this place before we had started our vacation. She had given us the name of the Portmagee fisherman who ferried her here, and she insisted that, no matter what, we needed to include Skellig Michael in our itinerary. She was right. Even if this place had a less amazing human history, people still would want to visit it.

Our half-hour climb ended at the cluster of beehive stone huts. The hives' small entryways and their open spaces invited the imagination to time-travel back to before people spoke English in this country, before they'd invented the printing press.

Perspective varies and matters, as became apparent to me when I'd looked up from the boat and saw our cottages in a way that I could not see from above or from anywhere else. I thought about how many things hinge on being at a certain place at a certain time, on knowing someone in particular, and being with that person at the right time. At any moment, we can see only so many of the causal chains that run through our lives, most of them apparent only in retrospect. This is true for nontraditional students, for their teachers—for everyone.

Rona, Vera, and I stopped at a wide spot near the top of the stairway. Despite the blustery wind, the view across the blue water to the mainland's coast made me forget any discomfort. We sat and ate without talking, and I thought about circumstances that had made a difference in my life. One of those was my relationship with my great-aunt.

In her thirties, my mother's Aunt Fabienne had surgery for an ear or nose problem, but the procedure rendered her permanently deaf. She lived and worked in Manhattan and visited my mother and me in Philadelphia for holidays. Her speech had become garbled after decades without hearing her own voice or anyone else's. I listened to her stories about her younger life, working as a lady's companion for Franklin Roosevelt's mother, about cruises to Europe with the woman, horseback rides with young Franklin. By far the most well-read of my relatives, she blessed me with books throughout my childhood, including two that I still owned, a dictionary and a world atlas, the maps of which, on brittle paper, bore boundaries and names that people changed long ago.

Fabienne's deafness intrigued me and no doubt influenced me when I applied for a job at the Pennsylvania School for the Deaf upon graduation from Temple University in 1970. I had no other employment possibilities at the time, and I was happy to have a job, even if it related only loosely to my major of psychology. Two years later, I knew that I did not want to pursue a career as a teacher of Deaf children, but I saw the possibilities in counseling. That fall, I began an MA program in counseling at Gallaudet, where I met Kathleen, whom I married at the foot of the campus statue of Thomas Gallaudet a year after my graduation and two days before hers. The day after my own graduation in 1974, I had begun working part time at Community College of Philadelphia, which hired me as a full-time counselor that November. That began a tenure that eventually would bring me back to the classroom and spawn a life of writing—which ultimately led to my residence at Cill Rialaig, eighteen miles across the water from where I now sat. *Thank you, Aunt Fabienne.*

She did not think about me as a future teacher and writer when she bought books for me, but those books and her engaging personality affected me. People might easily inflate particular unintentional connections when considering their path in life, but certain ones matter in the long run, not unlike what one might make of personal genealogy. Usually, the further back one goes, the less the impact and significance; however, an emigration to another continent or even a trip to Bermuda sets up a very different stage on which one's offspring play out their lives. Circumstances do not predestine; they do, however, set up possibilities and affect odds. And certain people make great differences in another person's life. A mother, an aunt, or a teacher can try to make great differences in a child's life, but at some point that child must pick up the ball and run with it. When we pick up the ball, we find that other people also occupy the field—teammates, opponents, referees. At that point, we also must realize that we cannot succeed in the absence of others—a point that my students needed and deserved to hear.

Even alone in my cottage on the distant rocks of Cill Rialaig, I'd had plenty of company in my head. A lifetime of recollected people, conversations, and experiences came through the windy doorway with me that first day, even if they did not make their presence known immediately. Mostly I had written fiction over the years, but here, I found my mind turning to memories of actual people who either had entered my life or had allowed me to enter theirs. None of these souls spoke to me through my computer, so I had to remember their voices, make sense of their conversations, and push the keys.

Sunday afternoon's far less demanding descent down the hundreds of Skellig Michael's stone steps afforded me a comfortable view of the blue waters that surround these two small islands. I reached the bottom of the steps and realized that our boat was the last one left. The rocky pinnacle was once again free of people. Skellig Michael's ruins remained fairly intact, not much different from when the last of the monks took their spare belongings many hundreds of years ago and sailed to exactly where we would head now, Ballinskelligs, where, a few hundred yards from the pier, they built an abbey, now also in ruins.

The trip back felt restful after hiking up and down Skellig Michael, and everyone felt about as happy about the day trip as possible. We spotted a pair of fins near the place where we'd sighted the sharks on the trip out. "Cill Rialaig means 'church of the regulars,'" Vera informed us. It was a reference to lay communicants who had moved to the village in the twelfth century, after the monks built their abbey in Ballinskelligs.

The village's row of cottages up above us beckoned after our long stretch away. I returned to Cottage 8, feeling inspired to resume my monkish dedication to my work.

Fall Semester, Week Nine

Monday, October 31, 2011: Philadelphia

Because I canceled classes at midterm to create time to meet privately with all of my students, they enjoyed a few days free of classes with me. They had plenty to read and write about before our next class and had to meet me for our scheduled conference, but I figured they would appreciate a bit of a break from attending class. Breaks seemed like a good idea, up to a point. Halftime in a rugby match lasted five minutes—enough time to catch one's breath, gulp some water, and argue with teammates about who should do what in the second half— but it did not last long enough for muscles to go cold or seize up.

I always wondered how this midcourse assessment would affect them. Would they return to class with a clearer picture of where they stood, or would doubt creep into their psyches as they approached the semester's second half? Would the break make them lose good habits or revert to bad ones?

Some students returned to class on the heels of a personal warning that if they missed another day, I would drop them from the course. Three of the original fourteen members of my 8:00 a.m. first-semester

Honors class had withdrawn from the link or had been dropped for excessive absences, and one other teetered on the brink; two members of my equally small second-semester Honors class had left.

Comments jotted on students' papers and related orally in midterm conferences directed them to aspects of their work that needed attention. Practically every conference had ended with some version of "Don't give up." Now I would see how they responded to the halftime rhetoric.

I was never surprised at the high number of students with failing or borderline grades at the midterm. One wincing glance through the semester's first essays documented the fundamental problem so common among writing students: a general lack of the skills needed to do college-level writing. And college writing demanded much more than basic command of writing's rules and practices. It had to do something to the reader.

What is this sentence/paragraph doing to you? Such questions during writing seminars quickly drove students to fits. So few of them came to college with strong writing experience. Writers measured their efficacy in the effects of their words upon readers. To teach writing students otherwise led them to believe that writing truly did not exist in the real world of experience; it just became classroom stuff.

I wondered how many of my students had learned as much. Teaching involved more than merely sharing knowledge—as if that did not provide challenge enough—it also concerned behavioral change, exposure to new beliefs and values, and, in some cases, even a rewiring of how people thought, saw, and did things. Much looked grim at midterm time, but we still had time ahead of us.

The ninth week of the semester ended with a guest lecture to our combined Honors sections by Philip Miraglia, a psychological clinician with over thirty years of experience. Drawing out the audience, he filled the board with the seemingly disparate elements of knowledge that he used in his work. By the end of the lecture, he had created a pyramid, showing the skill areas and course content areas that undergirded the work of a psychologist. He had provided the students with an easy-to-remember graphic display of the utility of all of a psychologist's training. Students could see the relationship among research, assessment, statistical analysis, theory, and so on in his work, understanding how all these things interrelated and served a purpose. He talked about what he had learned in various educational and professional environments, so they grasped that he had never stopped learning.

Beaming, the handful of future psychology majors in the classroom followed Phil down the hall offering their thanks, but they were not alone in their appreciation of his lecture. Office-hour regular Sid and Penn-bound Donald commented to me that they now could clearly see how the seemingly irrelevant aspects of a broad college education fit together, how they combined to enable a person to operate in a professional capacity. Phil's presentation fit into the arc of the semester perfectly. Vince and I thanked our old friend for teaching the best class of the semester.

In my Monday follow-up session with the 8:00 Honors class, Jenny noted that she could make connections between work and education that she hadn't made before. "That seems to be such a big part of learning," she mused.

Matt commented that she'd just made another such connection, causing Jenny to redden.

"Connections about connections," Matt added. "Trippy."

We all laughed. I thought it might be the best moment of the semester so far.

On the Saturday afternoon following Week Nine, I graded essays on the sunny deck with Jack and Roux so that they wouldn't terrorize the plumber while he installed the new dishwasher I had bought. Surely a new kitchen appliance would improve the desirability of our old house?

When Junior left with our broken old dishwasher, I returned to the basement and Memory Lane. How many birthday cards from Mom did you save? I was getting faster at this process, but it took both a physical and emotional toll. We had invested in industrial-size plastic bags, and on trash days our neighbors had the treat of seeing a line of cans and bags stretching from our driveway to the property line.

Resting between trips from basement to garage, which functioned as a holding area until trash day, I lingered over a fat envelope from Syracuse University, bound with string, into which I'd stuffed graduation and Christmas cards. Syracuse was one of the graduate schools to which I'd applied in 1972. I had no recollection of whether or not they had accepted me; when I learned Gallaudet had accepted me, I ended the process.

Sitting on a paint-splattered stool, I wondered how differently my life would have turned out if I'd ended up at Syracuse. Although Kathleen was a senior at Le Moyne College, a short distance east of the SU campus, during what would have been my first year there, the chances of us ever having met seemed beyond remote. In so many ways, our lives would have turned out differently had we not ended up at the same graduate school. I shook myself from my reverie and opened up a new trash bag. Into it went sports medals, tidy little elementary school yearbooks, and relics from ancient vacations. I managed to run through the names of all of my elementary school teachers before looking inside the eight report cards. Other things I could quickly toss, but I paused to see at what grade the straight A's started becoming a mixture of A's and B's. I tore each report card in half with some measure of dignity and slipped them one year at a time into the bag.

Early in the semester, it became apparent that quiet and barely responsive Will must not go anywhere without his faded Phillies cap. From the heat of Indian summer through the early tastes of winter, the wan-looking lad arrived and left wearing the relic, and the cap remained on his head through classes and conferences. One day when he was absent, I noticed a bedraggled cap that looked very much like Will's on the little bookrack beneath an unoccupied desk's seat. It was still there the next day, though again Will was not. I didn't notice Will coming into the room on the day that he did return, but when he responded to the attendance question, I looked up and saw that he and the hat had been reunited. Unfortunately, he hadn't brought his assignment with him.

The next day, I got another attendance surprise. As she had promised, Chelsea returned to class, bringing photographs of her newborn twins, along with her completed writing assignments. My attendance sheet showed that her delivery caused her to miss a total of four classes. She had not missed a day before that. She explained that she'd had to stay in the hospital for several days because of complications.

Across the room sat Adam, a Chinese American student. Two weekends ago, his girlfriend's e-mail had informed me that he'd gone through the windshield of his car and would miss that Monday's class. Two days later, my eyes widened when he entered the classroom and walked up to my table. He handed me a note explaining that he couldn't write or speak just yet because of the stitches. He hoped that I would allow him just to sit in class.

Other students, like Will and Ryan, held themselves to a very different standard. Additionally, others struggled but remained barely afloat. Afafa and Lourdes visited me together during an office hour, and we went over each one's paper in turn. I encouraged them to work with a particular specialist on the patterns of errors in their writing that appeared to stem from having English as a second language, and off they went. I hoped that they still had enough time to pull things together, but so far their results remained below the threshold for passing. Their collaboration pleased me, but I hoped it did not amount to the blind leading the blind. Fortunately, they had made their way to a lab specialist skilled in helping ESL students.

The structure of the second-semester Honors course required students to work together. Several students in my 8:00 Honors class had started getting together to go over material, and I told that class about the experience of Barbara Jordan, who attended Boston University law school shortly after it opened its doors to blacks. She had performed strongly as a high school student and in college, but her first semester of law school threw her for a loop. Like so many of my students, she learned that her formal and informal education was not the same as that of her better-prepared classmates. It seemed to her that practically all of them had grown up in a family of lawyers, that they knew all the legal lingo before they walked into their first law class.

She lacked her classmates' scaffolding experiences. Much to her credit, she recognized her disadvantage and focused on what was under her control. She accepted the fact that she'd have to outwork everyone around her to catch up.[1] However, good habits that had brought her success before did not work at BU. She operated on three or four hours of sleep. She was doing all of the right things, but she was doing them alone.

At the pre-semester social, she had observed the white students sizing up each other and determining whom they wanted in their study groups. They did not invite black students to join. Consequently, that fall, she and her black classmates studied alone. In her first semester, while she toiled away alone in the library, her white classmates in study groups got more bang for the buck by collaborating. In her second semester, when Jordan and some of her black classmates formed their own study group, they found that working together made a difference.[2]

I described how such groups could work. Students broke down long reading assignments into chunks, with each group member taking responsibility for leading the others through that material. All study group members read everything and prepared questions on the readings, but each student was responsible for briefing the group about the minutia in only one section. Reading a text as preparation for teaching differed greatly from any other kind of reading, as I knew from years of experience. Students working alone must bring that kind of intensity to bear on every page, whereas those working in a study group only needed to apply it to a fraction of their work. Students who joined a study group made connections that often outlasted the semester, and these provided weaker students with structure and support that accelerated their engagement and ultimately their performance.

"Pick a time and a place," I'd said to several weaker students in the 8:00 Honors class, "and tell classmates what you're interested in talking about. You might be surprised who shows up."

As Week Ten ended, I stayed up late on Friday night and worked through Saturday morning to catch up on grading, then spent the rest of the weekend doing a line-by-line edit of my book of short stories so that I could send a final copy to the editor on Monday.

Editing begat more editing, as it always did. Time not spent on grading or editing I devoted to preparation for a move that still hinged on our getting approved for a mortgage. Because we kept from talking about the move with friends other than Vince and Joan, Kathleen and I stole our moments and looked forward to the news that would let us break our silence. And while we waited, we sorted. I discovered yet another box of textbooks and notebooks that dated back to my undergraduate days. Paging through them forced me to confront an unflattering portrait of myself as a student.

While I had the positive influence of associating with friends and peers in high school who also planned to attend college, I had lacked both the desire and discipline of Chelsea and Adam and the imagination to find alternative ways of learning. I resembled the students in my class who would rather not get too involved, but I had not started out like this, as those torn report cards reminded me. Even late in elementary school, I did well and scored high enough on the La Salle College High School admissions test to be accepted by that respected Catholic college-preparatory school.

My good elementary school habits did not make the move to high school intact, and, once there, I considered myself less talented than my classmates. However, my lower performance came about, no doubt, because of decreased effort on my part. At thirteen, like many early adolescents, I felt inferior, alienated, and unmotivated, and I experienced a certain fatigue from having taken the dutiful path in elementary school. Unlike most of my students, I attended a good high school, for which my mother paid tuition, but I slipped through the cracks. As a teacher, I had tried to connect with students like me, to provide some reinforcement for moves in the right direction.

I had blended into high school's woodwork, happy to go unnoticed, lest I try to do something for which I felt unprepared or too embarrassed to attempt. When my mother had been the same age, she'd already begun full-time work and was partly supporting her siblings as well as herself. Meanwhile, I was wondering how I would save enough money to buy the latest singles by Gene Pitney or the

Ronettes. I did my schoolwork, but not with enough overall oomph to gain that electric sensation of first learning and the satisfaction that came with it; likewise, I put forth insufficient efforts to earn extrinsic rewards in the form of high grades. Consequently, I struggled.

And, under the influence of the new sixties zeitgeist all around me, I began to doubt everything I had ever believed in. With Kennedy's assassination, any magic in life seemed to disappear. I became jaded, as teenagers in any era do, but the condition was rampant in the sixties. I muddled on, still confident that I had enough native intelligence to get by. My miscalculation resulted in rejection by the colleges to which I applied. In the fall of 1966, I enrolled for classes at the recently established Community College of Philadelphia, a lifeline thrown into the water for floundering students like me. My relegation to the only school that would have me, however, did not make me want to do more.

Although I stopped feeling like a loser when I began classes at CCP, I kept the view that barely getting by would be just fine. Socially, the environment felt comfortable. For the first time in my life, I attended school with young women and non-Catholics, including a significant number of black people. Suddenly part of what everybody today would call a diverse student body, I found myself surrounded by students from economic backgrounds quite similar to mine. I never doubted that I had enough intelligence to be a successful college student, which I defined as C grades with maybe some B's thrown in. I lacked ambition and held a very vague sense of direction, certain only that whatever I did for a living better not involve math and science.

This perspective, along with my belief that surely my intelligence would stand up to anything these community college people could throw at me, guaranteed that I would end up with average grades, at best. To my shock, this approach produced a first-semester GPA barely above a D. I had failed biology and gotten D grades in history, which I loved, and in math. Nothing redeemed the semester.

This debacle showed me how close I had stepped to the edge of the precipice. Still, I felt motivated to move away from the edge but not much more. My belief that prospective employers would be more than satisfied with a mediocre transcript as long as it added up to a degree profoundly limited me.

And so my college years went. I knew that my bottom-feeding practices saddened my mother, but nonacademic aspects of my life consumed me. I think she assumed that I always did my best, and she considered that enough for her. Although I enjoyed learning things and had some genuine intellectual curiosity, I drifted along with my Instrumental Lite view of education. I worked but not with the consistency that students must display to achieve the kind of learning that correlates with high grades in most courses and at least decent grades in courses they find difficult.

"I pulled another all-nighter," I'd proudly tell Nevin, my high school friend who was majoring in electrical engineering at Drexel Institute of Technology (now Drexel University). A smart and hard-working student, he shook his head in disapproval of my late-semester surges. His efforts varied little over the course of a term. When I saw the finish line, I read and wrote like a demon, and actually found a certain pleasure in the experience. At the beginning of every semester, I turned over a new leaf, buying notebooks and telling myself that this time I would rush home, reread those notes, and dive into the assigned texts, but the next thing I knew I felt tired after working, or Nevin, having already done his schoolwork, called to say he'd discovered a lighted basketball court on his way home from Drexel, and off we went. I found distractions, although at the time I might have said that distractions found me. Much the same thing happened when I transferred to Temple for my last two years.

My lack of success made sense. I didn't do enough learning. It sounded like a child's explanation, but it captured the essence of the truth. My high school and college years did result in learning, just not enough. More to the point, though I developed skills and broadened my knowledge core, I had not yet done enough to see connections and relationships between what I had learned, or to fathom the meaning and value of such connections. Like so many of my students, I lacked a map onto which I could locate bits of learning and thus see that certain things actually *went* together. Unlike most of my students, I possessed good background but not enough, and I lacked consistency of effort.

For a student lacking a contextual map, history, literature, and American government courses seemed like three completely different jobs that I had to perform in order to get through the day, the week, and the semester. And like my students, I knew about jobs, having worked in the summers and after classes and done yardwork for family friends and neighbors. As a child and teenager, I too learned about work without ever leaving home. I had heard my mother turn off her alarm clock to go to the nonstop, back-bending, high-speed service job that occupied fifty weeks of her year until the restaurant finally unionized and gave her a third week off. The hard work often included less than civil treatment from bosses and customers, but she held onto that job like the man she deserved but never found. She missed a day's work about as often as the Philadelphia sports teams of my youth won a championship. She was skilled at her work, and all but the most self-absorbed customers and coworkers recognized her competence and good spirit.

At the dinner table, I heard her stories about customers like Norman, the giant cop who directed traffic outside at 15th and Chestnut

Streets; the annoying "Hot Soup," who never failed in twenty years to demand that her daily bowl of soup be more fully heated; and the generous Mrs. Miller, who, having heard from Hélene of my love of trains, gave me a switch-track or a freight car for my model train set every Christmas. I knew the names, mannerisms, virtues, and vices of her coworkers, some of whom became a string of aunts, always happy to see me when I passed part of my mother's Saturday shift next door to Schrafft's at the movie theater.

In many ways, work was her life, and though hard, and fulfilling only in the barest economical way, she gave it her all and counted her tips with a sense of pride. She performed work every day, whether at Schrafft's or at home. Although I harbored no interest in spending my life in such a working environment and holding the kind of job that had enabled Hélene's underdog survival, I learned that one's work made planning possible and that it provided one with friends and enemies, just like school. My mother hoped that I would find a job that I liked; she lived to see me do that but died before my work life evolved from the equivalent of girlfriend status to lifelong marriage partner. I felt emotionally prepared to work and anxious to find a position. I just had little idea of what position to look for.

In May of 1970, I graduated from Temple with a BA in psychology and landed my first full-time job in late August. With no teaching experience, no knowledge of American Sign Language, and a total of one education course, I was obviously the man that the Pennsylvania School for the Deaf wanted. I'd say that I performed the best bit of salesmanship of my life, but with one week until the beginning of the school year, they desperately needed to hire a warm body to teach academic subjects to their vocational school's high school–age students.

Having lost her hearing later in life, my mother's Aunt Fabienne had never learned American Sign Language, relying on her uncanny ability to speech-read in both French and English. Later, I learned that I was not to expect her skill among most Deaf individuals, especially the pre-lingually Deaf. Because so little of spoken language became visible on the face, speech reading turned into a guessing game, making my aunt's skill something of an aberration.

I sought a job at PSD partly because I had a family connection with deafness, partly because I did not see teaching as terribly distant from my major, and partly because I had the school on my radar, having grown up in its shadow. The salary of six thousand dollars a year outstripped what I made at the A&P, and I was happy to dip a toe into a college-based field. I began learning ASL immediately, even though no mandatory requirement to use it in the classroom existed at that time; in fact, until recently, the school had used the speech-reading oral system, which banned the use of ASL. All of the students signed; teachers who wanted to communicate with them signed.

My students did not take college-track courses, and some were older than typical high school age. When the semester began, I had a twenty-one-year-old student—my age, a commonality that I kept to myself. I donned a jacket and tie and tried to act like a teacher, a difficult acting job under any conditions, and absurdly impossible for someone who could not communicate with the students. My sharp learning curve kept me up at nights. The frenzy that had engulfed the final weeks of my student semesters became my lifestyle. No doubt the ghosts of my former high school and college teachers had a good laugh watching me stumble through lesson plans and fumble with mimeograph machines. My first students had not taken me outside and strung me up on the nearest tree, for which I remained eternally grateful because I probably deserved it.

Of course, my employers required that I take classes, leading me to on-site ASL classes and weekly drives to Trenton, New Jersey, for graduate courses in Deaf education. As the months passed, my communication skills improved. I also started to feel less like an actor; I began to feel like part of the place. I enjoyed my connection to the other teachers, most of them the age of my own teachers just a few months earlier. I found myself bothered by students who acted exactly as I had, an irony that I kept to myself. Now I wanted them to respond, to do their part, because, after all, I was standing on my head to help them. I attended their football and basketball games. At one away game, a student on the other team's sideline referred to me as "sir," causing me to trip. Drawn from all over the eastern half of the state, our students lived in dorms for months at a time, and one Saturday when I had no rugby game, I squeezed several of my football players into my Volkswagen Beetle and took them to a Temple football game. Haltingly, I served on the prom committee. I felt frustrated when they didn't do well in their classes. In short, I became invested in their work.

Two years of this on-the-job training taught me a lot, not least of which was my increasing realization that although I enjoyed working in the field of education and serving that population, I wanted to play a different role. I found myself tacking back toward my major but now in the arena of education. During my second year at PSD, Gallaudet announced the start of a graduate program for counseling the Deaf, and having improved my signing skills I jumped at the chance. Presumably, my two years of teaching experience trumped my academic record because they accepted me. I moved to Washington, DC, and joined a class of about twenty, composed of both Deaf and hearing people.

Being in graduate school thrilled me. I had never lived away from

home on my own before. By this point in my life, turning away from
the dark side of studentship would have qualified as an Augustinian
recovery; however, my Bad Augustine had not quite fully renounced
his self-defeating ways. I attended classes and did the work, but again
not with full commitment. My personal consciousness at the time
had reached its loopiest. I had decided that experience had more
importance than grades, so I did not even open my first grade report.
Somehow, I learned that my fall semester grades, as inconsequential as
I considered them, had registered on the low side. Fortunately, some
of my "experience-based" learning went in useful directions, but again
I found myself looking up from the bottom of my class.

Diversions and distractions at this point in my life included playing rugby, which I had discovered during the early part of my teaching stint at PSD. In Philadelphia, I had found myself in the right
place at the right time and became a charter member of the Blackthorn Rugby Football Club. The sister of one of the club's founders
dated my friend Paul Muessig, and she recruited six of us in one fell
swoop. My life changed.

I had always enjoyed the rough and tumble of sports, but my lack
of finesse had hindered my progress in soccer or basketball; whereas in
rugby, particularly playing in the front row of the scrum, I found the
better fit that had not appeared in any sport I'd tried while growing
up. The freedom from constant control by militant coaches during
games appealed to my anti-establishment leanings. Unlike baseball
and football, the game flowed, and players were expected to follow
a certain code that included sorting themselves out, there being
only one referee to manage the thirty players swirling around him.
Inclement weather never warranted postponing a game. A player had
two minutes to recover from an injury or the game went on without
him. Despite the game's undeniable wildness, sometimes bordering

on brutality, it also possessed an international culture that included wearing a jersey with a white collar and calling the referee "Sir." And, of course, players from both sides gathered after the match to drink beer and sing songs, including the filthiest ones I'd heard in my life. One game and after-party hooked me. My social circle changed, and through my two years of teaching at PSD, I spent more and more time with people I met through rugby.

As I recounted in the syllabus article that explained reciprocal determinism, playing rugby provided the environment that caused me to sing in front of others. Indeed, during my PSD and Gallaudet years, I was learning a great deal, though not always of a professional nature. Once I moved to Washington, DC, I began playing with the men's club down in Annapolis, but after one semester, I formed a club at Gallaudet. No rugby club primarily for the Deaf had ever existed in the United States. Living and working in a dorm, I recruited undergraduates and grad students and anyone else I could talk into wearing a gold-colored jersey. Even a PR department staff member joined. One of my Deaf players also had fairly significant cerebral palsy, and another had visual problems. A ragtag bunch, we lost more than we won, but founding the club was one of the best things I did at Gallaudet. I got to know students and Deaf culture, and our band of signing and hooting streakers provided a lot of rugby clubs and bar owners a sometimes jaw-dropping introduction to people they otherwise never would have met.

New players needed to learn much about the game, and as a first-time coach, I had a lot to learn too. Receiving Georgetown's kick-off on the nearly grass-free surface that served as their home pitch, I learned that teaching always involved priorities. I bit down on my mouthguard, caught the ball, ran into the first of the on-charging Georgetown pack, and turned to put myself between the ball and arriving tacklers. In the nanosecond when properly trained forwards would bind on me, forming a moving human wall to protect the ball (and prevent opponents from trampling me), the rest of the opposing forwards arrived at full speed, while my fledgling teammates stood around, waiting for a clue from their player-coach. They couldn't hear me if I screamed. With both hands clamped around the ball, I could only plant my feet, glance at my teammates' puzzled faces, and wait the briefest of eternities for the inevitable. I had no awareness of going down, merely of suddenly *being* down. From my face to my feet, my body became imbedded in the top layer of stony dirt, under an immense pile of opposing players intent on using their boots to get at the ball that somehow remained under me. Binding on kick-offs should have been the first lesson I taught the forwards and would become my first order of business at halftime—if I lived that long.

Such extracurricular community involvement did, however, take time from studies, and again, I graduated low on the totem pole. At Gallaudet, I also met Katheen Kempf, who immediately began providing what Albert Bandura might term environmental influence in important ways and of salvific impact—a source of knowledge and support that I hoped would endure as long as we breathed. None of my experiences with the rugby club or with this student from Hoosick Falls, New York, showed up on my transcript, but they provided some of my best learning.

I did not become a good student until, after years of working as a counselor at CCP, I found myself wanting to do something different. I'd started performing music by then, which had also resulted from playing rugby. I had written in various forms all of my adult life—songs, comedy sketches, newsletters for the rugby club—and I loved singing and learning about traditional folk music. I approached Kenneth S. Goldstein of the University of Pennsylvania's Folklore Department, a world expert on bawdy songs, among other things. We formed an instant natural connection, and he encouraged me to take a few courses and consider applying to the PhD program in folklore. I had a two-year-old child at home, worked full time as a counselor, and performed with a band, so my time was guarded, precious, and carved from a schedule that would have knocked the younger Ned as flat as I was on that rugby pitch in Georgetown. As a result, I did not miss a minute of class.

I had long ago entered into academic culture and now had the opportunity to work in it as a well-prepared student. Finally I threw myself into my studies, and my grades showed it. I loved folklore. I knew that I always would, whether or not I worked in the field, but I found writing about it my favorite part. Writing seemed to be the way that people in the field figured things out. I saw it happening in the academic work I did for the courses.

When I took a course in creative writing at Temple the next year, I experienced the challenge and the lure of workshop classes. My classmates had talent and drive. We each mined different terrain but became comrades. I came to think of the members of this temporary community as my fellow code crackers, as if we were tucked away in the recesses of Bletchley Park puzzling away at Nazi ciphers. Learning the basics about writing poetry and fiction from Elaine Terranova and watching my work improve over weeks of classroom workshop, I knew what I wanted to do next.

Taking my first sabbatical leave in 1986 when I was thirty-seven, I began the two-year low-residency writing MFA at Vermont College. Living on half-pay for a year, I cared for our new daughter while Kathleen did her own retooling, studying for her nursing degree at Community College of Philadelphia. No longer waiting for the semester's point of no return, I read and wrote like a madman from day one. Twice-a-year residencies became a total immersion experience, as intense as any end-of-semester writing binge when I'd drunk coffee all night, but minus the desperation.

Being a new father played no small role in my transformation. I wanted a lot: to pay the bills, to write, and to spend my days and nights with our little family. Someone else or a less engaged Ned might have felt like he was being pulled in opposite directions, but I learned how to plan and how to squeeze as much life into an hour as possible. It felt good.

At the residencies, I made friendships that would follow me and enrich my work and my life. In my first round of graduate school, I had studied with a certain sense of mission and been surrounded by good classmates and teachers, influences that no doubt helped me at least survive the experience. However, in crafting my own fiction, the personal nature of the work gave me a greater sense of mission than I had known previously. I was like a carpenter who finally used his tools, skills, and time to build his own home. We *all* were. Obviously, the work was largely solitary, the inspiration personal, but the learning experience proved intensely social. We influenced each other, learning through our interactions.

Sparked with a bit of knowledge and experience, I wanted more than ever to write, which meant that I began to read compulsively and to talk about writing with classmates, teachers, and anyone else who shared my passion. Guided by a series of accomplished writer/teachers, I stumbled through draft after draft of stories that either grew in ways that surprised me or died leaving me wiser. I cherished conversations with people who knew more than I did, and tried to listen more than I spoke. Writers taught. Teachers wrote. In short order, I found myself also wanting to help other writers, and off I went. When my sabbatical ended halfway through my MFA program, I taught an 8:00 a.m. writing class before my counseling hours began. My rush to satisfy my soul had led me right back to teaching.

When I transferred into the English Department at Community College of Philadelphia in 1989, I returned to the classroom in a different state than the twenty-one-year-old who had stumbled into PSD's Wissinoming Hall playing the role of teacher. Looking back in 2011 at more than two decades of teaching at the College, I realized that I had never completely stopped acting, as improvisation is part of the job, but now I acted with scaffolding support that I'd lacked as a fresh college graduate. And I knew that I always had grasped connections, just not usually enough to add up to actual learning, the kind that sped the learner on. When I began teaching at CCP, I knew firsthand the practices, pitfalls, and pains of being a very bad student, but by that time I also had learned how a person *could* learn, even one who'd been a loser for a long time. Exchanging a counselor's caseload for class lists, I realized that I had much to learn about teaching, but I also knew that I was ready.

I was fortunate to have found a role I could inhabit so long and a job that provided sustenance for my family and gave me enormous stimulation, satisfaction, and meaning. I hoped that my students would find the same, and the last part of our semester focused on these very things.

Though ordinarily personality did not experience seismic shifts, readings in the first half of the semester showed students that sometimes people underwent changes in their approaches to life: in ways of seeing and ways of behaving; indeed, the possibility of such change was at the heart of my intentions for the course. Such change accounted for my standing in front of them, leading them on this academic and—when I was most successful—personal journey into the workings of learning. And such change could enable students to similarly play roles previously closed to them, in their work, their play, their families, their communities.

I'd been blessed to find this work and to do it year after year. Now I was on the far side of what might well be my last semester, nearing the point in the term when students complained that life shifted into a higher gear and threatened to go out of control.

The culminating work of the semester called for students to make use of all of the explanations for learning they'd studied in a paper focused on Murana Bill, the main character of Susan Dodd's out-of-print novel, *No Earthly Notion*. One by one, they'd been introduced to Vygotsky, Bandura, and company. What would happen if they all sat down in the same room at the same time to talk about Murana while applying the concepts they'd learned to her story?

My second-semester Honors students had already selected the focus for their own culminating projects. The class's collective task was to develop a guidebook for prospective parents, and each student had picked a particular stage of human development and a team of theorists/experts. Drawing from sources that sometimes disagreed, students had to organize and present information and suggestions that they considered valuable to a prospective parent.

Unlike students in the first-semester courses, their thinking must take into consideration the complexity of nature versus nurture. This was not an opinion paper; instead, students served as producers of a kind of orientation program. I reminded them of what I'd told them the first day: "You're the writing staff. I'm your editor. Together, we will piece together a book-length manuscript."

An early snowstorm reminded me that we had entered a different season of the year, even if the calendar said otherwise. Bundled up against the weather, I drove to work with Anna on one of the rare days that our schedules coincided, and together we laughed, listening to sports radio. Nearing the campus, I found a free parking spot on the street, and we quick-stepped the four-block walk. I felt the same slight heaviness in my chest that I had felt last December but said nothing. The funny sensation in the cold weather was in line with what the pulmonologist had explained when he'd prescribed an inhaler for me.

"You all right, Dad?"

I hadn't realized that I'd looked or acted differently. "Yeah," I said, "but I'm not going to be starting for the Eagles any time soon." I didn't like appearing that out of shape to my daughter—the last thing I wanted to do was alarm her. And even if I'd been alone, I would have felt shame for letting my health and fitness slip.

Driving alone two days later, I found a spot on the same block. Hustling to campus, I quickly found myself panting and felt that heaviness again, prompting me to try a huff of the inhaler. It didn't seem to make a difference. I'd waited long enough to do something about my fitness level. With winter coming on and facing a home schedule that involved the daily movement of large bags of trash and occasionally furniture, I could not afford this sort of thing. It was time for less eating and more sweating, and I vowed to get back on the exercise bike. Moves in those directions always paid off in unexpected as well as expected ways. The specialist might have something better to prescribe, so I scheduled an appointment to see him later in the month.

On Saturday, November 12, after catching up on grading and completing a final line edit of my manuscript of stories, I dutifully spent forty minutes on the exercise bicycle in my study listening to Pat Metheny before dinner. When I checked e-mail at the end of the day,

I found a message from a student in our first-semester Honors class. "My daughter was not feeling well on Friday so I did not attend class and her uncle was just killed last night." He went on to ask what work he needed to do since he would miss Monday's class in order to attend the funeral. My reply offered encouragement and my condolences, but what could I say that would make anything better for this young man? *Is he surprised that such a horrible thing could happen to someone in his world? No.* Other e-mails I received fit in more with the sort that a professor at any college might expect from students, but his message stuck in my mind as I went through my end of the day activities. Again, troubles chronicled in our fictional case studies had intruded into the lives of our students.

The semester's race had reached the far turn, and the pace increased. Students would turn in a major essay this week and set their sights on the semester's climactic assignment. The band would play Friday and Saturday night of Thanksgiving weekend. We might hear about our mortgage application any minute.

Week Eleven moved quickly. We finally reached the school deadline for dropping classes. Three students withdrew from the class, including Ella, whose aggressive tone in e-mail belied her pleasant in-person demeanor, and Will, whose baseball cap had better attendance than its owner. And I had lost three students from the two Honors sections, deadline attrition that disappointed but never surprised me. The remaining students knew that they must stay on board for the rest of the term. Thursday morning, I got a haircut then drove to my appointment with the pulmonologist. I was relieved to learn that my respiratory test results did not concern him. We talked about strategies for helping me get through the bracing schedule ahead of me.

"I'm back to the bicycling," I told him.

"Excellent," he said. "I'll have you do a cardiac stress test, just to rule out any possible problems in that area." I knew the drill from having taken one in 1996. I was grateful that I did not have any serious pulmonary disorder. This was nothing that diet, exercise, and the right medicine could not control. I drove home visualizing the schedule for the last few weeks of the semester, thankful that it wasn't anything that would interfere with my crazy but exciting workload.

18

Spring Sabbatical,
Day Twenty-One

Monday, April 23, 2012: Ireland

For three weeks, I had lived in Cill Rialaig village, only the second time that I'd spent this much time in a place other than home or a dorm since the Vancouver dishwashing summer between my two years at Gallaudet thirty-nine years ago. As with my life, more of my residency trailed behind me than lay ahead, with the difference that I knew that in eight days I would leave this cottage.

Mostly I'd kept company with my laptop, with breaks provided by the rattling uphill or downhill passage on the gravel of the farmer's little truck, followed by the quick clop-clop of his charging Border Collie in pursuit; breaks also came courtesy of the two or three radio stations that I could locate. Marty, host of the morning show, had grown on me to the point that I made sure I caught his daily reading of the mysterious Hugo's latest correspondence. The accents I heard on the radio were as varied as the ones on an American national call-in show. Listening to voices in shops or on the radio, I often mistook their lilting English for Irish.

In the company of the radio's unseen voices, I ate my meals in the cottage and enjoyed the music and the different voices, and, of course, the ever-present sound of rain on the glass roof above the table. Deprived of fellow diners, I ate with an opened newspaper beside my plate. I had purchased several issues of *The Irish Times* and *This Post* or *That Journal*, as much for the newspapers' great fire-starting value as for the information therein, but every night, I pulled out some section of a now-dated newspaper and read it through. I flipped to the weather section, wondering if I might have purchased the special issue that forecast drought, a blizzard, or heat lightning. Nary an Irish soul would bat an eye if newsstands suddenly offered *The Daily Rain*.

Invariably, I also spent part of mealtime exploring the map of Ireland that I had brought with me. I studied the region in which I found myself and looked at areas I had visited previously, but I found the entire map of interest.

After doing the dinner dishes I returned to the studio table and called Kathleen. "You're taking breaks, aren't you?" she said. She knew I was in binge-writing mode.

"I read for pleasure," I assured her.

"Sure you do."

"Maps mostly," I said. "Remember Muff?"

"Who?"

"The town named Muff. You noticed it on the map when we were here."

She laughed. "You're not anywhere near there."

"No, but did you know that there's a Sneem here, and a place called Pluck, and of course Ballybunion."

"Ouch," she said.

"You wouldn't want to live in a place called Snave Bridge."

"I guess not," she said. "You're not letting your brain rest, are you? Even when you cook or eat. Meditation might help."

"Ballybunion, Ballybunion, Ballybunion," I chanted.

"You're delirious, and I've got dogs to walk, honey," she said. And I had sheep to count. We said goodbye. I saved my current writing file and climbed the ladder to the loft bed, where I would lie waiting for the rain to lessen to a level that allowed sleep. The expression "good sleeping weather" came to mind. Surely, I thought, the Irish must rank among the most well-rested people in the world.

Monday morning, I woke, but I heard nothing but the scattered crying of lambs and the gargling of their parents. *No rain?* I peeked out the small loft window and saw a sky that finally invited me to make the climb to the top of Bolus Head.

I started up the winding road, pausing to turn and snap photos of distant Waterville across the blue bay. A descending car stopped, and the Englishman on holiday cautioned me to keep a grip on my hat when I got to the top. I was pretty sure that everyone else in the village already had made the pilgrimage to the windy high point above the wave-splashed extremity of rock. Rona had done it almost every day. I continued past the sign meant to discourage drivers that I had seen on my first night here.

Not far beyond, I spotted Rona's red hair. She had found a windbreak in the rocky cliff side and had stretched out in the sunshine. I called to her, and when she beckoned me, I climbed the fence and walked down to the spot she had taken over on her last full day at the village. This relatively windless nook provided the perfect place to savor the warmth of the sun and to look down at a solitary fishing boat and the crashing surf. I left her to her solitude, knowing that if I sat down my legs would not want to keep going up. When I reached the fence at the roadside, I heard her shouting my name. "You don't stay on the road to the end!"

"No?"

"Just after the white farmhouse, there's a farm trail on the right. It goes up," she yelled, raising her hand in zigzag fashion. "Climb three gates!"

I headed off, wondering if I would have stumbled onto the place without her help. I had heard rumors of ruins at the top, stone barracks used by British soldiers to train for action in World War I. I moved at a pace that enabled me to take in the subtle differences in the magnificent views along the way. It had taken me three weeks to find a day to do this, and I didn't know if the weather during my remaining week would invite another visit here. I drank in the views and the air. Even at my comfortable pace, by the time I reached the farmhouse, I had unzipped my outer layer and pulled off my sweaty Phillies cap.

Birds called to one another, and the clear water in the roadside rivulet splashed its way downhill. Taken slowly, the climb was exhilarating. A sky that someone might rightly call partly cloudy struck me as sufficiently sunny. I found and climbed the first livestock gate then followed the rutted switchback path that fit her description.

I climbed another barrier and continued straight up toward a third gate. The mountain on my left looked like it would loom over me, no matter how long I climbed. Finally, I glimpsed blue water in the distance. The slip of ocean ahead urged me on, but a sudden gust of cold wind halted my progress, while I reset my cap and pulled the hood of my sweatshirt up over the top of it. My legs felt fresher, stronger than when I'd begun.

Thirty feet short of the gate, I saw that the water view sprawled to the left, where I spied a small island. A few steps higher, I made out the unmistakable Skelligs. I scrambled over the gate then caught my breath, looking at the sea far below. Stretched out before me I saw the most Irish of blues, and I wondered how the flag of this island nation failed to include this amazing blue along with the obligatory kelly green. Dark sky after dark sky watered this island into a quilt of every pleasing shade of green imaginable. The blues of the ocean and the sky, turned to grays under those dark skies, waited for their chance, and the daily dousing kept them a treasured rarity.

I mounted the green metal ladder and pressed on, looking up at what must be the final ascent until I saw another fence, which led me to another, which curved its way to where I could see the remaining stone columns of the old British Army barracks on my left and the double-Skelliged ocean to my right. If I could not have seen that I had reached the top, the wind's howl would have told me. Far below to my right lay the rocky outcropping of Bolus Head jutting out into the surf.

The field to my left lacked sufficient flatness to have served as parade grounds, and I wondered about the daily activities of the soldiers training for "the war to end all wars," presumably bivouacked here and learning skills that they hoped would prove useful in the hellish reality awaiting them. Here, they could not have been further west from the fields of conflict and still have been in Europe. Their westward view from here, the same as mine now, must have invited thoughts of emigration and escape. I wondered if they had learned anything about the by-then monk-less lighthouse island eighteen hard-rowed miles away.

Ages ago, Irishmen must have scanned the waters from here for invaders, like the ones that periodically wiped out the Skellig Michael monks *du jour*. The view here had changed little since humans first climbed these hills. The Skelligs sat silently before me, their iconic shape inviting thoughts of what one must feel when coming upon the Great Pyramids. I could make out the fairly flat uppermost nook of Skellig Michael, where the monks built their huts. Turning, I glimpsed the same bay that I viewed from the cottage, the green and gray peaks and finally the curlicue of inlets that led to Valentia Island. Even without the history lurking all around me, these views would have been compelling.

I had heard about this place since I arrived, and now had snapped dozens of pictures in ten windy minutes, but neither words nor photographs could capture the actual experience. The climb's rewards easily outweighed the effort. The place's visual beauty stunned the senses. One reached such a place only after climbing the pilgrim's path.

I turned slowly, recalling my mother's view of the life lived by educated people. As in my educational journey, I had reached what felt like the top of the world alone, but not without the help of many people. Here in the midst of breathtaking natural beauty, my mind shot back to the rewards of learning. I couldn't have foreseen what I found on that lifelong climb either. It too had been worth every step. And it wasn't over.

After the long descent that concluded my hike, Vera stopped by the cottage to inform me that the villagers would gather tonight to toast Rona's departure the next morning. After dinner, I joined the seven artists and Vera's newly arrived husband, Ken, in #6, the village's meetinghouse. It was the first time our group had convened here.

Unlike the other cottages, this one had a large hearth, in which a fire raged. I brought bottles of beer to the refrigerator and placed a lighted candle beside the several already lighted smaller candles, which, along with the crackling fire, provided the room with dim but cozy light. Unlike the cottages in which we slept, this one lacked a glassed roof section; it was configured as a Famine Era building, outfitted with furnishings that evoked that period. A wooden cradle sat against the front wall, and a crucifix hung above the empty chair that I claimed within the circle of artists. Somehow, large families had lived in these small quarters. The heat from the fire did not reach to where I sat, at least not enough for me to remove my coat.

Soon, I realized that my neighbors had started playing a game of musical chairs, taking turns in the warm seats closest to the fireplace. Moving around every ten minutes or so kept everyone tolerably warm and in the conversation. This chimney was not nearly as effective as the one in my cottage, and a thin layer of smoke hovered in the air. Toasting Rona's stay and wishing her good fortune, we went about getting to know each other. For the first time, I met Alan, a Dublin painter, who'd been here for a week.

Rona mentioned the welcome change of *not* experiencing the buffeting winds up at Bolus Head today, especially on her last walk there. My eyes widened, but I held my tongue. She even walked all the way down to the water's edge before returning to the village. We agreed that today's weather had been the best of the week. "And we've only had rain twice since I arrived," commented Vera, whose stay had begun over a week ago.

"Twice?" I said, wondering if my cottage lay in a microclimate.

A nodding of heads suggested that the others agreed with her.

"It's rained every day since I've been here, except today," I countered, "even the day we went to Skellig Michael."

"Oh, that wasn't rain," Vera said. "Just a bit of a shower. Sure, you can walk through them in a T-shirt and not even know it."

She seemed serious. Apparently, liquid falling from the sky did not meet Ireland's definition of rain unless it hurt. Surely, as Shaw famously suggested, we came from lands separated by a common language, but I also recognized that, in at least some ways, I *saw* differently. I suggested that like Eskimos speaking of snow, the Irish might have a far richer vocabulary for the subject of wet weather than I was used to.

People refilled their glasses. United by our common appreciation for this place and for the opportunity to live and work here for a few weeks, we jumped from topic to topic, laughing with the ease of old friends.

In the morning, I smiled, thinking of the previous night's smoky, laugh-filled gathering. Finally we had gathered, drawn together by the bittersweet focus of someone's imminent departure. Did the others see their own work as building upon previous creations of theirs? Had this environment sped the process or triggered new ideas? I had asked none of my questions. Yet I'd seen my fellow villagers at play and heard them expound on mundane matters. If we'd had time, like family members who eat together daily, we surely would have touched on other matters, but I thought back on the night's great *craic* with gratitude and satisfaction. Perhaps if I ever had the good fortune to return here some day, I would make the experience more social.

Fall Semester, Week Eleven

Saturday, November 19, 2011: Philadelphia

With the weekend's grading under control, I headed out to the Chestnut Hill farmers' market to purchase cranberries, collard greens, and smoked turkey for Thanksgiving cooking. With my purchases secured, my mind spun as I pointed the car back toward Mount Airy. I had ten classes left with each group, and I visualized the remaining sequence of activities for each section.

Rumbling over Germantown Avenue's cobblestones, I fumbled for the cell phone ringing in one of my pockets. Despite heavy Saturday traffic, I risked a stop by the police after seeing Kathleen on the caller ID.

"The envelope arrived!" *The mortgage people.*

"It did?" I stopped for a red light at Willow Grove Avenue.

"I'm opening it," she blurted.

I heard her ripping open the bank letter's envelope, then laughing.

"It says here that you're retiring," she announced. "And that we're going to Maine."

The light changed, and I stepped on the accelerator. "Maine!"

I roared, feeling an electric charge shooting through my body. "We did it!"

By the time I arrived home, it had dawned on me that we might get to nothing else on today's list. We had tiptoed around so many people we cared about, and now telling them about our no longer secret plan jumped to the top of that list. Striding up the drive to the front door, I also realized just how much needed to be done before this cluttered and needy house could go on the market. *Impossible.* Panic swept me, almost instantly replaced by a delirious but determined optimism—what we'd felt both times we'd learned that Kathleen was pregnant. As on those truly blessed occasions, this was excitement and stress that we wanted. We would find a way.

Kathleen was talking excitedly with her sister on the phone when I walked into the kitchen. I called Vince and Joan to share the news then prepared my own phone list.

I called Michael, who I knew had no inkling about our intentions. The retiring part didn't jar him—he had already retired and had waited to share the experience with me—but the Maine part did. "I'm devastated," he gasped.

"I wanted to tell you right away," I said then explained that I had to let others know. He understood and wished us the best. When he called later, asking if he could do anything, I mentioned that I'd asked bandmates Michael Bailey and Jerry Howard to meet me at the Chestnut Hill Coffee Company at four. He showed up, along with Mike and Jerry, both curious about the mysterious invitation that probably sounded more like an ultimatum. "I'm not leaving the band," I assured them. They expressed their amazement and happiness for us. I watched Michael repeat the wincing reaction he must have had when I called him. His reaction was the hardest one to absorb. We were brothers, and each of us would feel the separation, no matter how often Kathleen and I returned to Philadelphia. But this was not his doing, and I wondered how long it might take for him to feel better about our move.

After making our calls, Kathleen and I felt like we had finally exhaled. We then walked to the homes of our immediate neighbors and stunned them with our announcement. *Twenty-five years on this block.* Each time, they greeted the news with wide eyes, hugs, and congratulations, and Kathleen shared some tears.

Sometime while eyeing the suddenly expanded to-do list, I felt the finality of what we'd been exploring, considering, weighing for months. Signing an agreement of sale had been our de facto decision-making moment—or had it been applying for the mortgage? For a moment, I felt like someone had made the decision for us, but I knew when I'd tasted this joyous sense of commitment before: the moments when we'd seen the results of the 1980 and '84 pregnancy tests. It appeared that again the gods were smiling on us.

But like a team that had won the game that put it into the playoffs, we could not celebrate for more than a moment because the more important second season loomed ahead of us now. Most of what we'd done to the house had simply eliminated nonessentials, but the heavy-duty work needed to get the house looking like one that would entice other people to buy it must start now. The real estate people had taught me a new word: *parge,* as in, we needed to parge our basement. This process involved sealing up the basement walls and preparing them for painting, which would give them the clean, intact appearance that we always suspected could happen but that we had never considered necessary.

Then there were the other rooms. "You will not have time to do it yourself," Bob told me, and looking at today's calendar, that became obvious to me. To put the place on the market in the timeframe our move now called for, we must bring in work crews. Settlement on the condominium would take place January 6—quite the Epiphany, I thought. We targeted a moving date nineteen days after that. I now knew for sure that the remaining three and a half weeks of the semester truly would be my last days teaching at Community College of Philadelphia. We had miles to go to reach our goal, but we held a high level of motivation. As so many of my students said at the beginning of the semester, nothing would stand in my way.

"Tell us something else about Mr. Vince?" Matt asked at the beginning of the 8:00 a.m. Honors class on Monday of Thanksgiving week. Through the semester, I'd concentrated on exposing Vince's obsession with swimming, spreading a mixture of truth and tall tales, and leaving them to guess what was real. "Who do you suppose holds the Roxborough YMCA record for most laps swum in their pool?" They groaned their disbelief. But it was true. "And not just for his age group."

In the writing seminar, we examined drafts of their next-to-last paper of the semester, which I now knew was also my penultimate assignment.

During the break before my other two classes, I scrambled around, telling the news to colleagues. What I had anticipated as awkward actually felt comfortable. Everyone seemed to understand the logic of our move and appreciated how much it meant to us.

"Cindy, it's official," I told my department head. She suggested that she not go public with the news until the following Monday, so the news wouldn't get lost in the shuffle of Thanksgiving. I entered the classroom with a jump in my step.

Monday's last two classes yielded a bountiful harvest of revised essays, enough to keep me busy at home for days. Classroom discussion covered a scholarly article and a newspaper piece both about positive psychology—the study of psychological well-being or happiness. We would compare the pieces next Monday, which, considering the week's overwhelming schedule, seemed impossibly distant; however, I knew it would arrive whether I was ready or not.

The final and summative writing assignment encouraged students to use, among other tools, their recently acquired knowledge of positive psychology in considering the fictional Murana Bill.

"You get paid for working at the daycare," I said to Charisse. "You are rewarded."

"Extrinsic reward," someone added.

"And you can use that pay to buy ice cream," I said.

"The first route to happiness," Charisse offered.

"You've told us that you get very involved in your work there."

"I love it there. The time flies by."

"You're engaged in it," I said. "You get gratification from that involvement."

"And you get meaning from it," Ian called out. "You're doing something for others."

That was how classroom discussion went when a critical mass of students became engaged in our work. This time around, we had a session like this in the 8:00 Honors class and in one of the two unlinked classes. Two classes got by with very few leading questions and no conclusions from me, while the other class needed me to lead them, inch by painful inch, to the point that terms and examples filled up the board, with lines connecting the ideas.

"Do you get satisfaction and gratification from teaching?" Douglas asked.

"Both." But I now knew with certainty that that didn't mean I should do it for the rest of my life.

Students knew that I would take sabbatical leave next semester. I could tell them my bigger news after Thanksgiving. Again, I had gotten involved in their lives. I had never ended a semester as a neutral observer, and this one, which I now knew was my last, had proved no different. I savored the privileged intimacy, mindful that this was my last run.

In the dark, I knew from Kathleen's long regular breaths that she'd already fallen asleep. My mind raced from the afternoon's class to ingredients that I still needed to buy for Thanksgiving to the song lyrics that I'd mangled the last time the band played at the Mermaid: our Country-and-Far-Eastern Zen truck driver song that I'd written years ago. "We're getting closer every mile that we drive, taking in more than we pass by. The shape of a hill, the turn of a phrase, nose to the windshield as inward we gaze." I'd thought my retirement/Maine question consisted of looking outward and forward then realized that it also meant looking at what we'd be leaving.

But the process's Zen hook that I was now grasping in the dark bedroom concerned looking inside me. "Is it harder to leave or try to go back? And what can you leave and what can you pack?" The damn song's title was "Almost Home," more irony than I could handle at one in the morning on a weeknight.

Kathleen appeared to be handling it better than I was. Beside me, she sighed gently and regularly. But right now she might be dreaming of being eaten by a giant lobster, obviously a stand-in for rational misgivings about this cockamamie move. Beneath the bed, Roux stirred. I knew that Jack lay at the foot of the bed, sleeping lightly, lest any plumbers appear. That was how the spouse who had made me laugh every day since 1975 had explained our sleeping arrangement to visitors.

Is there no way to slow this brain down?

And now we'd decided that moving Kathleen and me and our dogs five hundred miles away from Stephan and Anna could benefit the bunch of us, at least for the foreseeable future. When I'd climbed into bed, the notion made complete sense, but here I was, teetering on the edge of an opening hole.

Who did I think I was? No way was I getting out of this long night without one more crisis of doubt.

I'd be leaving Michael, Vince and Joan, and the band. And all the living and the dead here. Friends in Philadelphia had become so much a part of our lives that they might as well share our last name. They, the human branches that we'd grown in our decades in Philly, had helped define us. *If I move away, there might not be much left of me.*

My heart was beating like Jerry's drumsticks when we rushed through "Six Days on the Road." I went to the bathroom for a drink of water in the dark, then carefully stepped around Jack and climbed back into bed. We had time to deal with these nagging fears. Tonight was not the time. I evened out my breathing and hoped for the best. At least I didn't have to get up early to face a class the next day.

Tuesday morning, I rushed off to the dental office, where I learned that a chewing sensitivity I had recently experienced came from cracks in either one or two teeth. I wrote down the time for a follow-up appointment the next week. After lunch, I headed to the hospital for the stress test, toting the file that held a stack of essays. The wait did not take as long as I'd prepared myself for, so I got only one paper done before they took me back.

Dressed in sweatpants and sneakers, I sat beside the treadmill as instructed while the lead technician and the nurse practitioner listened to my heart and watched what it did on screens I could not see. I concluded that they must obtain baseline readings before they put me on the treadmill. The NP asked the lead assistant about the whereabouts of Doctor So And So, receiving a shrug in reply. In contrast to the jolly crew at the dentist's office, this trio seemed downright somber.

"She's somewhere in the building, right?"

"I'm sure you'll be able to find her."

This did not seem to put the NP at ease. Through it all, their three sets of eyes had not left the machines.

Do their hushed tones have anything to do with my sitting readings?

Directed to get on the treadmill, I rose slowly, a gaggle of wires drooping from me, and placed my feet on the stationary sides of the machine. "I've been on these things before," I assured the nurse practitioner, then listened to her detailed instructions about how to step onto the moving part. *Do I look so out of shape that you don't believe I've ever exercised?*

"We're going to begin very slowly and with no incline," she informed me.

I nodded.

"At any point, if you feel the slightest bit uncomfortable, let me know, and I will stop the machine."

You didn't see me running to class yesterday. The track began to inch along, and I stepped onto it. "I'm good," I said.

The pace increased to a normal walking rate. "Any pain or pressure at all?" the technician asked from behind a monitor. Her face did not reveal a picture of any of the three kinds of happiness.

"Definitely."

"You do?"

"No," I said. "I definitely will tell you if I do."

"We're going to give you a bit of an incline," the nurse practitioner said, and I comfortably eased into it. She looked pained.

"Still good?"

"Yes."

The track raised a bit more. Soon I started to breathe harder.

"How's that feeling?" she asked.

"I'm working now," I said, "but no pain."

The two women exchanged furtive glances.

"Nothing different?" the second one said.

When they informed me that they now would stop the machine, I thought I heard the same gravity in both voices. No one needed to tell me that I had not aced my test, yet I felt no worse than when I'd scampered to class the day before. I stepped off the machine and sat down as directed. "Not bad at all," I said, "just feeling out of shape." The assistant gently detached the wires while the other two women moved between machines, occasionally punching keyboards, all in silence.

"A doctor will speak with you soon," said the dour NP. They led me to the small waiting area on the other side of the glass wall, where I took a seat, nervous but more confused than anything.

In five minutes, a young doctor approached and confirmed the obvious, but she provided some measure of clarity. I had a blockage or blockages that needed to be dealt with soon. *When? Tomorrow is the day before Thanksgiving. Friday and Saturday, the band has gigs.* She scheduled me for a cardiologist appointment the following Wednesday.

I drove home feeling numb. *Soon. Appointment in a week.* I could not call Kathleen until she finished work. *You must sort this out, but you don't have to do it this instant. Let it catch up with you, not the other way around.* I plopped into the rocking chair on our little enclosed porch.

In solitude, I tried to square the medical staff's sense of urgency with an eight-day wait—not to have the test or whatever they had in mind, but just to see the cardiologist. Cars blitzed to and from the stop sign at the corner as I rocked gently, growing less comfortable with how slowly they were moving with my heart blockage.

I called my teaching spouse. As always, talking with Vince helped slow everything down to where I could see more clearly. And, as always, he waited until I asked him for his opinion before he offered it, which he did with gusto. Waiting a week to start something that must be done *soon* didn't make sense to him either.

I hung up and called the cardiologist's office. On hold, I thought about the boxes we had to fill and store. The jobs before me multiplied in my head. They took my call, and I braced myself for disappointment. With less than one day's warning, I needed an appointment for the day before Thanksgiving, everyone's ultimate get-away day of the year. They squeezed me into somebody's schedule for late the following afternoon. Now the medical issue felt less like an emergency and more like a task.

No stranger to such matters, Kathleen immediately grasped my situation and its implications. She rolled into organizing and sustaining mode without hesitation. "I'm not sure why this doesn't seem to be freaking me out," I said, "but I'm glad that you're on my side."

She smiled, probably knowing that she already was having a positive impact on my attitude. As usual, she was a step or three ahead of me, which I realized the next day when we sat down to go over details for the coming week.

On Wednesday, the day before Thanksgiving, I led discussions about Susan Dodd's novel *No Earthly Notion*, the basis for the final writing assignment. I explained the assignment to both unlinked classes; I would do the same for the first-semester Honors class next week.

Vince knew about my medical complication, but otherwise, I had a new secret to keep at work, one with possibly greater significance than the one I had held so long this fall.

At the appointment that afternoon, I learned that the discomfort I'd felt the previous winter and during two recent scrambles to campus was angina. I never would have called the sensation painful. Thinking back, I realized that it felt something akin to pressure, but I probably would not have chosen that word to try to express the feeling. All of a sudden, the exhaustion I'd felt in the swimming pool a year ago and last summer while splitting wood made more sense. Apparently, I had unconsciously ducked bullets all year. Just as I was revealing my retirement news, my body had let out its own secret. If untouched, my heart would crash and burn.

People said that the way to make God laugh was to announce your plans. I had schemed and put things in motion, as if nature and nurture were under my control. As if I could rely on having tomorrows ahead of me. *Nothing would stand in my way?* I'd looked at the odds as blithely as did my least realistic students. But the semester wasn't over. Diet and genetics had put me on a fast track to a heart attack, but now, I had a chance to do something about it.

Before leaving the doctor's office, I scheduled an appointment for a cardiac catheterization the next Tuesday. If they found one or two blockages, they could perhaps place a stent, but if they found more than two they would have to perform a bypass. The stent possibility would get me out of the hospital before the semester's end, but if I needed a bypass, with its attendant recovery time, my last class as teacher at Community College of Philadelphia would take place on

Monday. In my head, I was screaming *stent, stent, stent!* like some crazed *Wheel of Fortune* contestant.

At home, I called Cindy and the folks at Human Resources, learning that if I missed more than three classes in a row, the college would have to put me on disability. Other instructors would have to take over my courses, not something I wanted to imagine. Even if I needed only a stent or two, I still might be put on disability. *If you dodge the bypass, there's no way you're missing more than three days.*

I had to eat light at Thanksgiving. The doctor said I could do the gigs, but I had to sit, not stand. No lifting or carrying gear, jumping around on stage, or full-throttle singing. He prescribed a series of medications that I was to begin taking immediately, including one for the tiny nitroglycerin pills that I had seen dying movie characters vainly reach for. If I started to feel angina during a set, I must take one then head up to the ER. For a moment, I wondered if this all were one wild, vivid dream that just kept twisting along. I felt steady and ready, not afraid or intimidated. *Why am I not shaking?* I had no answer but knew that I needed to keep moving, like the dream.

Telling the kids, I felt the same calmness, though that didn't seem to transfer to them. When their shock settled, Stephan tried to joke, saying that he hoped this news did not suggest a trend. Anna held onto me for a long time without saying anything.

Because Kathleen and I got engaged the night before Thanksgiving in 1974, we always celebrated that night as much as the actual anniversary of our wedding, if only by sharing a toast of beer. This year's celebration involved even lighter fare, especially with Kathleen facing a morning shift.

No longer surprised by suddenly enlarged to-do lists, I began to prepare to hand off my courses for at least three days and, if needed, for the rest of the semester. Knowing this might happen, I had brought home extra copies of all my syllabi, and now I started annotating the eighty-page beasts for a substitute. This meant modifying the schedule, so that I could use the Monday after Thanksgiving to get as much done as possible. The evening passed quietly.

With Kathleen working a full day on Thanksgiving, the holiday barely interrupted my work. The best news on Thursday came when English professor Mark Hughes, whom I had recruited to replace me in the Honors courses during my sabbatical, called to tell me he would happily take over my current Honors sections for as long as I needed him. Just when our secret plans had seemed to come to fruition, our lives had been hijacked, leaving us with no choice but to make the most of the ride. There might be shock to feel, but we were too busy to fully feel it.

Friday morning, Kathleen drove me to a clinic to have my blood drawn. En route, I took Valium, primarily for its antiseizure quality but also for its value in dealing with anxiety. If not medicated prior to an invasive medical procedure, including a simple blood test, I experienced a vasovagal seizure-like episode. With the medication on board, I approached such encounters calmly, rather than with dread. I let Kathleen drive to and from the clinic, then spent a quiet afternoon grading essays and constructing set lists that would feature every instrumental the band knew, every song that Michael Bailey sang, and as few of mine as we could get away with.

On Black Friday, a larger than usual Friday night crowd showed up at the Mermaid. I arrived at the bar on the late side and set up about half of the percussion equipment that I normally used. "It'll have to be Ned Lite," I told the sensitive Sacred CowBoy souls.

"We're calling it The Last Waltz," John said.

"I like Ned Man Walking," Jim added.

In both sets, a moment came when we needed to keep the crowd going, and I sang Chuck Berry's "You Never Can Tell" and Randy Newman's "Mama Told Me Not To Come." The night rolled on. The energetic crowd did not seem to notice that I was essentially performing with one vocal cord tied behind my back. The small bottle of nitroglycerin stayed in my pocket for the entire night.

Saturday drew a larger and louder crowd. At the end of the show, I announced, "We'll be back in March," to the revelers. Despite my limited capacity, the band had put on a good show, and I escaped with another relatively early night.

I spent Sunday finalizing my materials for Monday's hand-off.

We'd reached Week Thirteen. After I explained the final writing assignment and went over what would happen in each of the semester's remaining seven classes, I told the students my first piece of news. Facing the possibility that I might not see them again, I wanted to tell them what I could. They already knew that I wasn't going to be on campus next semester, and now I told them that I was about to retire.

"Good for *you!*" Charisse called. They chorused a mixture of disappointment that I was leaving and happiness for me to have reached this point. I thanked them for their efforts all semester.

"Tomorrow, I will have a cardiac catheterization," I said. "They'll either fix the problem in my arteries then and there or operate again in maybe a week."

Now they looked like they were watching a man who'd just started raving in front of their eyes.

"It's going to be all right," I said. "I plan to be back here in about a week. The substitute you will meet on Wednesday knows all about our texts and assignments. But if the doctors determine that I need another surgery, that teacher will take you through your last couple of weeks. You'll do everything that it says in the syllabus."

Several students looked frozen in their places.

I was not lying to them. I expected to bounce back in short order, and I believed that my high level of confidence was what was getting me through this unexpected presentation in a calm and, I hoped, convincing state. "I'm glad I could tell you myself. And I can't wait to see you next week."

Charisse announced that she would pray for me. Chelsea chimed in. "That's awesome," I said. "And I'll pray for you."

"Because we're going to need it," a male voice from the rear said.

We all laughed. We had laughed together before, but this roar topped any other of the semester. "Thank you," I said, still laughing.

Half the class lingered at my table at the end of class. Gratitude overwhelmed me, but I knew that I must hurry to the classroom across the hall.

At the end of the day's teaching, which I kept remembering might have been my last, I stayed late to line my desk with piles of materials for Mark. On the way out of the building, I stopped by Cindy's office to drop off materials for the other two people who would cover my classes.

For once, I faced an evening with absolutely no papers to grade and no academic plans to go over. I had officially put house matters on the shelf, and I had happily surrendered list-making to Kathleen. Thanks to her hour-by-hour planning, I enjoyed a nice dinner and a quiet evening, further relaxed by the knowledge that she had tomorrow morning's logistics all worked out.

No food intake made my morning regimen simple and easy; the day's first hour went smoothly, as expected. Michael would pick us up and take us to Abington Memorial Hospital for the morning's surgery. At the appointed minute in Kathleen's neatly printed plan, she and I should step outside the house to meet him. Accepting his offer to drive had made perfect sense. I did not need the schedule to know that I would take my Valium ten minutes from now.

Waiting for Michael, I admired the front of the house, painted by our friend Alex. I remembered him showing Stephan some of his tricks of the trade. Five minutes later, Michael still had not appeared. History seemed to have won out over his best intentions as well as the vow of promptness that he had made the past weekend.

Of course Kathleen had built extra time into her plan. However, when we hit the ten-minute mark, she unlocked our car, and I climbed into the passenger seat. Just then, Michael screeched to a stop at the edge of the driveway, yelling out his open window what I assumed were key details about the many unexpected problems that had cursed his morning. We sighed and moved to his car.

"Straight down Mount Pleasant," Kathleen said calmly, as if we were leaving an hour early.

"Bastards!" Michael screamed, slamming the steering wheel.

"It's okay," Kathleen purred.

Michael growled under his breath but drove at a reasonable pace.

A car at the first cross street we encountered ran a stop sign. "BASTARD!" Michael roared, riding his horn.

"This can't happen, Mike," Kathleen said soothingly. "You need to pull over now. I'll drive."

Michael came to a complete stop at the sign then turned to Kathleen, horror on his face. "Please," he said. "I'll be good."

"No more, Michael," I said from the rear seat, knowing that if I laughed, Kathleen would direct all of her repressed wrath my way.

Michael pulled out slowly. "I promise," he said, his eyes locked on the street ahead.

After checking her watch, Kathleen handed me my Valium, and I knew that shortly I would care even less about anything.

When the IV technician smoothly inserted the needle into my hand, I subtracted seven from 165, eight from 158, nine from 150. The medicine I had on board should be more than enough to prevent me from experiencing one of those episodes, but keeping my brain occupied with simple arithmetic calculations felt like a good insurance policy. While I watched other patients on stretchers coming and going, Christine Galante, an on-duty nurse and John's former sister-in-law, stopped by to check on me, and then it was my turn.

When I awoke from the anesthesia, I found myself in the recovery room. Soon, a nurse shuttled me to the telemetry unit, where they would monitor my recovery for the next several hours. Various wires connected me to beeping monitors in the room and to others down the hall in a central control room, which I pictured as NASA's center in Houston. The surgeon told me that he had needed to place only one stent during the procedure, the best of all possible outcomes. Kathleen's beaming smile reassured me that I was, in fact, hearing correctly. The other arteries were hardly clear, but they did not warrant stenting. Dietary changes, exercise, and medicine should enable me to live a normal life. "No bypass!" I exclaimed.

"We're so lucky," Kathleen said, between sobs.

"I can't believe how good I feel," I said. "I mean right now, physically."

A nurse, known as "the sheath puller," introduced himself. He was here to remove from the small hole in my groin the device that enabled the doctors to use a catheter to see inside me and to repair me. Michael said he must make a phone call and left the room. The nurse lifted me enough to slip a small white towel under me, clamped an arm on me, and asked if I was ready. I looked across the room at the window. "One, two, three," he said, and pulled out the sheath.

"Get it all?" I asked.

"Want to see?"

"No, I'm good."

"Wasn't so bad, right?"

I told him he was great at what he did, wishing I could better articulate my thanks.

"Your job for the next five hours," he said, "is to keep your right leg perfectly still, in order to prevent bleeding, which, because of the blood thinners you're on, would cause a problem."

On the phone, I told Stephan and Anna that I felt fine. Kathleen talked Anna out of driving to the hospital. "He'll be coming home in the morning." During my surgery, Kathleen and Michael had returned home so that she could drive back in our car. This way, Michael could leave whenever he wanted. She planned to stay with me as long as possible. Michael entertained us with news of his model railroader buddies who had gone on tour.

I tried my first hospital meal. "Heart healthy," Kathleen said, as I tasted a piece of chicken. I ate most but not all of the food, feeling a bit cocky about my new healthier ways.

When my five hours ended, the unit nurse decided that I should keep my leg still for one more hour just to be safe. Everyone who entered the room studied my beeping monitors, looked at my feet, and uttered some variation on "Everything looks great."

Michael returned from another telephone break. He looked like he had not slept for three days, so Kathleen sent him home. He promised to stop by the Mermaid on his way home to tell the owner, Joanne, how well I was doing. The regular nurse told me that I should take another rest, to make sure that the bleeding had stopped but that before I knew it, they would allow me to stand up and walk to the bathroom.

Kathleen talked about the joys of spending an entire summer in Maine. "And spring and a chunk of this winter," I said. I was stunned at how good I felt. *Tomorrow is Wednesday. I might be able to go back to class on Monday, only miss tomorrow and Friday.*

The nurse checked my numbers and feet again. She smiled. "We're close."

Kathleen sent updates by phone to both kids. I lay still and let my mind wander. *No bypass.* I felt like we had won the lottery.

The nurse returned as promised. "You'll probably be happy to walk to the bathroom after that long wait," she said. "I'm going to check on the person in the next room, but you don't have to wait. Nice and slow, when you're ready."

Kathleen helped me shift my leg to the side of the bed, reminding me to go slowly.

"I am not a flight risk," I assured her.

Holding the side of the bed as instructed, I reached a standing position, feeling triumphant. Out of the corner of my eye, I glimpsed a blood-soaked towel on the bed and instinctively shot my gaze up to the bathroom door. *Slow. Steady and slow.* Without letting go of the bed, I extended one foot.

"Good," I heard Kathleen say, from behind me.

"I feel dizzy," I said. *I will stand here until the feeling passes.*

"Hold on," she said. She said something else, but I could not make it out.

I turned back to her. "Really dizzy."

I came to, back in the bed, with the 7th Cavalry storming all over the room. Strangers in scrubs darted about, looking at monitors and wires, talking loudly to each other. Kathleen sat in the chair under the window, nodding to me.

"Ned, *Ned*, can you hear me?" a woman yelled.

"Where am I?"

"You're in the hospital. You're back in your bed." She called out something to other people then swooped over me, her face hovering right above mine. "Stay with us now!" she yelled. "Do you hear me?"

Okay, something serious has happened, but the hubbub sounds like dialogue from a bad hospital drama. "Yes."

Kathleen remained in the chair. As a wife and a nurse, she knew that she must let them do what they must do.

The action continued to swirl around me until I finally realized it concerned me. I watched the excitement, aware that they, not I, played the main roles in this drama. Eventually, a few people exited the room. The ones still with me seemed to slow their pace, and everything became less frantic. A new doctor or nurse remained right with me. I stared back, hoping that my expression conveyed that I was with her too.

"Your heart stopped beating for more than ten seconds."

"Oh."

I felt like I had just learned about an earthquake that I missed. In time, the doctor laid out the new plan for me. I would be returning to the OR the next day.

Kathleen must have sensed that she could approach the bed because she crossed the room and took my hand in hers. I was glad that she did not cry, though I knew that with no other people present, she would have had no such control over her emotions. They rolled my bed down the hallway, Kathleen half-jogging alongside, still gripping my hand. I felt spent but was not in any pain. I did not doubt that the plan they had was a good one.

Sometimes when I was watching a tense movie, even though I knew that the story would end well, I still found myself clenching up, believing that I was in the scene with my life at stake, but riding the elevator to the cardiac surgical unit, I had no feeling that the night's mystery would end badly. We still must walk through all of the episodes of this unfolding story without knowing what lay around the next corner, but I did not feel agitated the way I did watching a scary movie. I told Kathleen that both of us would get through this. "I'm not just saying that." She looked like she believed it. I hoped so, because I had no doubt.

After such a whirlwind conclusion to my stay in the telemetry unit, my room on a different floor seemed sedate, even calming. Kathleen could spend the night. As far as I knew, this type of heart stoppage had never happened during previous seizure-like events, even in my GP's office, while I had lain wired up and under my doctor's watchful eyes. A heart surgeon told me that I had "high vagal tone," another new term, and which I understood to mean that the cranial nerve controlling my major bodily functions like breathing and heart rate shifted easily into extreme fight-or-flight mode. It was a reaction over which I had little or no control, and which could cause sudden and radical shifts in heart rate or seizure-like episodes. Certain sensory stimuli, like invasive procedures, or, earlier in the telemetry unit, the sight of a blood-drenched towel, could trigger reactions like tonight's collapse. The possibility of such future events did not please the heart doctors, of course. "We're going to squeeze you into tomorrow's surgery schedule sometime," the doctor said. "You're going to get a pacemaker." The new hardware would keep my heart ticking, even if I had another vagal incident.

I would not be going home on Wednesday. Tomorrow would be the first of my three allowed absences before they'd blow up my plans for finishing my last semester in the classroom. But a straightforward surgery and an uneventful recovery should mean that I would be home on Thursday. I could miss class Friday and Monday. Even with this misadventure, returning to class next Wednesday still looked doable. I kept up an optimistic outlook.

In the morning, a tall, lanky surgeon strode into my room and told me what he would soon do. He would do my surgery sometime in the late afternoon when the hospital could find a time amidst all the previously scheduled operations. He sounded like he could do anything he put his mind to, and my procedure would be just one stop on the man's routine for the day. He reminded Kathleen of the characters on *The Big Bang Theory*. I pictured him shedding his scrubs at the end of a day of successful surgeries and dashing off for a spirited round of Dungeons and Dragons over Cokes.

Kathleen settled into the chair beside my bed, and we both managed to sleep a bit. She updated the kids and Michael. Many of this unit's patients had just had bypass surgery; periodically, I glimpsed one of them shuffling up or down the hall. I figured I was still way ahead in this game.

"Are you anxious to get this started?" Kathleen asked.

I told her that I'd rather not have the *doctors* rush. Several times, I noticed the wall clock at a moment when one of my classes had just begun or ended.

When they rolled me into the operating room, I was greeted by a masked Chris Galante, who, as part of the OR team, helped prep me for the procedure. She told me what would happen, and her presence did much more in reducing my anxiety level to a nonfactor. I thought of her as a star player on my team. Lying in the chilly operating room, I recalled some of the people who'd told me they would pray for me: the North African Muslim student in the Honors class, a trio of my 11:15 students—still the same good citizens I'd seen the first day of the semester—all of Kathleen's Vincentian priest and brother patients, and Janet from next door, who had given me a beautiful Hebrew prayer card. I felt the surrounding presence of all of these people. Chris's wise kindness worked like the assistance of Vygotsky's skilled guides, and waiting to undergo something that normally would frighten the dickens out of me, I realized that I could handle my part, even without a load of Valium. I had confidence in the doctors and nurses who would do it, and largely thanks to Chris, I found myself not only optimistic and confident but also at peace, even before I went under the anesthesiologist's spell.

After the procedure, I woke up to learn that it had gone swimmingly. When I realized that this part of the adventure had ended, my sense of good fortune carried me through the night, the next morning, and the happy ride home.

At home, I faced the oddness of having no schoolwork to do. I knew I could handle grading or preparation, but others had taken all of that into their hands. Vince offered to announce my arrival home to my students.

"I'm definitely teaching next Wednesday," I told Kathleen.

"Only if you don't make me kill you," she said. She did not allow me to do any sorting or packing, so on Friday, I got the most rest I'd had since the semester began. I felt like a kid who got to stay home from school for one day more than he needed. I watched television shows that I never would have even thought about watching at this point in the semester, and I had time to think about what I had read about teaching and learning in the last year. I also tried to imagine the students hard at work.

Three classes had completed reading and discussing *No Earthly Notion*. The novel's Murana Bill, a solitary and undemanding soul, experiences great loss but finally acquires a friend whose influence opens her up to possibility. Readers observe Murana's new ways of dressing, talking, and thinking, and by the time her friend Lucille dies of cancer, she can move on in her work life and in her personal life, not a wholly different person but one with altered and healthier character traits—or not, depending on one's perspective about the degree and stability of the changes.

Students received a photocopy of Susan Dodd's out-of-print novel, legally reproduced and used through the generosity of the author, whose friendship I had appreciated since we met when she taught at Vermont College. "Can we write on these?" a student had asked.

I nodded. "These are yours to keep."

A former student named Shirley once invited Vince and me to attend the end of year academic awards ceremony, at which the College recognized her with an award from the support program that had provided her first-semester courses, including the ones Vince and I taught. Standing beside the podium while the award presenter read the story of Shirley's success, which included, at her request, reading the name of every one of her teachers, this middle-aged woman beamed up at Vince and me, seated way back in the upper level of the auditorium. We heard about her accomplishments since that first semester. For the duration of the presenter's speech, Shirley stood beside her like the Statue of Liberty, holding aloft something, which halfway through the speech I recognized as the copy of *No Earthly Notion* that I'd given her. The rest of the audience must have had no idea what this woman held. No one mentioned the book. Smile intact and still clutching the novel, she received her award and quietly returned to her seat on the stage.

Chatting afterwards, she thanked us for providing scaffolding at a critical time in her life. In her concluding essay on Murana Bill, she had incorporated the wealth of knowledge about psychology that she had gained from Vince's course and from our reading. She would never part with such a cherished relic from her first successful foray into foreign waters.

Our student achieved what researcher Susan A. Ambrose considers an elusive and key aspect of learning (and a goal of teaching): she'd successfully applied or transferred knowledge. [1] Transfer was exactly what I was going for in the semester's last essay.

Rearranging the schedule before my hospitalization had enabled me to introduce the final article in the syllabus and discuss the final assignment. My students were no longer novices. The semester's sequence of increasingly complex writing assignments built upon what they'd done in earlier assignments. Students perplexed by the task of applying Vygotsky's ideas in their first major assignment generally got better at it, using some or all of those concepts in every subsequent paper. And each paper introduced new concepts to be incorporated into their analysis. By this stage, applying those concepts learned in September and October likely did not faze my freshmen writers.

The character Murana Bill had changed, but would those changes have rendered her a good next-door neighbor? Students needed to account for Murana's changes, using the means provided by theorists and giving them credit along the way. Then they needed to discuss the traits that they would want to see in a neighbor—using terminology drawn from the study of personality and from positive psychology. They would not invent theory, but they would decide which concepts would prove useful here and employ them, as a surgeon used previously learned techniques in the operating room. They might well discover the limitations of various concepts, and like the surgeon they would need to use what worked best and avoid what didn't. They could imagine what Bandura, Vygotsky, Steinberg, and Rotter might have to say about Murana's changes and about her development into the kind of person that they might want to have as a next-door neighbor.

"Definitely that Goleman," Ian had suggested during the last class before my surgery. Others nodded.

They agreed that Martin Seligman could be useful. The usually quiet Bill raised his hand. "I served his table Saturday night," he announced.

Over the last three months, they had learned that social aspects of learning mattered, that they represented what might be called the nurture aspect of one's life. While trusted colleagues guided my students through workshop discussion of the papers about Murana's changes and about the constituents of neighborliness—help that I very much appreciated—I rested at home, an arrangement that did not please me. But I was going back.

20

Spring Sabbatical, Day Twenty-Two

Tuesday, April 24, 2012: Ireland

After I washed my breakfast dishes, I sat at the long worktable amidst all of my materials, accompanied by the rain patter on the glass roof. When I'd gotten my bearings in the current computer file, I surveyed the paper landscape on the table. I had written a draft of events up to my return home after my hospitalization and realized that I was nearing the end of my journal entries and other notes just as I began the final week of my sojourn in Cill Rialaig. Before I knew it, the clock had passed one, the time I stopped for lunch.

I turned on the kitchen light and threw open the tiny window that looked out onto the road. Leftover beans and rice had never smelled so enticing. The radio was blasting as I clanged silverware and cooking utensils in the little kitchen. I had not spoken all day except to my computer screen, and the infectious melody worked like strong ale. Few human pedestrians strayed by my cottage and I was long past any shyness about what they might hear if they did. *Is that the ghost of Lou Monte or some lunatic painter singing in there?*

Again, "Rosina! (The Menu Song)" reached its chorus. I drifted off book. "I make you a dish—without any fish," I crooned. "I cook you a treat—without any meat!"

I was getting by with limited ingredients, but the lack of spices and herbs was another matter. With just about a week of meals ahead of me, I allotted myself several shakes from the miniature bottle of Tabasco sauce that I'd found in Caherciveen that first day. *Could you trust a town whose supermarket sold only one brand of hot sauce, and that in bottles the size of an airplane whisky?*

When I'd dried the last dish, I turned off the radio and admired the little kitchen's practical use of space, to which I'd accustomed myself three weeks ago. I took a cup of tea out to the stone table and bench, exchanging greetings with Dirk on the way. He lived in France but had grown up in Germany. Dutch-born Yvonne lived in Ireland. They had taken over from an Irish painter as residents of Cottage 1. I couldn't remember when Vera replaced Deirdre. Avril had cut short her stay due to illness. The mostly phantom dancers had completely vanished. I imagined that Rona had left for the airport hours ago. All of the villagers who'd been here when I arrived had returned to their regular lives. Soon, I would too.

Watching the white caps on the water below, I heard the uproar of the farmer's truck and turned in time to see his dog speeding along behind. A sheep dog's work was serious, and one didn't disturb them. *How can anyone not admire such commitment?* The guy who stopped to greet most of the dogs on the street back home had to accept that meeting this hard worker probably was not in the cards.

I felt relieved that I was keeping a journal in Cill Rialaig. Already I'd used it to make sure I kept a clear picture of the writing's progress and of mundane matters that I knew I would want to recall. Without the journal, my memory of these days and nights would have endured but with disappointing vagueness.

What do you do *there?* I'd fielded variations of that question in e-mail exchanges with Vince and another friend. I was living and working in weird isolation at the edge of the world. I couldn't get away with telling them that I thought about food. *What's it like?* "Beautiful." "Cool." "Amazing." Flat, flat, flat. *Extreme Writing?* I deleted every effort to describe or explain the experience and the place, and ended up promising to take photographs and to return with the beginnings of what might eventually become a book.

What did I do *here?* I wrote about what I did last semester. No, about what I did for forty years. I thought about what I just wrote. No, about what I was ready to write. I'd spent three weeks doing what rarely happened during a semester: following my nose. What I saw or heard—in books, notes, or memories—led me. Last semester that had happened only in those few days at home after the hospitalization. Here, it was my routine.

What *was* it like here? Living and working at Cill Rialaig was a bit like my summers, the most productive writing season of the year. However, summers began with weeks of academic prep work and continued with painting projects. When things calmed down, there was the routine daily involvement with family, neighbors, and friends. And Phillies games, food shopping, and cooking.

A Cill Rialaig Project residency had elements in common with a religious or spiritual retreat. Plumbing the depths of the soul? Yes. Unexpected discoveries about oneself and one's work? Check. But the focus here was on producing artistic work, not primarily on finding one's center, as if that weren't enough.

Was it like vacation? That must be what it looked like to the outside observer. Beautiful scenery. Every dawn began a free day, with one's everyday job and other obligations gone, gone, gone. But artists came here to reorder their ordinary lives around the work demanded by their art. While vacation meant escape from work, this experience was all about work.

Was it like field research? In my thirties, I was fortunate to have Kenneth S. Goldstein as a mentor when I considered pursuing a degree in folklore. Before and after semesters of teaching at the University of Pennsylvania, Kenny collected traditional ballads—songs that told a story—while living among English-speaking people in the British Isles, Australia, and Newfoundland. Henry Glassie, another folklore professor then at Penn, scoured a corner of Northern Ireland for oral stories. The place was thick with them and seemed to be a hotbed for fresh tales. Simply stepping off the plane in Ireland, one seemed to join saga after saga, in medias res, and some of these had found their way into my work. Here, I was finding non-Irish stories among my memories and in my notes, but mostly I was trying to make sense of them, then turn them into something else, a work of nonfiction.

Was it like a pilgrimage? The Cill Rialaig experience certainly had elements of a pilgrimage, complete with walking, climbing, and self-discovery. Every day, I paid homage to the gods of inspiration. The pilgrim's way deeply concerned discovery, finding. Life in Cill Rialaig did too, but it also involved making, creating.

Was it like monastic life? Cottage 8 was not quite a monk's hermitage, yet life and work here offered something akin to the single-focus contemplative life practiced by the Skellig Michael monks. I was more of an on-site monastic than an on-the-move pilgrim, but I lacked an abbot. Actual monks generally followed the Rule of Saint Benedict, but like my fellow villagers, I followed self-imposed rules that I could change at whim. Noelle Campbell-Sharp had accorded us complete freedom, as long as we paid our electricity fees and didn't pillage the cottages. I recalled Vera's explanation that Cill Rialaig meant "church of the regulars," a place for monk-like lay people. The aptness of the residency's name was undeniable.

What do you do *there?* Each of my fellow villagers would give a different answer. And therein lay one of the beauties of Cill Rialaig Project.

I arrived with one goal, to tell the story of the previous fall semester—but I knew that doing so would occasion intellectual side trips, digressions into related issues, questions, and stories. The first day here, I'd been surprised at the sudden realization that my story would include the Cill Rialaig experience. Soon into the writing, I also learned that I could not tell the story of the fall semester and of the residency without also telling Hélene's story. Which spooked my own story out of the bushes. I was primarily a fiction writer, so this was not my comfort zone. I was accustomed to taking snatches of my own experiences, usually stories in which I'd served either as bit player or observer rather than as principal, to use as grist for the writer's character-making mill.

For three weeks, I had followed the surprises. When asked about my progress, I described the work as "plowing." I knew that it was work and that I was at the beginning of the process. "I'm boring through rock," I e-mailed Kathleen.

I loved home and everything that entailed. I missed Kathleen. Yet I might have made less progress in six months of work at home. In the bargain, I'd removed myself from spouse and family, home and *my stuff*—familiar grounding routine, television, internet access, and live and telephone contact with friends. In exchange, I'd gained almost unfettered use of a month's time, monastic isolation on the raw edge of Europe, and inspiring natural beauty. *My once-in-a-lifetime experience.* Early in my month here, I'd realized how much I already wanted to make it back here, at least once more. I'd expected more in the way of connection with the other villagers, but we all seemed to have opted for near silence. "You're engaged!" my students would howl.

Less than a week remained of this very good deal, and that was good. Working in this time and space mattered. The trick lay in knowing how long to remain in this quiet smithy. Soon I would reach the end of a very rough first draft, and I sensed that I was nearing my limit for deprivation in the other areas of my life.

The next day brought a carbon copy of Tuesday's chilly dampness. I made a stir-fry, fashioning a sauce with a dollop of the peanut butter I'd brought with me from home. At nine in the evening, I called Kathleen, up to her elbows in dog care and her work. Both of us expressed readiness for this to end. "You're coming with me, if I ever come back here," I told her.

Fall Semester,
Week Thirteen

Friday, December 2, 2011: Philadelphia

Friday night brought a carload of friends for a primarily nonsocial visit. The parents and younger brother of Anna's oldest friend paid their respects to me before marching up to the third floor with the rest of my family to begin loading out for Anna's move the next day. She had nailed down the move-in date before my hospitalization. Not helping one of the kids move seemed inconceivable to me, but I sat in bed and listened to them tromp their way down the stairs with boxes and furniture. I offered encouragement to them as they shuffled past our bedroom door on another trip downstairs. The house became lighter with every step, but even if this continued straight through the holidays, the place still might feel full.

Saturday morning found me sitting up in bed, indulging in the pleasure of reading and answering e-mails from friends, coworkers, and students.

"I love giving good news," I announced, when Kathleen entered the bedroom with the newspaper, fruit salad, and more drinks for me.

"Don't even think about going back on Monday," she said.

"Monday seems a little early."

She shot me a savage look.

"Wednesday," I said, "like we agreed."

"And 'we' included the *Big Bang Theory* surgeon and the discharge nurse."

"Right." She'd been great all week, taking off from work to run point. Yes, I was feeling on the slow side, but so far, so good. We were on the cusp of Week Fourteen. "Two days to teach this week and two more next week spreads out the last four days of the semester, but it will be plenty."

"Plenty," she agreed.

"Hey," I said. "I think I figured out why the whole hospital thing didn't freak me out."

"What's that?"

"Everybody and everything was prepared. Doctors, nurses, me. It was probably like what you experienced going into exams as a student. Confidence. Trust. I didn't have that going into a lot of exams. This might be worth sharing with students."

She looked at me funny. "You're thinking of this now?"

"It makes sense," I said. "I could have made student life a lot easier on myself. It's not too late for them."

She kissed me and went back to work.

I stood at the bedroom window and watched Anna pull the loaded truck out of our driveway. Kathleen followed her in our Civic. Back in bed, I picked at my fruit salad. My diet had turned Spartan since my meeting with a nutritionist.

While the family unloaded the truck at Anna's new apartment, I paged through several sauce-stained cookbooks, making mental notes about which recipes could remain in the lineup. When I finished scanning this handful of books, I would add them to the last box of cookbooks and seal it, the only packing work I was allowed to do for the moment.

When the movers returned, I expected stories and bags of take-out food—as much a part of any moving day as trucks and dollies. I brought the scrutinized cookbooks to their box in the half-dismantled study then gazed out the window at the untouched woodpiles. Practically all of these books had come to us during our decades in this house. Like any cared-for child, I grew up not needing to know anything about cooking other than what time supper was served. My mind ran through the string of apartment kitchens from my childhood. In short order, faces and voices filled those remembered kitchens. Strangers might have passed through my mother's living room, but no one left her kitchen still a stranger.

Mothers famously used food as an expression of love, and mine definitely fit that category. Like starving lions, my high school and college friends arrived at our place without warning. No problem. My mother would put on the coffee and bring out cups and plates. Portion control? With two swift blade strokes, she cut an apple pie into quarters. "Boys, there's another pie in the Frigidaire," she'd say, then excuse herself.

She cooked whatever I wanted, learning to prepare dishes like pasta, which she had never eaten as a child. These she called spahh-geh-tee or maah-cah-row-knee, rolling the R and stressing every syllable. Creating, sharing, and eating crusty pies and perfect roasts, post–Midnight Mass *réveillon* feasts, and everyday suppers gave her one of her few pleasures, yet her hectic pace kept her from gaining much weight over the years. Feeding herself by pouring Ensure through a tube into her stomach for the last year of her life seemed like cruel and unusual treatment.

Although the greatest fan of her cooking, I never asked a question or paid much attention to what she did, and I never cooked a thing until I left for graduate school at Gallaudet. After a year of eating cafeteria food, I started cooking for myself in Ely Hall's second-floor cubbyhole that they called the RA kitchen. Somehow, I replicated her chili and her beef stew. Kathleen joined me for some of those meals. When she finally ate my mother's stew, she exclaimed, "This is just like Ned's!" Osmosis or genetics only went so far, so I wished I had paid much better attention. But her influence entered in there somehow. I knew her feel in the kitchen. And I knew how things were supposed to taste.

I learned from her that an unshared kitchen creation made no sense. Holiday feast or work night supper, Michael never refused a dinner invitation and always added wine or cannoli from Café Roma. "Mike's on the food plan here," Anna told other guests.

No holiday rivaled Christmas Eve, when Kathleen and I produced a Seven Fishes feast for as many people as could squeeze in at our table. "Dad," Anna protested, "you only *think* you're Italian." Hélene would have loved those dinners.

The surgeon had saved me. Kathleen and I were moving to our favorite corner of the world. I would get to finish the semester with my students. But I felt punched in the gut. *Hélene.* Was I about to lose yet more of her with this move? Countless parts of the city conjured her up for me, as did so many of the items around me. I would be leaving emotional triggers and touchstones behind, painful but treasured connections. Decades ago, I'd grown so accustomed to the wave of sadness that accompanied even the happiest thoughts of my mother that it never surprised me. "It won't go away," the younger Ned said to friends who'd just experienced their first loss of someone that close, "but you get used to it." I'd always found comfort in the latter thought, but the former truth hounded me.

Acute mourning evolved into an ebb and flow between two quite different though not exactly opposite emotions. The tidal counterpart to loss's deep sadness was not its emotional opposite: sublime joy, such as what one felt at the birth of one's child. Joy came and went by its own logic. Grief's pendulum swung not to joy but to peacefulness, an emotional state that involved appreciation and acceptance. I'd learned that such balance could be enough, and that it could be pretty darn good. It was the expected course of things. I had not lost my spouse or child. Many people must learn much harder things.

I closed my favorite book about Italian cooking and slid it across my desk beside the others that would accompany us to Maine. I filled a small box with the memory-charged cookbooks I'd revisited, sealed the box tight with tape, and labeled it. Atop the pile of books and papers on the more disheveled side of the desk sat the two large manila envelopes, depth charges that I'd put aside during the basement trunk purging. Enough. I was done for the day.

On Monday, Kathleen returned to her job, leaving me on the second floor with a radio, my charged cell phone, color-coded instructions, meds, and a small cooler filled with drinks and food. She walked and fed the dogs, so they could wait to go outside again until her early return. I sipped the juice Kathleen had left as if it had the qualities of a fine wine. Today, the good people who had covered my classes would tell my students that I would come back on Wednesday. That left me today and tomorrow to continue healing. My general weakness was undeniable, but I knew that it would pass. In time, I moved to my office desk, ready again to let what I saw around me drive my thoughts.

The manila envelopes rested on top of the mound of papers on the desk, looking as innocuous as the folders, novels, and notebooks around them. In the last thirty-five years, I had known just two addresses—a stark contrast with childhood's wanderings. Combining my memories from adult conversations with Hélene with written identifications on the back of photographs, I had reconstructed the "missing years" of my life before Philadelphia, which involved a near circling of the forty-eight contiguous states.

During the twelve years of my primary and secondary education, my mother held the same job but moved around the corner from a small apartment on Tioga Street in North Philadelphia to the first floor of a house on 21st Street, a second-floor Germantown apartment on Johnson Street, two different Mount Airy apartments on Meehan Avenue, followed by two stays in an apartment above the Hamilton Bank up the block on Germantown Avenue, separated by a year or so in an apartment further down the avenue in Germantown. When I attended high school, she bought a small row house on Sydney Street, a stone's throw from Mount Airy's Holy Cross Church.

As with most struggling people, she did not change address by choice or as steps toward joining the middle class, except for the move to the row house, which, in the end, her disability rendered unsustainable. She spent her last years in the familiar environment of another second-floor Germantown Avenue apartment, her life again punctuated by the rumbling of the 23 Trolley on the cobblestone street below. In our earlier years of moving around, property owners raised rents, ended leases, or sold to other buyers, causing my mother to scour the newspaper and query her friends for a quick and perhaps better situation.

I sensed her nervousness, but it never caused me a moment's worry about our welfare. She knew how to handle life, and she did it with energy and stoic amusement at the twists and detours that it threw in her path. Her crudest comment, "The Devil shits on me," came in a whisper: a confidence imparted with a twinkle of the eye, as if making me her crony of long-standing, which I suppose I was. I had no question as to whether or not this woman would survive. I must have assumed that all parents faced such daily obstacles, though I did not dwell on the nature of her status as a single parent. Throughout her travels and moves, she maintained a sense of normalcy for me. An accident or illness could have stopped her in her tracks. Through a combination of good fortune and persistent indomitableness, she avoided being pulled under by the threats that came her way.

Raising our two children, Kathleen and I constantly talked to each other about what they and we had to deal with. One night, I said to her, "I can't imagine doing this alone or trying to make decisions like this without being able to talk about it every day."

"How did she do it?" she said.

Growing up as an only child of a single parent, I had Hélene as my confidant, which does not mean that at every developmental stage I revealed to her my innermost thoughts; however, I probably shared more with this good listener than most growing boys do with a parent. She always remained interested but not in a suffocating way. I recalled reading in graduate school about listening skills. What the books held up as useful practices for professional counselors described Hélene in practically any conversation.

Not long after I had been hired at the College, my mother began taking classes at our old Snellenburg campus. I was married and living a ten-minute drive away, but I'd see her in between classes, talk with her on the phone, and see her at her apartment for Sunday dinners. I remembered hearing about her wonderful English teacher, Mr. Hummel, and about that psychology professor who wasn't quite so wonderful. I remembered the pride she took in mastering beginning Italian with Dr. DeMarco, and learning about Michelangelo from

Bobbye Burke. I remembered the palpable joy of *first learning* that came as something of a surprise to her, a blessing, as she would put it. She was getting a taste of the life she imagined educated people enjoyed, and it couldn't have been more delicious.

The relics that I'd found in the basement trunk, though tied to various parts of Hélene's life, skewed oddly toward one particular era. It contained a treasure trove of Community College of Philadelphia lore: notebooks, corrected writing assignments and tests, her photo ID card. She had lived into her sixties, had worked in various parts of Canada and the United States, yet so much of what she saved came from her few semesters as a part-time student at CCP.

In a way, she was speaking to me from the grave, thirty-some years later, still telling me what she considered important. That day in the basement, I scanned her notebook scribblings to get a sense of her as a student. Appointments for conferences with her teachers, reminders to go over particular sections of a textbook. Her counselor's telephone number—Vince (before he transferred to the psychology department). She needed and loved the place that she had attended over thirty years ago. It enriched her already vital life of the mind.

Since then, the College had moved to a new campus and had operated there long enough to see need for significant upgrades. Articles in magazines and newspapers argued that community colleges played an essential role in the nation's overall education plan. President Obama urged support for repairing and upgrading existing community college buildings. My mother could have told him as much thirty years ago.

"I'm doing great," I told Kathleen when she phoned partway through my first day alone. She was afraid that I might do too much, but I assured her that I was just sitting at my desk. "It's the pause before the storm of final classes, papers, and exams," I said.

When I hung up, I reached for the larger of the manila mailers. I recognized my mother's handwriting: "Divorce Papers." Inside, I found a legal document's carbon copy. I held the parchment-like paper and read for the first time the typewritten words in Hélene's divorce settlement. I knew that my mother had taken me to Oklahoma with the intention of living with my father. She had made the space his parents had provided her as welcoming as possible, and she had cared for me at the farm until he arranged for the divorce. She did not contest the ironic charge that she had refused to live as his wife.

According to the document, the court awarded her custody, and he agreed to pay $40 per month in child support. Of course, the second part turned into another falsehood that she lived with, rather than risk losing custody of me. Perhaps her fears were ungrounded. Perhaps he would have contributed to our welfare if she had pushed, but she operated under no illusions about the capriciousness of human nature or about the trustworthiness of society and the law. She would rely on no one but herself.

Forty dollars. I flipped through her W2 forms for my school years. My elementary school tuition came to over four hundred dollars in 1959. The W2 did not include tips, but her wages for the year totaled just over one thousand dollars.

I stared at the W2 forms and at the divorce document. She never complained, just got up, went to work, and made everybody around her smile. I had known the story for years, but the dollar amounts gave a searing clarity to my understanding of what she'd accomplished. God *and* the Devil always were in the details. For me, it had always been more about her than about my father, at least the parts of the story that affected my life. We all had our limitations; judging family members as if they operated with the same ones guaranteed disappointment and bitterness. Nature and nurture proved an odd couple indeed.

In 1970, news of my father's death at forty-three came not long after the heart attack that put an end to Hélene's work life, and weeks after I'd pulled my least likely end-of-the-semester rally, which sent me to Temple University's graduation. Hélene would have to rely on disability support and had little money in the bank. I had just begun my search for a full-time job that related in some way to psychology.

"Do you want to go to your father's funeral?"

I had opened a savings account as a young boy and had only withdrawn money once, the previous fall, when my mother and I had bought our first car. I knew that the price of airfare would remove a major chunk of what remained in my account or hers. "Well, yes," I said.

"Good," she said. "Because you should." She paid for my flight to Oklahoma that day.

Once there, I was welcomed by Ned's wife and by my half-brother Mike, whom I hadn't seen since I'd visited as a ten-year-old. I slept in the cozy home they'd shared with my father. Their genuine warmth made me realize that the three of us shared something, no matter how different it was from the families I'd seen on television.

I genuflected at the coffin and made the sign of the cross, no doubt the only Catholic present. Sitting near Ned's widow and my half-brother, I felt an awkward pain as they broke into tears. For them, the loss was fresh, and I felt close to them in that moment and wanted to console them. Watching them and others around us crying, I mourned anew a loss that I'd accepted long ago, but it did not make me cry. I said a prayer for them but also for my mother back in Philadelphia.

The funeral procession seemed to include half of the population of Oklahoma. I was struck by how much he'd been loved, and knew that meant that he'd given love. He'd found a consistency in the life he'd made with his second family.

Now I was reaching retirement age; he'd died so much younger than I was now. Going through these papers, I concluded that perhaps both he and I had learned and changed when we'd reached a certain age. But as always, thoughts of my father quickly brought my mother back to mind.

She rarely was still. She hustled between rooms and tasks. If she lived with access to one square yard of dirt, she grew vegetables. She laughed at comedies on TV and at the silliness of my friends and me. The volume of her speaking voice rose, her pace quickened, and she reached lower and higher pitches when she telephoned family in Quebec. The free hours on Hélene's day off must have flown by her, but my enduring memory was of her singing and cleaning, while some aromatic dish in a *chaudron* perked away on the stove. In a more perfect world, my mother might have become a teacher, nurse, doctor, or writer and impacted numerous lives. Some might say that she *should* have been bitter, that she had every right to be angry and malcontent. All of us knew a gap between our potential and our accomplishment, but as a single mother, waitress, and homemaker, no significant gap existed for Hélene. I'd thought it impossible to appreciate Hélene's strengths any more than I had, but I realized that I now did.

I remembered walking alongside her to the park with a baseball and glove. Years later, the hairdresser who owned the salon next to the park told me that he had marveled at the sight of this woman who had never seen a baseball game trying to teach her son what she thought a boy in this country should know. Growing up in America and in her care, I gained blessings and advantages that I did not always recognize. I did learn from her that one should not wait for that perfect world. I wished I had more quickly emulated her passion for good work. She deserved better from me. But I also learned from her that you never stop loving and hoping. Not out of some great act of will, but because that is the nature of genuine love. It lives on, and it includes the capacity for hope.

I remembered talking with my mother during her CCP time about her psychology course. She showed me an article about a Jewish woman who'd survived a Nazi concentration camp. She admired the woman's enduring optimism. "She never became bitter," she said over the noise of a passing trolley out on the avenue. Then she opened her psych book to the section that explained Maslow's concept of self-actualization.

"Yes," I said. We drank our tea and talked about the idea of a person fulfilling her potential in ways that mattered, for them and for others. I smiled and agreed that the Jewish woman fit the model. Wishing myself back to that moment in her little apartment, I heard myself exclaiming, "That's you, Mom!" But I had not done that.

The day in my study drew near its end. When Kathleen returned from her shift, I would tell her about a day of progress that involved no lifting or moving of heavy objects—at least not physically heavy ones. In for a penny, in for a pound, I thought, and reached for the other manila folder. Inside, I found a tidy little envelope from an unfamiliar name on Rex Avenue in Chestnut Hill, addressed to "Ned K. Bachus." I had always used my Confirmation name, Christopher, as my middle name; Kathleen and I kept our phone book listing as "NK Bachus," an easy way to identify junk mail and unwanted telephone solicitors. The writer had used the phone book, but the "Ned" suggested a closer connection. I realized that it had been opened but had resealed, after decades of lying under the weight of other documents.

I studied the robin's egg blue envelope postmarked a few weeks after Hélene's death. The handwriting on the envelope revealed the precise control of a calligraphy artist; each descending line of the address began a graceful step further to the right than the line above it. I felt the thickness of the folded pages but did not pull them out. I had read this letter in 1979, had thought about it a few times in the last several weeks, but still remembered nothing of its contents or source.

Perhaps my inability to remember was because the letter had come from someone who knew Hélene but not me. I removed the carefully folded sheets and opened them. "Dear Ned," the stranger's letter began. "I loved Hélene Bachus from the moment I first saw her in Room 225 of the hospital." The line arrested me. *How could I have forgotten?* The hospital volunteer.

Long-interred shock filled me, as it surely had the other time I read this line thirty-three years ago. "She had the most *beautiful* face with a luminous ethereal quality. I knew when I saw her that she wouldn't be here on earth too much longer." The directness of her language froze my breathing. Reading another line, I could see the Durham Street kitchen table where I'd once opened this envelope, the afternoon light slanting through the back window, Kathleen's desperate expression as I pushed the letter toward her, then sobbed into my hands.

I breathed out and steeled myself. "Over the years, you get to recognize the transparent look that the very ill get when time is running out. It makes you weak in the knees, especially when, like your mother, they show tremendous patience and courage." Months before, Hélene had asked the Red Cross Gray Lady what she would do about treatment if she were in her shoes. The volunteer's reply that life was always worth fighting for resonated with her, even after all she'd been through. The woman recounted being with Hélene as she endured an injection of some sort, "but she didn't bother or make much fuss about it. Instead, she was grateful for all the kindness shown her."

Calling Hélene a favorite of all the nurses, the volunteer described her as "lovely and exceptional," underlining the words. All of this I had known about Hélene, but this sensitive stranger's words reached some new place in me. No emotionally safe time existed when I might read this letter. I wanted to run up a white flag. Enough.

But I read on. "The last time I saw your mother was in Caruso's Market where she was buying some food for a happy Sunday breakfast with you." Now, I too entered this omniscient narrative, an offstage figure. But she was telling Hélene's story.

"She was so frail, and I don't know how she ever would have managed to get back to her apartment. I drove her home and carried the marketing up the stairs for her. She showed me her apartment—it was lovely. The place was immaculate and warm and comfortable." She regretted not having seen Hélene during her last hospitalization, wished she had been able "to tell her what a wonderful person she was and how much we all loved her. I hope she knew." She spoke about what Hélene *did* know, about the place that Kathleen and I occupied in her heart.

In 1979, I recognized this woman's gift for understanding both my mother and how much I needed to hear that from her. Written sentiments from other people stayed with me, but the power of this one had sent it into hiding in a safe place. Holding up the last page of the letter, I remembered this unmet stranger, Betsy Warwick, like some god, inhabiting the grieving young man, and I felt her inhabiting the teacher on the verge of retirement, still knowing me from both inside and outside. I sensed this as palpably as one felt severe heat or cold in a room.

She had to know that I could make it through her searing song only once before securing it like a time capsule, to be forgotten but ultimately discovered when I might hear it with the ears of someone Hélene's age when she was dying. *Surely I wrote her back.* Why had I not tried to meet her? Perhaps she knew that such an encounter would have been more than I could handle, that her work was done. I would never write anything that did so much. Few people had. I looked at the woman's graceful signature. Below, in parentheses, she added, "Mrs. Nelson D. Warwick," and under that, almost as part of her signature, a hastily drawn sketch of herself that was dominated by the nurse's cap with its cross. Below it all, "the old Gray Lady" provided the final touch.

What else had I forgotten? In the basement that afternoon, I'd peered into the opened trunk, steeling myself for hard decisions about souvenirs and relics, telling myself that I could remember what I needed to remember without dragging every knick-knack, frayed baseball card, and report card with me to however many more addresses I had ahead of me. If I could not retrieve some insight, experience, or emotion without boxes full of moldy triggers, I didn't need that memory. Right? I knew that I should plan on reserving *some* room for relics, but I would not know which envelope or small box contained an emotional depth charge. I would keep this letter not because I wanted or needed to revisit that flash of sadness but because, like the little note attached to my baptismal gown, it contained something that might capture her essence and importance for Kathleen, me, for our children or perhaps future grandchildren. And because it would keep me writing.

I thought of my student Chelsea who had just returned after giving birth to twins. She too appeared to be made of different stuff than most of the people around her. My advice to community college students concerning the dangers of relying on willpower made sense, unless you spoke of someone like Hélene or Chelsea. Hélene had sent my thoughts back to my students and their strength. They were writing an essay in which they considered the nature of a good neighbor, and they couldn't have dreamed up a better one than Hélene. So many of them were about to discover under duress just what they had inside of them.

I didn't feel as weak as when I'd sat in my desk chair this morning. I knew that I had at least another week of teaching left in these bones.

Spring Sabbatical, Day Twenty-Six

Saturday, April 28, 2012: Ireland

On my last Saturday in Cill Rialaig, I woke up slowly and donned the usual extra layers for outdoor activity. I plugged in my iPod earbuds and hiked downhill to find a beach that several people had told me about. My hike took me over a sheep gate, along a heavily rutted field's footpath that bottlenecked—after passing a series of moat-like puddles and pools—into another empty field, ultimately reaching a five-foot-high earthen wall that might or might not divide private properties but certainly marked the end of grazing land.

I clambered up the barrier and jumped down onto rocks that sloped down to the promised beach. Pulling my camera from my backpack, I took shots of wild flowers, rocks, the curving strand, and distant buildings. The water looked so different down at this level, friendlier, and calming. I settled on a rock, turned on a Richard Drueding album, and sat back, marveling at the blue sky's curative effects. I had taken more photos than any day except on the trips to Skellig Michael and Bolus Head.

Finally I started back across the fields to the sheep gate. Climbing over the gate and onto the road, I realized that the album was repeating and started up the hill, enjoying the same guitar tunes I'd listened to out on the rocks. Lost in the song, I startled when a vehicle pulled up from behind and came to a stop beside me. It was the farmer in his truck.

Turning off the music, I returned his hello.

He nodded and told me his name, which I could not make out. "T-A-D-G-H," he spelled, then asked what I had been listening to.

"Acoustic guitar," I said.

"I've seen you in the village," he said.

"Yes," I said, and realized that his dog was nowhere in sight. "It's a great place to work."

He told me that he once lived in what now was the second set of ruins down from Cottage 2. When he turned three years old, his family moved to his current home, even farther down the hill. "Have to be getting on," he said, nodding again.

He pulled away, and I waved, finally spotting his hard-charging dog. Apparently, she had been protecting the farm truck's other flank while we'd been speaking.

Later, when I reached the cottage, I spied Tadgh above the village, putting out feed for the sheep on the other side of the road. I extended my hike past the cottages and snapped a dozen pictures of his dog. "What's her name?" I called out. With effort, I just made out his reply: "Lassie." I asked if I could take a shot of the two of them together. He managed a crooked smile as he stood beside his partner. Capturing them on film made me feel more like I was nearing readiness to say farewell to the old sod and return to America. And it would help me remember yet another story.

Fall Semester, Week Fourteen

Wednesday, December 7, 2011: Philadelphia

The doctors would not allow me to drive for a while, but Anna picked me up on her way to the College. I reminded her of one of my trunk findings: a group photograph from Take Your Daughters To Work Day when she was about eight years old. There she stood, under the CCP banner. I remembered when first her brother then she discovered and fell in love with the College's escalators. They both attended CCP musical performances, lectures, and basketball games. She appreciated the irony of taking me to work for my final classes. Her position, though temporary, gave her some great experience. I told her how proud I was to have her as a coworker for my last weeks at the College.

I had missed three days of classes—a week's worth of sessions. My 8:00 Honors class discussed the three routes to happiness outlined in the Seligman article. Seeing that they had kept up with the work in my absence reassured me that of course these classes could run without me—especially with teachers like Vince and Mark at the helm. The discussion moved along without much need for direction from me, and I was aware that I was receiving at least two of the kinds of rewards they described—gratification and meaning. I let myself take this in, the way I hoped a rookie shortstop or retiring pitcher would pay acute attention to the crowd, the smells, the panorama of the crowded baseball park. I had taught in this dingy classroom for years, but now I scanned the long chalk ledge below the board so that I might remember the fraying erasers, the bits and butts of chalk, and the accumulating drifts of chalk dust. Heeding Kathleen's advice, I ended class five minutes early and asked a student to hoist the document camera atop the multimedia cart for me.

Guiding the 9:05 Honors English 102 group through a writing seminar on revisions of their culminating papers—chapters of what would amount to a small book aimed at prospective parents—proved harder. Workshopping previously unseen essays always was an exercise in improvisation, and I felt myself slightly off kilter after having spent the last week away from the classroom. Even though the students were just as welcoming and solicitous as the first group, navigating the hour seemed to take longer and left me exhausted.

Two hours later, I felt refreshed and ready to take on my afternoon double-header of unlinked 101s. I had arranged for them to report to the classroom I used in the morning, sparing me the schlep to their regular room in the building down the street. The document camera was still set up and would help me lead the writing seminar on the students' final paper. Charisse and Douglas hugged me when they saw me. Charisse presented me with a card they all had signed as Ian and Zhivka beamed. *How close did I come to not making it back here?* If I was going to get through this class emotionally intact, I must focus on the task at hand. I thanked them, trying to sound as normal as possible.

Their ranks had thinned considerably since the beginning of the semester, leaving an experienced and dedicated band in each class. Most of the students who gave early indications of inability or lack of engagement had left. Sometime before the deadline, Ryan had vanished, and I'd dropped him to make it official. Likewise, the 12:20 student whom I regularly spotted at his flirting station near the Winnet Building entrance had left; his consistent arrival so close to the end of my roll-taking fueled my suspicion that a more punctual classmate had assumed the task of texting him just as I reached the last three names in the alphabet so that he could bid adieu to his coterie of admirers. Not all of the finishers would leave with passing grades, but they still showed up with their papers.

Most of them seemed genuinely delighted to see me, a sentiment I admitted to sharing, although I doubted they realized how true it was. Of course I was happy to have recovered enough health to return to work, but the sight of them affirmed that I belonged here. I realized with great certainty that I had spent all these years in the right place. The time to move on had arrived, but I would leave knowing that I left at a good time. I felt blessed that I could finish this semester with these people. As happened every semester, I had gotten to know *these* students, and their struggles had become mine. I wanted them to finish well.

I flipped through the syllabus booklet until I came to this week's schedule and located today's attendance question. *Which theorists have been most useful to you in writing your final paper?* I'd planned the questions before the semester began and they generally lined up with material we were studying, but suddenly I felt like we could all use a break from routine.

"Rashid," I called, "best place to get a cheesesteak?"

"Gooey Looie's," he answered, and was greeted by a chorus of groans then laughter. I marked him present.

"Chelsea."

"Dalessandro's, definitely."

"Douglas?"

"John's Roast Pork in South Philly," he sang out. And on we went. It might be a long while before I had a cheesesteak, but I was happy to add my answer when we reached the end of the alphabet. "I'm with Chelsea *and* Charisse," I said. "Dalessandro's in Roxborough. But for me it's a tie with Mama's in Bala Cynwyd."

I switched on the document camera, and we turned our attention to the semester's final writing assignment. I felt the fatigue of having gone through two classes already, but talking about their essays felt normal, invigorating. When we finished combing through the last draft of the day, I thanked them. "You look so good to me," I told them.

I did not let the day's emotion overwhelm me until I reported to Kathleen at dinner. She experienced something akin to this at her job, having shared the news of our forthcoming departure with her coworkers and patients. Now she learned how much her work had meant to them. Unlike many of my connections with students, most of her work relationships, both with staff and with patients, endured longer than a semester. They did not like losing a great nurse, and for some of them, it felt very personal. We would return to Philadelphia several times a year for family visits and band gigs, and we vowed to keep in touch through e-mail and cell phones, but deep down we knew that some folks would slip through the cracks. When we did leave, we would bring with us what we had learned in our work lives, and we realized how much the people there, as well as others, had contributed to whatever knowledge or skills we would take with us from Philadelphia.

By the end of my first day back at teaching, I felt sufficiently drained to know that I must cancel the band's tentative booking for

New Year's Eve. I knew that even though I would regain some strength, a Mermaid gig's workout was more than I should take on at this point. We would have other dates. The relief that I felt after sharing this revelation with my bandmates convinced me that I'd made the right decision. Kathleen and I also canceled our plans for hosting the Seven Fishes Christmas Eve dinner, our most cherished social commitment of the year. Even with all of my classes now scheduled to take place on the same floor, I might have trouble making it through them. Friday would come soon enough. Finishing the semester, preparing the house for sale, and packing for the move would be plenty.

Sitting in my home office Thursday morning, I took store of what lay ahead. My students and I had three more class days ahead. Teaching had left me feeling weaker than I had ever imagined I could feel. During any other semester, I probably would have heeded the suggestion oft repeated by people at work that I let others fill in while I recovered. But making it through the first day made me realize that I could do this, and I had Thursday to catch my breath.

Although the doctors had warned against sorting or packing, I found myself tempted by the shelves and the stacks of books awaiting triage. I had already prepared my plans and materials for Friday's classes. I would not move piles of books or stack any boxes, but a file drawer full of old materials was right in my reach from the chair.

Teachers taught hoping to enhance certain traits in their students. I lingered over an article about teacher expectations, recalling four former students. One January evening during the semester break in 2005, these four veterans of the Transfer Opportunities Program (TOP), one of the academic support programs that evolved into the Honors curriculum, joined Vince and me over tomato pie and barbecue ribs to explore Marshall Gregory's ideas in the light of their experiences. Vince had not taught these particular students, but

I knew that he would serve as a great co-facilitator. They were to have been five former students, but at the last minute, Michelle had to cancel. The conversation ranged from Gregory's list of desired traits in students, which read like a Scouts manual, to his suggested ethical commitments for faculty: fairness, respect, charity, and civility.[1]

Reggie, a former valedictorian at an inner-city public high school who would go on to graduate from Temple, had quickly recognized his own improvement at becoming open-minded, introspective, and respectful of others. Seen by everyone around him as a good student in high school, the black man now in his late twenties said that he did not become a serious student until he reached CCP.

"Professor Gould had a knack for making complicated matters clear and graspable," he explained. "He did this in a way that made me feel like I belonged." I'd seen Clint and Vince make material come alive again and again, but more importantly, they helped students come alive.

Coming from equally gritty Norristown, Trevor, like Reggie, had come from a working-class Italian American background and epitomized the vulnerable nontraditional student during his first term at CCP. "Here I am, a dropout, a carpenter for fifteen years," he said. "What the hell can I contribute to this class?"

Taking a summer course in his weakest area, math, he scored two 60's and a 40 on his first three quizzes. In a conversation outside of class, his teacher Geoff Schulz gave him clear direction as to what he needed to do to pass. Expectation and confidence made up the subtext of Geoff's message. As Trevor told it, "He just kind of went down the list with me, and I wound up getting an A in that class." Trevor, now a Philadelphia public school teacher, recognized Geoff Schulz as demonstrating the four ethical commitments that Gregory sees at the heart of effective teaching.

Commenting on Trevor's story, John, a white man in his mid-thirties who graduated with a degree in history from Temple and now worked as a social worker, zeroed in on the make-or-break nature of Trevor's math class crisis: "If not for having a decent professor," John said, "who did concern himself with being fair, respecting his students and that kind of thing ... you never would have gotten this far. You're probably like thousands of kids in that exact same situation, having failed that first couple of quizzes and in their minds proved to themselves that, see, I *knew* I couldn't do it, and (who) then ... went back to whatever life they were unhappy with before." Clearly, Geoff Schulz taught Trevor more than algebra.

Chris, who now held a BA from the University of Minnesota and taught music, came to the College with determination, but he credited the academic peer culture in TOP with his growing ease in college. Responding to Trevor's comment about the social support benefits of their academic experience at CCP, the white man in his late twenties said, "You're going to college to learn, but actually you're going there in a very social atmosphere. It seems like the learning comes *with* that."

Trevor seemed to enjoy learning most when he could enjoy it with others. He mentioned a conversation he had with a non-student friend, a fellow carpenter, with whom he shared his excitement about his project on poet Etheridge Knight. "We wound up talking for about two, three hours about this project," he said. "We're digging into this poem, and it was great. I went to bed all high. I was charged up. My presentation was the next day, and I was saying, this is great. I nailed the presentation."

Several days after the session, after transcribing the discussion and reading it over, I realized how much of what the students said had to do with the interaction of students with classmates and with faculty.

After a disappointing semester at Temple, followed by a few years away from school, Reggie, like Trevor, faced an existential crisis. "I didn't know if I could handle it," he said. "And I had a talk with Gary Mullin. Looking over my test scores, he told me, 'You belong here.' And that really gave me a lot of confidence. It was really important to me to hear that from someone who's already established and someone who is where I want to be."

John pointed to a quote in the piece by Gregory: "to students all interactions with their teachers are both intellectual and social—and the social part of the interaction has *at least* as much to do with how well they learn as the intellectual part of the interaction" (emphasis in the original). [2]

Teachers like Gary impacted students, and when they combined forces, they maximized their social connection with students. Asked how different their experiences would have been if they had taken the same courseload as separate, discrete courses with the same faculty, Trevor articulated a whole-is-greater-than-the-sum-of-the-parts view of faculty collaboration. "It's not like we had individual teachers per se," he said. "We had a group of teachers. You acted as an entity."

Speaking of the faculty, John said, "You guys were all over the same spot basically, in between classes. Half of us would end up hanging out in your offices … and it increased the comfort level and everybody's willingness to interact with each other."

My colleagues and I in the Transfer Opportunities Program had the advantage of a unified and text-based curriculum, a consistent and common view of the nature of academic writing, and a pool of fairly high-scoring students; however, something as simple as having offices clustered near our classrooms turned into a critical element in our effectiveness as teachers.

Walking over to my office window, I stretched my back and looked out at the bare trees, but I kept thinking about what these four students had showed me about learning and teaching. I hoped that my students learned more than what I told them. Teaching them, especially when I did so as part of a faculty team, taught me things about learning that I had not learned when I'd been on the other side of the classroom. Being a member of a teaching team had enabled me to be more effective. Gary, Clint, and I probably accomplished more as teammates than we could have done individually with those students. And collaboration upped my game whether I taught alone or as part of a team.

Time after time, in both formal and informal education, my students, my faculty team partners, and I learned *with* others, and "learned how to play well with others." Immersion in collaborative practices fuels learning. The social conditions of my on-the-job teacher training mirrored my opportunities to learn and improve as a front row forward on a rugby team, as a singer/musician in a band, and as a novice scribbler in a community of writers. In each of these activities, I'd worked alongside people who could show me what I hadn't learned on my own and who taught me how to improve.

When I learned about Vygotsky's concept of learning guides I immediately thought about veteran prop Lino Giampaolo bending me like a pretzel in our first scrum, bandmates Jerry Howard and Michael Bailey helping me "find the one" in a groove, and writer-friend Jim Brady red-inking ten flabby bits of phrasing in what I'd thought was a finely crafted paragraph. In each case, with the help of a skilled guide, I'd moved from observer to guided participant to doer.

Similarly, Bandura's reciprocal determinism fit the interacting influences in my roles as rugby player, singer, and writer. Again and again, I saw that changes in environment, behavior, and cognitions/

beliefs impacted one another. Those learning experiences mattered, but in teaching—the work that I came to recognize as my calling—I grasped that the ability to function well with fellow faculty and students made a difference in my understanding of the process of learning. A single factor—other people's influence—offered learning's greatest hindrances *and* its best resources. And the same was true about teaching.

Learning had changed me. I winced when I thought about a colleague's belief that after fifteen or so years, teachers ceased improving. I wondered if he believed that his theory also applied to surgeons or artists. Perhaps he stopped improving, but I was convinced that my work now was better than ten or even five years ago. I hoped the same applied for my colleagues. If not, they ought to consider taking up some alternate activity.

Isolation bred more isolation, and professors long past their prime—if they ever had a period that others might recognize as such—haunted the halls of every college. Some of them brazenly flaunted their lack of engagement or accountability.

Experienced teachers were familiar with the variant forms of faculty mediocrity and ineptitude. One strain that irked me involved the professors who should have stopped long ago. Years, maybe decades, had passed since they taught a different course or modified the ones they taught. With no passion for ideas or desire to help others, only academic inertia, some yellowing notes, and a convenient teaching schedule kept them going. I saw them shuffling between office and classroom, and thought of *Night of the Living Dead* or, in their case, The Teaching Dead: these tenured pedagogical zombies who clung to their posts for various reasons until some change in their life forced them out or offered them something they considered worth a gamble. They liked the structure, and they didn't know what else to do. They did not know if they could live on Social Security plus the pension that had percolated for forty or fifty years.

Some faculty members did work years past ordinary retirement age because of real economic pressure, and they did a fine job. They liked to teach, and it showed. Sometimes aging faculty members became the life of the department, high-level classroom teachers, perhaps even faculty leaders. I saved my ire for the ones who intellectually died a long time ago but wouldn't fall down. Students deserved living teachers.

I was not leaving my job because of reduced capacity or passion. I was not ready to disengage. I was leaving to dive into other kinds of work and to do so in a fresh environment, an opportunity afforded by the College's retirement provisions—opportunity that existed largely due to the muscular advocacy of the faculty federation, our union.

I was nearing the end of my only academic term that would have no follow-up semester, but so far this semester felt the same as all the ones that had preceded it. Post-operative discomfort and fatigue limited but did not stop me. However, dismantling our entire routine and our castle did set this semester apart from previous ones. Piece by piece, we took it apart and would assemble the surviving pieces of it five hundred miles to the northeast a month later.

Anna drove me to work again on Friday. Immersing myself in a full slate of writing seminars exhausted me as much as it had Wednesday—hardly the encouragement I hoped for, but only nine days had passed since the surgeries. The familiar relief of arriving home for the weekend was heightened by the knowledge that I truly had entered the home stretch. Papers and exams would follow me home every day next week, but this weekend provided the calm before the grading storm.

The unlinked 101 classes on Monday of Week Fifteen focused on Raymond Carver's story "Cathedral," which would serve as the basis for Friday's exam. I had taught the story many times, and I savored the discussion in both hours as much as I always had. I brought home stacks of final writing assignments from both unlinked 101 classes and began grading.

I entered my office Wednesday morning, mindful that with exams set for Friday, this would be my last day of actual teaching. I had wondered if this moment would feel different, but I soon realized that, as with concert performance or athletic competition, as soon as one engages, such emotional overlays fall away to the concentration demanded by the moment. I felt focused, not maudlin or sentimental.

All of the remaining students in the 8:00 Honors first-semester class showed up.

"Did you know," I began, "that if Mr. Vince removed his shoes and socks, you would see webs between his toes?"

They laughed and pounded their desks.

We discussed traits of the Carver story's two main characters, another familiar conversation. I knew I could go on leading this discussion, watching the students' reaction to these quirky characters, and the quiet, odd act of redemption to which the literally blind man leads his figuratively blind companion, but I was comfortable with making this my last classroom visit to this favorite story. I could not think of a more fitting one with which to end. Even a slug like the story's Husband turns out to possess the capacity for transcendence, however fleeting his redemptive moment becomes. The possibility of such achievement kept teachers and students at their work, and some would develop the necessary love, passion, and discipline to do a good job of it, even if they ended up needing more than one pass at it.

I graded all day Thursday until Kathleen came home from work around half past three. It was my mother's birthday and the day before Kathleen's mother's birthday. We'd always considered this two-day reminder of our mothers as the beginning of the Christmas holidays. Some years, we'd put the tree up on the 15th or 16th as a tip of the cap to Hélene and Olga, but boxes packed for Maine already occupied space in the living room where the tree usually stood. This would be a treeless Christmas.

"I've been wanting to show you this," I said, when Kathleen had removed her coat and sat beside me at the kitchen table. She'd seen every other trunk discovery, and, after talking about the gown, old photographs, and Hélene's precious things, we'd saved what we wanted and packed them into boxes. I handed her the thick little envelope addressed to Mr. Ned K. Bachus.

She looked confused. Her eyes took in the fifteen-cent US flag stamp, the Philadelphia cancellation, and the address. Removing the sheets of stationery from inside, her look of puzzlement gave way to a grieving frown. She sighed. "I thought about her all day," she said. She picked up the envelope again and quickly turned it over. That puzzled expression returned as she read the writer's name and address.

"Hospital volunteer," I said. "That September."

She said nothing.

"We read this in 1979," I said.

She shook her head and said she would go to the living room to read it. I nodded as she walked off with the letter. I organized my piles of essays and returned them to their tattered manila folders. I'd planned to end the afternoon's grading when Kathleen came home. We still had dinner to deal with, and I hadn't even asked her about her day.

When Kathleen brought the letter back, she placed it on the table and stretched her arms around me. Holding her, I felt her shuddering against me and patted her back. "I didn't remember this letter," she said. "Did you?"

She'd stopped crying, but her eyes were red. I told her no.

"You're the same age she was when she died, you know."

"Yes," I said.

"I thought about that when they were flying around the hospital room, trying to bring you back."

My impulse was to joke, to say *Well, I didn't*, but I thought the better of it.

Breaking off abruptly, she held up one finger then headed upstairs.

I was empty, worn out from grading. *I can't talk about this now. Why did I start this?* I gathered all of my grading materials and the letter and brought them upstairs to the study. The untouched essays outnumbered the ones I'd gone over once and taken notes on. I dropped heavily into my desk chair.

Kathleen appeared in the doorway. "Come on," she said.

I followed her out to the car, which she drove up Germantown Avenue to Chestnut Hill, then turned onto Rex Avenue. "We're not doing this," I said.

She pulled to a stop across the street from Betsy Warwick's 1979 address.

"She's probably been dead for decades," I said.

"She doesn't have to be here. You do. What are you going to say to her?"

The leaves on the walkway blew up towards the house. I studied the curtains on a second-floor window. I imagined her upstairs at a writing table, thinking about a dying patient. "Thank you," I said. I closed my eyes.

Kathleen pulled out slowly. In two minutes, I grasped that she was headed to George Washington Memorial Park.

When we'd buried my mother's ashes beside a sapling at the memorial park thirty-two years ago, I surely didn't expect that anything could make me smile. Kathleen, a priest from Hélene's parish, the park's manager, and I stood beside a small hole at the base of a young tree that had recently been planted along one of their winding drives. As the priest offered a prayer, I noticed the foliage on the sapling: maple leaves. A piece of Canada, I thought, and could not suppress a smile.

Now Kathleen and I stood beneath a mature maple, visiting Hélene's marker and tree for the last time as residents of her adopted city. Soon we would live within striking distance of the village where she was born ninety-five years ago that day, some consolation for giving up the option of visiting here any time we wanted. "We'll come back," Kathleen said. I ran my fingers over the lettering on her marker. When we drove away, I felt sure that she approved of our plans.

On Friday, the students filed into the classroom for their final exam, my last partners in the teaching/learning dance. Student attrition's grim consolation meant that by adding a few extra desks, I'd been able to fit the students from all of my classes into one large classroom for their final. My brief announcements before I turned them loose on their blue books offered me my final opportunity to speak to them as a group. I reminded them that they should make use of the full two hours allotted, that they could consult their dictionaries, that I would periodically post the remaining time on the board. "It's been an honor to teach you this semester," I said. "Thank you for working so hard." They smiled back. A few students offered their own thanks and wishes that I enjoy my retirement, but I knew that we could not let this turn into a love session. "Good luck," I said.

At my table, I resumed grading the writing assignments, but I could not resist looking at my students. Jenny appeared to be sketching out ideas on the loose-leaf paper that I'd given out. Ian, his brow furrowed, studied the prompt. Having already filled a page of her blue book, Zhiv flipped the page over and dug in on the next one.

If I closed my eyes, their near silence might lead me to conclude that the people around me were not doing much of anything; the quiet belied their ferocious efforts to end the semester well. My course had stressed to them the social nature of learning. I'd encouraged them to take advantage of the help available to them. But when it came to performing for evaluation, students generally had to stand alone.

Just like every other semester, we had reached familiar ground. In two hours, they would have spoken their last lines in the script and played the final out of the ninth inning. Every fall and spring, students and teachers signed up for a four-month work arrangement: a semester. It seemed like so little time, a most un-Hélene-sized slice of their life.

I watched my students scratch away, filling their blue books with words that they hoped would fairly represent their good efforts, meet the standard, and earn them good grades. They had no idea how much I wanted that to be the case. Long ago, I'd entered the teaching life practically by default, having taken a last-minute opening for a job that I had not planned on taking or had trained for, but in short order, I had found myself wanting my students to succeed. As a rookie teacher, I'd first tasted an unnamable but powerful interest in the learning, changing, and betterment of people who were not my relatives or friends—not a passive curiosity but a strong and surprising drive to be part of their experience. As a first-year teacher responding to this impulse, I could not have known that I'd want to keep hearing and answering this call throughout my life.

The moment my first child was born, I felt amongst the many other powerful reactions a similar but even more powerful pull, a magnetic connection to this tiny, ruddy-faced, round little being. Kathleen's tears were joyful, and I knew that what we felt was love. In time, I recognized that what drew me into coaching rugby and soccer but especially into teaching and into the lives of students belonged to the same family of emotions.

Once, at the end of a semester, I met with Max Eirich, my friend and mentor, to determine grades for a link of students we shared. "It's happened again," I said, shaking my head. "I want them to pass so much."

He nodded.

I told him what I could not or would not say to anyone else. "I love them. They drive me nuts, but I can't help it."

"I know," he said. "This is one day when we earn our money."

And we went on making hard decisions, no matter how much we understood about the pain and injustice of our students' lives.

At such moments, I felt the full weight that bears down on the teacher, and I realized just how *large* a semester could become. The students had so much at stake, partly because our time together was finite. This work mattered, it had meaning. To do this kind of work for the kinds of students who found their way to community college classrooms was to hit the grand slam of teaching reward. I'd had the unique privilege of returning as a faculty member to my alma mater, which had played a prominent role in the lives of my entire family.

The first student finished an hour and a half later, and one by one the rest of them wrapped up their work over the next half hour. When students approached the table with their completed work, I made sure they'd put their name on the cover and placed their sheets of paper and blue books upside down on my desk. Then, as I'd done at every other final exam as long as I could remember, I shook hands with each student. Several whispered good wishes to me.

When they'd all left the room, I realized that I had forgotten to share with them what my surgical experience had taught me about taking exams. Maybe I would write about it in Ireland. Writing a book about the semester might be a way to get one last class in.

Vince and I made copies of the Honors exams and final writing assignments so we'd each have a set. At home, I took notes on each paper and exam, then sorted them into tentative piles of A's, B's, and so on. I reread them, shifting some from one pile to another. This process always took me more time than I thought it should. Borderline performances twisted me in circles. Over the week, the pile of in-between papers shrank. I found dealing with the students I shared with Vince easier. He called on Monday, and we discussed the grades for the first-semester Honors students' exams. By Tuesday night, we both were ready to settle the second-semester papers. On Wednesday, we hashed out the first group's course grades, took a break, then settled on the second-semester students' grades after dinner.

Four of our original first-semester Honors students had departed long ago. LeSean, whose high water mark was C-/D+, ended up receiving a D in each course. The two next-weakest students earned a C and a B. Five students finished with a pair of A grades, including Jenny and Matt. Nine of our ten finishers received a C or better.

Eleven of the fourteen students who started the second-semester Honors class made it to the finish line, with ten of them earning an A or a B in writing and in psychology. Sid, whose ferocious revision and editing continued throughout the semester, earned an A- on his final paper, pushing his course grade for writing up to an A. Four students who held a B at midterm finished with A's.

Ten students who began the unlinked English 101 courses had disappeared before it ended, including Jim from Judge. Diego, who joined the semester after his vacation, did not turn in two major assignments, failing the course. Three others vanished after modestly successful first half performances. I would never know for sure what nonacademic factors caused their departures. Nor could I know how many students who ended up passing came close to bailing out at some point during the course. Chelsea, even with her hospitalization for the birth of her twins, met the attendance requirements and finished with a B in the course. Kind-hearted Charisse pulled her grade up to a B. Zhivka, the feisty Bulgarian, and Ian, the young Marine, both turned midterm B's into A grades. Adam, who'd dragged himself to class after being in a car accident, nailed an A, and was considering my invitation to join Vince and Mark in Honors the next semester. I'd tried to recruit Ian and Zhivka, but the courses didn't fit their work schedules. Afafa battled to a C grade, but her buddy Lourdes again fell short of the mark. Recording her unsatisfactory grade for the second semester in a row was the most dispiriting moment in my day's work, but there was nothing I could do about it now. Twenty-one of my forty-two starters finished with a C or better, including Douglas, Luther, and Bill. Rashid, who survived three shootings and imprisonment and who held a low C at midterm, pulled a B on his final assignment and a C+ on his final exam. His final course grade of B struck me as one of the most impressive performances of the semester.

On Christmas Eve, I posted the final grades online, triggering a rash of electronic appreciations and complaints. For once, Kathleen and I did not spend this day stuffing calamari, peeling shrimp, or frying smelts. Mixed in with responses from my final round of students,

I received a message from a joyful former student who had just completed her first semester after transferring to Saint John's University in New York. Her e-mail provided me with great consolation for having to cancel the Seven Fishes festivities. Perspective, I reminded myself. I had much to give thanks for.

Checking e-mail at 5:28 p.m., I found a message from a student who had not passed. She assumed that I did not accept one late assignment, causing her grade to fall short of passing. I responded, explaining that I had indeed received and credited the particular assignment, despite its lateness. Her final exam did not reach a passing level. "You will need to register for English 101 again," I wrote. "You truly did make progress this semester but need to continue improving next semester. Please continue to work with your learning lab specialist. I believe that helped you improve your skills. If you continue to work with her, your chances to pass will be much greater."

Three minutes later, she replied: "its impossible I don't know what kind of professor are you..you could at leat pass with a D I don't mind I know im ready for English 102. But thx"

I chose not to respond, but twelve minutes later, I received a PS: "thank god you are retired because you r the worst professor I ever meet"

This rousing exchange of holiday greetings angered Kathleen when I read it to her, but I gave in to a sudden impulse to laugh. The student had turned in all of the assignments, worked with me outside of class, and connected with the lab specialist I had recommended. Unlike some of her classmates, she had put her best foot forward, but clearly this educational arrangement, including my part in it, had not sufficiently met her needs. My reaction to her response's dark irony passed quickly. In time, her misdirected frustration would fade, hopefully replaced by more successful practices, but first she must recognize the depth and breadth of her needs. My efforts had led to insufficient improvement; that much, I did regret.

Semesters ended as they began, in their own time. I had sent in the grades, none of which were incomplete. After New Year's, I cleaned out my office at the College so that Mark Hughes could move in before January classes began. Again I found myself filling trash bags, struggling to reduce the paper that remained from my teaching years to a mere few boxes.

My former student Nina stopped by to deliver a gift from her and her Moroccan classmate Asmaa, who was unable to leave work to accompany her. They'd been students in our Honors class last spring, or perhaps the previous fall? Somehow they'd learned about my retirement. Arriving at my office with a gift surprised me even more and touched me to my soul.

The short, sunny Italian American student beamed as I pulled off the gift wrapping. I read the engraved message on the black granite paperweight to the end: "To teach is to touch lives forever. You have touched our lives, and we are grateful to you. May your retirement years be full of peace and happiness. Your Students, Asmaa and Nina." I felt an emotional aftershock. She smiled and shook my hand. "You two are incredible," I stammered. I must have thanked her five times but felt hopelessly inarticulate.

Driving home with boxes that included this gift from my two students from opposite parts of the world who had become friends, I suddenly reddened, feeling even more moved by their gesture and their words. I recalled the engraving. "Your Students." Those two words were enough.

Spring Sabbatical, Day Twenty-Six

Saturday, April 28, 2012: Ireland

For close to four weeks now, I had tended the cottage's peat fire and huddled with my notes and books over my table, returning after walks or food breaks to my laptop's keyboard. The previous night, I had reached the end of my notes. Now I had my first tortured pass at telling the story of my final semester, a draft that had not existed when I'd arrived—a mess, for which I was grateful. I could see the work ahead of me.

For more than three weeks, I had blasted my way, however arduously, through the stubborn rock of the empty screen before me. Now, the time to revise had arrived, time to see again as if for the first time, even as I knew writing never was that simple. A Vincentian priest friend, Father Aidan Rooney, described the nature of life: joy, sorrow, all of it—all at the same time. Somewhere, somebody felt one extreme or the other—only in the ego's isolation did it seem otherwise. Aidan's cosmic sense of things fit writing and learning as well. We multitasked, even when we tried to focus on one thing at a time. I knew I had much work ahead of me with this manuscript, but I felt like the sculptor who had chipped away enough fragments to see what he originally envisioned inside the block of stone.

After dinner, I brought a cup of tea and my computer out to the stone table and bench on the other side of the road. The view in every direction seemed to go on forever—mountains, blue water, clusters of tiny homes. I pulled out my cell phone. It had been too long since I'd last spoken with Michael. He'd been one of the people who'd barged into the cottage day after day.

Not long after Kathleen and I settled into our first apartment, beginning our life together in Philadelphia, Michael and I signed up for a group guitar course. Alone, either of us probably would have been able to resist the temptation to react to the teacher's annoying affectations, but together we discovered our inner third graders. By mid-course, we'd migrated to the rear of the classroom.

"If the two giggle-boxes in the back of the room will kindly stop fooling around, we can learn the G chord!"

We stopped registering for classes together but never forgot the woman who'd "almost met Burl Ives."

I dialed Michael's number. "You awake, Mike?"

"*Now* I am," he whined from Philadelphia. "You still eating porridge over there? Or is it time for haggis?"

"That's Scotland, next island over," I told him. "It's great here. You'd love it."

"What are you writing about today?"

"Same old, same old," I said. "It's about learning. And about people who figured into my learning."

"What a relief. At least you're not libeling me."

"You'd only be in the book if you contributed to my learning."

"Every time you open your mouth, I feel like you're yanking my chain."

"I try, Mike. I try."

Few people had been more influential or supportive in my life, and distance apart didn't seem to matter. In no time, we'd made each other laugh and smile. When we traded our final insults, I knew that things he said would come back to me throughout the day and make me laugh all over again. I hoped the same was true for Michael.

Zipping my jacket, I plugged in my earbuds and listened to Keith Jarrett, whose evocative keyboard jazz oddly fit the ancient rugged Irish scene around me. The cold wind reminded me that I would not remain sitting very long. I needed my sunglasses to see the computer screen. Occasionally peeking up from the keyboard, I drank in the pastoral panorama and let my mind wander. Every writer or artist I knew would savor just one day in this place.

On Sunday, I let myself wake up slowly. I opened the curtain to a gray blustery sky and worked until lunch. I pulled on my layers and headed out for a walk, intent on taking a picture of the imposing "unwelcome" sign up the hill. The gusts shoved me ahead, making me feel like a stumbling school kid. I turned back long before reaching the sign and tilted my head down against the biting wind. The cottage had never felt more like a refuge. I started a fire, rationing the peat and newspapers so that they would last one more night, then prepared fusilli and fashioned a marinara sauce, using the last of my Tabasco sauce, garlic, pepper, and red wine, saving enough so that I would not have to cook again. Jack the taxi driver returned my call, promising to pick me up on Tuesday morning at eleven.

At home, the sky would have become dark by this hour, but after dinner, I sat on the cottage's loveseat and watched through the studio's glass roof as clouds moved by furiously. The colors changed as the sunset progressed, as clouds flew by, and as the sheep munched their way across the top ridge. Suddenly, a blinding blast of late sunlight turned the gray clouds to white. I would not have been surprised if Brunhilde had rushed across such a sky.

I started the morning of my final full day at Cill Rialaig with tea and my last portion of oatmeal. The gray sky, no longer strictly ominous, offered comforting familiarity. I visited the meetinghouse's library to read up on local myth, geography, and history, lingering over books about Irish music and culture. In my month here, only one meeting had taken place in this building, a fine session of *craic* that I would always remember.

After lunch, I stretched out on the loveseat and looked up at the hillside through the glass ceiling. As usual, the sheep picked their way to the right, while the clouds rushed by towards the left. After watching several showers come and go, I decided to try one last time for a photo of the "unwelcome" sign, arming myself with camera, gloves, hat, and scarf. The winds had tantalizingly subdued—encouragement that I could not refuse—and further up the winding hill path I went.

Of course, tasks seemed quite different the second time around. Before I knew it, I again reached the same edge of woods where I'd startled the pair of roosting pheasants on the first walk I'd taken here. I concentrated on everything around me, as if by some superior act of photo-telepathy, I might store in my mind every starkly beautiful sight and sound around me so that I could play them back some time in the future.

Spying what looked like a gravestone, I clambered over the fencing and approached an ancient flat stone sticking up out of the sod. The harsh elements had softened the outline of a circle and cross that some long-gone soul once carved into its face. Already this hike felt worth the effort.

In no time, I reached the sign that said, "End of route: please turn around." I took a photo and strode past it up the twisting road, hoping my former students were doing much the same when they encountered such messages.

Already I felt like I'd negotiated this second hike much faster than the first. This time, I climbed the first two pasture gates with ease, then strode up the switchback cattle path at a good pace, pausing to take in the bay behind me. Pressing onward, I spotted the green metal ladder that enabled people to scale the barbed wire fences where the path I was on joined the official hiking trail. A step later, I glimpsed the Skelligs off to the left. I felt the sweat gathering beneath my clothes as I climbed up the fence-side path towards the barracks' ruins.

Today, typical of days at Bolus Head, had turned dreary, a quality I now considered superior to the crystalline blue skies I'd tramped beneath a week ago. I had held out for another perfect day to see Bolus again, not realizing that imperfection suited the place. People should experience Bolus Head during fast-changing weather, under operatic cloud battles.

Slices of brilliantly lit sea illuminated the otherwise dark waters between Bolus and the Skelligs. To the monks of a thousand years ago, this stunning light must have seemed heavenly. The wind announced its presence with a mighty roar, so I tightened my scarf and pulled my cap down tighter. I pressed my little camera down onto the top of a fence post and snapped shot after shot. I'd been here before, taken in these sights and sounds, but as with my later forays in education, this return trip felt different. Standing in the wind, I felt gratitude for everyone and everything that had figured into my journeys. My approach to life's treks changed with the loss of my mother and the arrival of my children. Kathleen had been central in both experiences and in every journey since. She was the intended audience for these photos. Some day, I would bring her here, another adventure.

I let my eyes wander across the 360 degrees of austere and whistling beauty one last time. Off in the distance, rippled fields climbed up from the water's edge, eventually giving way to cottage-dotted vales with winding empty roads. I saw no one else. Since the dawn of civilization, humans had journeyed from known to unknown places in order to learn more. And they had told tales about their adventures. I had come to the Blarney Stoned land of the tale well told and had spent nearly the whole time alone, except for the company of familiar ghosts, who mostly rattled on in a Philly accent. Here to *write* a story, the damned things had rained on me without end for four weeks, whether I went outdoors or hunkered over my computer inside Cottage 8. Being alone didn't matter. I couldn't open a computer file or eat a meal without them interrupting. *Stories.*

The four former students who'd shared with me their thoughts about learning came to mind. Their community college stories sprawled into tales at four-year institutions then jobs. Community College of Philadelphia's influence extended beyond their time at 17th Street, and it also impacted the lives of their partners and families. Their lives made the community better. The reach of community college was as impressive as the unblocked view at this windswept height. It was a story worth telling.

When I'd listened to the tape of those four students talking about learning, I was struck by the fact that, again and again, they told stories about their experiences in order to make their points. Our trip to New York to see Christopher Walken in the musical production of James Joyce's "The Dead," Clint Gould's eye-opening discussion of Camus's *The Stranger*, a girlfriend's patience at listening to classroom tales— for these students, telling stories about their education did more than inform the story's listener and deepen the connection between teller and listener. Telling the stories helped them understand the changes they had experienced, their own growth. It demonstrated their awareness of the importance of their enculturation. It provided evidence of that enculturation's success.

We relate to stories. We become involved in them. Stories engage us. In everyday life, all of us rely on stories to explain, but we are less likely to realize that we use story to try to understand, to learn. I thought about the late fiction writer Andre Dubus's observation that "we did not know the truth of the stories until we told them. Or, more accurately, until the stories told themselves, took their form and direction from the tactile language of our memory, our pain, and our hope."[1]

Rocking in the wind, I wondered how many stories had been told or created on this lonely spot. Always, it's the same the whole world over. On Saturday nights, we gravitate toward stories in movies and theater. At the dinner table after holiday meals, we share stories. When we meet old friends or make new ones, we tell stories. Teachers do it with colleagues, and students do it with classmates when they reconnect after breaks.

It was time to go back to the village. Walking down the series of descending ridges, I photographed views to the right and left. Off in the west, near Waterville, dark clouds dropped their watery load. Walking past the last point that afforded a view of the Skelligs, I slogged down the narrow road, my slightly soggy boots slapping the mud, drawn on by gravity and gratification.

Back in the cottage, I listened to a radio interview of Christopher Gabbitas of the King's Singers and studied the movements of the sheep grazing on the hillside above my glass ceiling. While the sheep worked their way through their usual salad bar, Gabbitas described his love of traditional English folk song and Renaissance music. It made such sense. I wanted to see and hear more, but also I wanted to go home.

I remembered the wide-awake night before I'd failed the stress test. Who did I think I was? I'd told my former student that your actions showed you who you were, but I hadn't thought of it again until I came to Ireland. Lorene Cary's journey through prep school showed her who she was. Some of my students learned this every semester. Of course you changed, but it was hard to find the time to consider the significance of such change.

It was hard to consider home, identity, and work except from some distance—be that distance physical, temporal, or psychic. Cill Rialaig had provided just the distance I'd needed to see how each influenced the other, but hadn't it also become a sort of home?

As one of the CowBoys' songs went, "It's not here. It's not there or somewhere between. Just a speck in the mirror and a light turning green. We're all—almost home."

Only one name had been on my airline ticket, but I had not traveled unaccompanied. Packing up the books that nearly cost me an overweight luggage fee, I thanked them for their assistance. Spear and McGrath had shown me the importance of students' entrance into academic culture. Gregory reminded me that relationships could underline or erase our best intentions. But just as teachers wanted students to do more than merely accumulate basic skills and knowledge, they also should want to make academic culture a welcoming place for students—not by dumbing down curriculum or by buddying up to them, but by sharing their passion for their fields of expertise, their appreciation for the interconnectedness of ideas, and their recognition that, for better or worse, students and faculty became integral parts of each other's stories. In the end, if teachers welcomed students into the academic life, they would enrich both the students' lives and their own.

I recalled Trevor, John, Reggie, and Chris, who had shared their stories with Vince and me that night in my kitchen. Transcribing the tape of that discussion, I had found myself often writing "(laughter)" because to ignore the guffaws, chuckles, and belly laughs would have left out a vital part of the discussion's meaning. If we bothered to listen, humor ran rampant through our lives; it played a part in our stories, and it indicated how we connected with and understood one another. I heard that laughter when I remembered conversations with my mother, with Kathleen and the kids, and with special souls like Michael. I felt privileged to hear it in conversations with countless students, and I hoped that other teachers heard it too.

Watching the stars starting to dot the sky above my glass roof, I conjured up my fellow teachers across time and space. Although no longer employed as a teacher, I still thought like one. I had worked with and learned from great ones. I thought of Vince Castronuovo, the greatest classroom teacher I had ever known. I thought of Mark, the fine teacher who replaced me back in Philadelphia, and I thought of all the teachers who played the game the right way, as baseball people liked to say. Unlike people in some occupations, I didn't have to look outside my work to find meaning and purpose.

If you taught, your students entered your life and your stories to some degree, and you entered theirs. You could do so by accident, or you could do so with purpose. You could do it with the conviction that you had something worth sharing. You could do it with respect because they, like you, wanted to learn. And you could do it with some measure of joy, for it was good work.

In the morning, I used my last slices of brown bread to make a peanut butter sandwich for the bus rides that eventually would end at the airport hotel. I turned over my food supplies to the Finnish artist Ula, who was grateful for it all but was doubtful about what one might possibly do with peanut butter. I stripped the bed and piled the linens and towels near the door. By the time I had swept the floors and closed my luggage, I had enough time left for just one cup of tea. Jack knew that the bus left Caherciveen at 12:05, a twenty-minute drive from here.

I stepped outside at 10:50 to enjoy one last view of the bay. Standing in the car park, I saw a man outside one of the other cottages and assumed he was the person I'd heard had arrived several days ago. He headed right my way. He was Johnny from Dublin.

"A painter?" I asked.

"No, I'm a screenwriter."

With ten minutes of my time at Cill Rialaig left, I'd finally met another writer at the village. He had arrived here Friday and would leave tomorrow, a quick visit by someone the director had already invited back. We chatted about the economic climate for writers. He made his living by writing screenplays, and I saw the gravity of his situation. To eat, he must find a market for his work, and to survive in the market, he must build a reputation and demonstrate consistent skills.

Besides his desire to create art, the screenwriter wrote to eat. As a teacher, I had a very different kind of writer's life. A long time ago, I heard someone say you should only write if you have to—if the part of your soul that's in charge insisted on it. I admired Johnny's grit. I'd never wanted to quit my teaching job in order to write full time. I didn't expect that I could support my family from whatever kind of writing I'd do, and I wanted to *teach*. Once they gave me a classroom, I found more and more reasons why I wanted to keep it. I wrote during the summers, wishing they would not end, but also knowing that the first week of the semester would bring me right back. I had the best of both worlds.

Johnny knew I was a Yank from the moment I opened my mouth.

"Where are you from?"

"I'm from Philadelphia, but now I live in Maine." It had become my preferred answer to the inevitable query. When overseas, people often asked you this question, but none of them expected or wanted an answer that could fill a blue book. I always would answer that I came from Philadelphia—that much I realized after only a few months of living in Maine, where natives considered non-natives "from away."

At five after eleven, Jack had not appeared. Johnny visited Philadelphia once, for one night. He talked about cheesesteaks. As I savored my last blasts of Cill Rialaig wind, we discussed the essential elements of a genuine Philly cheesesteak. I saw that he got the idea of cheesesteaks, so I informed him about hoagies, Philadelphia's poor stepbrother to the more acclaimed cheesesteak. After ten minutes of explaining why some people preferred oil to mayonnaise on their cold cuts, I pulled myself away to call Jack's phone number. "I'll be there in five minutes," he told me.

He arrived in exactly five minutes, and I said goodbye to Johnny. We rolled down the hills and I asked him if we had enough time for me to pop in at the gallery to say goodbye, to which he assented. Mindful that I dare not miss the 12:05, I opened the door to a staff meeting in progress. "Yo, excuse me!" I called, the Philly in me coming forth. I gushed out a sincere but probably incoherent thank you to the dozen people seated in a rough circle.

Jack pulled out of the parking lot and set off at a good pace. An official looking photograph of Jack stared back at him from the windshield. He knew his business. This might well be his second or third run to Caherciveen today. But not even his mother would find the image captured in his portrait reassuring.

"You don't have any sign on the outside of the van, do you?"

"Not allowed!" he exclaimed. I'd struck a nerve.

Because you're crazy and they won't let you? Before *my* crazy mind could go further, he explained to me the difference between taxi and hackney licenses in Ireland. Taxi drivers must work in cities, and people could hail them on the street. People must call a hackney ahead of time on the phone—or ring them on the mo-bile. Hackney vehicles could have no exterior signage, and a hackney license cost less than a taxi license. Jack the hackney driver made his explanation clear as a bell, and made equally admirable driving time. Before I knew it, Jack the hack had not only treated me to a final lesson about Irish practices but also reminded me that, yes, I was a bit anxious to get back home. I had to insist that he take a tip. If I was lucky enough to return here someday, I knew which hack I would be ringing.

"Ah, you'll come back," he said.

"I hope so."

"Are you a painter?" he asked.

"Writer," I answered. "And a teacher."

Epilogue

Community colleges are far from perfect, but they are worth fighting for. Their mission and their record should matter and be a source of pride to all Americans. So too should be the welfare of nontraditional students, who today appear in classes at all levels of American colleges and universities, and who work their way into the lives of countless teachers. Helping nontraditional students is a big part of the community college's mission. May that never change.

When I was writing in Ireland about my community college life, something made me think of Melvin Udall, Jack Nicholson's character in *As Good as It Gets*. Sitting at my computer in the little cottage, I became accustomed to unannounced visitors in the form of remembered moments and wild mental associations. Every day, former students appeared and held my attention. But this one day, I realized that if I could summon all of them and have a moment with them, I would say, to paraphrase Melvin, "You make me want to be a better teacher."

I hope they don't find my sentiment too corny.

Recently, I visited Community College of Philadelphia and found that the last few classrooms with chalkboards had been converted into up-to-date, high-tech, whiteboard-walled classrooms, the kind of upgrade that one would expect at a leading community college. Otherwise, this old curmudgeon was very pleased to see my "other place" rolling along, a flagship in the least sexy niche of American higher education.

As a faculty member, year after year, I witnessed what community college does for people, particularly for students who are economically most in need. Largely unnoticed by the media or citizens not directly involved with these schools, community colleges are used by droves of Americans as launching pads to academic and career achievement. This slice of the higher education pie is considerable; in 2014, nearly half of American undergraduates attended community college.[1] According to the American Association of Community Colleges, over seven million Americans were enrolled in community colleges in fall 2014, not counting the five million others who took noncredit courses there.[2] People from all over the country and of all levels of society prosper at community colleges. When community college looks in the mirror, it sees all of America looking back at it.

Popular appraisal of the quality of community college education tends to grossly undervalue it. Faculty and students of our nursing program never felt that way, especially when yearly results of the state boards exam were announced. Typically, the pass rates for Community College of Philadelphia associate's degree nursing graduates matched those of the bachelor's degree nursing grads at the University of Pennsylvania. They crowed even more loudly when our students' pass rate exceeded that at Ivy League Penn.

I taught English. But really I taught independence. Community college teachers across our fifty states do the same. Every time former community college students return to campus with stories of a higher degree, a good job, and maybe a new address for their family, their teachers know beyond doubt that those students had learned independence. On such visits, students and I might have discussed writing or literature, but we surely talked also about independence.

It was at the heart of every story about their careers, their children, their plans. Independence means that you *can* plan.

Returning students usually visited alone, but their stories almost always featured a cast of characters. We must take our exams, undergo hiring interviews, and perform many job tasks in seeming isolation, but the journey to financial and personal autonomy rarely is unaccompanied. I wouldn't have arrived at my approach to teaching independence had I not worked with and learned from others, an irony that I hope I always appreciate.

Success and redemption stories play out one student at a time, one semester at a time, at the more than 1,100 community colleges in our country. When Americans consider academic and career success, or the forces that strengthen their communities and that counter poverty, crime, and dependency, most of them think about everything other than community college. On the whole, they know precious little about community college—and what they do know may be entirely wrong.

I hope this book shines a bit of much-needed light on the place that changed my life and the lives of my family. Our story is hardly unique. Chances are that such community college stories are unfolding right near you, and that thanks to community colleges your neighbors or family members lead better lives. The ripple effect of community colleges benefits all of us. Community colleges deserve and need public and government support. Learning about them is a first step.

Writing in Ireland helped me grasp the Zen-like truth that one never really leaves one's calling. Maybe as this book is published, I will begin to think less often about the work and about my students, but I'm not counting on it or hoping for it.

Reading Betsy Warwick's letter again in Maine sent me to the internet, where I ultimately located her son Dudley, not much older than I am, a real estate appraiser who still lives in Chestnut Hill near the Rex Avenue home where he grew up. On the phone, he told me that his mother had died some years ago, that he'd recently lost his wife, and that it all had been very hard this last year.

When we met during my recent trip back to Philadelphia, I showed him his mother's letter and gave him a photocopy of it. I watched him delicately turning the pages of his mother's letter, his eyebrows creased in concentration, thinking that for him this must be like watching an old home movie of his mother that he'd never known had existed. "Oh," he said, smiling, "this is Mom all right."

I tried to express my appreciation for his mother's kindness to Hélene and to me, and for his willingness to meet with me. "Our mothers," I stammered, sure that a second ago I'd known what I intended to add. He nodded, and I let it go at that.

I hope our paths cross again.

On the frenetic morning that Kathleen and I moved to Maine, our friend Michael Napoletano, who never wanted us to leave Philly, made sure we got out in one piece. The moving van had departed. A small stash of belongings that no one wanted sat beside our packed Civic. Michael loaded these nonessentials into his car for a last trip to the dump, then, like a captain on a sinking ship, stood alone in our driveway waving to us as we pulled out. Later, we learned that the same afternoon, he found out that he had cancer. Our dreams of hosting him in Maine had to change to caregiving stays in Philadelphia after his stem cell transplants. He died in April 2016. I hope he knew how much we all loved him.

Kathleen and I miss him everyday. That he never will see or be part of our new life in Maine is something we are trying to accept.

We live in a little town that in some ways reminds Kathleen of where she grew up—the kind of place that the city boy she subsequently married had intuited from model railroad layouts, with their mountains, lakes, winding roads, and cozy nooks. Of course this little corner of the world is challenged by life, like places everywhere else, but we feel fortunate to live here.

Our feelings about mid-coast Maine life are captured by the reply I heard from a new friend, when I asked if, after having been born and raised in his beloved Argentina, and having lived in Los Angeles, he liked living in Maine. "Like it?" he cried. "I want to *die* here!"

Much as we love Maine, we also love our regular returns to Philadelphia, savoring every musical outing with the band, Blackthorn rugby game, reunion with old friends, encounter with former students, and most importantly every hour spent with our grown children. We feel fortunate to have two places we can call home.

I may no longer be standing in front of a classroom of students, but I know that I will always be a teacher, just as Kathleen will always be a nurse. Wherever we wake up, we hope we are following our calling.

Acknowledgments

Thanks to Ireland's Cill Rialaig Project, which granted me a month-long stay in a cottage on the Kerry coast, where I began writing this book.

My deep appreciation to you who kindly read parts or all of the manuscript and offered your advice: Kathleen Bachus, James P. Brady, Vince Castronuovo, Christopher Fahy, John Firmani, Judy Gay, Jim Gorman, Mark Lyons, Paul McGarvey, Jill Parchuck, Jess Rinker, and *muchas gracias* to the eagle-eyed and owl-wise Raquel Pidal at Wild River Books and her gifted and giving associates.

Thank you to Simone Zelitch and Quinn Eli, who advised and encouraged me when I first conceived of this project.

Thank you to design wizard Tim Ogline, and to photographer Paul McGarvey and photo editor Michael Bailey.

With their complementary talents, Wild River's Kim Nagy, Joy Stocke, and Raquel Pidal saw this project through with wisdom, passion, and grace. Each of them proved essential, and in combination their gifts seemed to multiply. Writers should be so lucky as to work with a team like this.

I am indebted to all of my teachers, students, and colleagues who changed me and made me better in my work, and I thank them.

Finally, I couldn't have written this book without the support of my friend Michael Napoletano, my children, Stephan and Anna, and most especially, my wife, Kathleen.

NED BACHUS

About the Author

Born in Quebec and raised in Philadelphia, Ned Bachus taught at the Pennsylvania School for the Deaf for two years before attending graduate school at Gallaudet College (now Gallaudet University), where he founded the first rugby club for the Deaf in the United States. A founding member of Blackthorn Rugby Football Club, Bachus has been inducted into the Blackthorn RFC Hall of Fame. During his four-decade career at Community College of Philadelphia, he won multiple teaching awards, including the Christian and Mary Lindback Award for Distinguished Teaching. His fiction has been anthologized, published in literary magazines, and presented at the Writing Aloud Series at Philadelphia's InterAct Theatre, and has earned him fellowships from the Pennsylvania Council on the Arts and a residency at Ireland's Cill Rialaig Project, where he began writing *Open Admissions*. His Fleur-de-Lis Press book of short stories, *City of Brotherly Love*, received a 2013 IPPY Gold Medal for Literary Fiction. A singer-songwriter, his songs have been recorded by numerous artists and performed on National Public Radio programs including *A Prairie Home Companion*. He sings and plays percussion as a member of the Louisiana-style roots rock band Sacred CowBoys. He was named honorary member of Alpha Sigma Pi, a Deaf fraternity, and of Phi Theta Kappa International Honor Society.

Endnotes

CHAPTER ONE

1. American Association of Community Colleges, *Data Points:* "Who Attends Community College?," 2015, http://www.aacc.nche.edu/Publications/datapoints/Documents WhoAttendsCC_1_MD.pdf

CHAPTER FOUR

1. Martin S. Seligman, Acacia C. Parks, and Tracy Steen, "A Balanced Psychology and a Full Life," *The Royal Society* (2004): 1380.

2. Ibid., 1380.

3. Kenneth Hoyt, "Career Education and the Teaching/Learning Process," *Educational Leadership*, 1975: 32.

4. Seligman, Parks, and Steen, "Balanced Psychology," 1380.

5. Ibid., 1380.

6. Ron Suskind, *A Hope in The Unseen* (New York: Broadway Books, 1998), 190.

CHAPTER SIX

1. Malcolm Gladwell, *Outliers: The Story of Success* (New York: Little, Brown and Company, 2008), 40.

2. Laurence Steinberg et al., *Beyond The Classroom: Why School Reform Has Failed And What Parents Need To Do* (New York: Simon & Schuster, 1996), 19.

CHAPTER SEVEN

1. Gerald Graff and Cathy Birkenstein, *They Say / I Say: The Moves That Matter in Academic Writing* (New York: W.W. Norton & Company, 2006), 1.

2. Ibid., 1.

CHAPTER EIGHT

1. L.S. Vygotsky, *Mind in Society: The Development of Higher Psychological Processes* (Cambridge: Harvard University Press, 1986), 86, 90.

2. Ibid., 86, 90.

CHAPTER TEN

1. Albert Bandura, *Social Foundations of Thought And Action* (Englewood Cliffs, NJ: Prentice–Hall, Inc., 1986), 12, 18, 23–30.

CHAPTER ELEVEN

1. Steinberg et al., *Beyond*, 13.

2. Ibid., 138.

3. Ibid., 139.

4. Dennis McGrath and Martin Spear, *The Academic Crisis of the Community College* (Albany: State University of New York Press, 1991), 95.

CHAPTER TWELVE

1. Steinberg et al., *Beyond*, 169.
2. Ibid., 166.
3. Ibid., 170.
4. Colin S. Diver, "Knowledge for Its Own Sake," in *College Unranked: Ending The College Frenzy*, ed. Lloyd Thacker (Cambridge: Harvard University Press, 2005), 133.

CHAPTER FOURTEEN

1. Steinberg et al., *Beyond*, 92.
2. Ibid., 92.

CHAPTER FIFTEEN

1. Lorene Cary, *Black Ice* (New York: Alfred A. Knopf, 1991), 144–145.
2. McGrath and Spear, *Academic Crisis*, 5.
3. Richard Rodriguez, *Hunger of Memory: The Education of Richard Rodriguez* (New York: Bantam Books, 1983), 44, 48.

CHAPTER SEVENTEEN

1. Barbara Jordan and Shelby Hearon, *Barbara Jordan: A Self-Portrait.* (New York: Doubleday & Company, 1979), 91.
2. Ibid., 92.

CHAPTER NINETEEN

1. Susan Ambrose et al., *How Learning Works: Seven Research-Based Principles for Smart Teaching* (San Francisco: Jossey–Bass, 2010), 111–112.

CHAPTER TWENTY-THREE

1. Marshall Gregory, "Pedagogical Disjunctions, or, If I Say I Want My Students To Be Mainly Learning X, Why Do I Think Mostly About Teaching Y?" *Journal of Cognitive Affective Learning*, 1 (2004): http://www.jcal.emory.edu/viewarticle.php?id=27 (accessed December 19, 2004).
2. Ibid.

CHAPTER TWENTY-FOUR

1. Andre Dubus, *Broken Vessels* (Boston: David R. Godine, Publishers, Inc., 1991), 92.

EPILOGUE

1. American Association of Community Colleges, *Data Points:* "Who Attends Community College?," 2015, http://www.aacc.nche.edu/Publications/datapoints/Documents/WhoAttendsCC_1_MD.pdf
2. American Association of Community Colleges, *Fast Facts:* "Headcount Enrollment (Fall 2014)," February 2016, http://www.aacc.nche.edu/AboutCC/Documents AACCFactSheetsR2.pdf